Angkor's Temples in the Modern Era

WAR, PRIDE, AND TOURIST DOLLARS

To Karen

Angkor's Temples in the Modern Era

WAR, PRIDE, AND TOURIST DOLLARS

John Burgess

RIVER

BOOKS

First published in Thailand in 2021 by
River Books Co., Ltd
396 Maharaj Road, Tatien,
Bangkok 10200 Thailand
Tel: (66) 2 225-4963, 2 225-0139, 2 622-1900
Fax: (66) 2 225-3861
Email: order@riverbooksbk.com
www.riverbooksbk.com

Editor: Narisa Chakrabongse
Production Supervisor: Paisarn Piemmettawat
Design: Ruetairat Nanta

ISBN 978 616 451 046 3

Front cover: Detail of image by artist Lê Phổ on cover of *Angkor*, a tourism
promotion booklet published by *Gouvernement Général de l'Indochine, Office
Indochinois du Tourisme*, circa 1931. © Lynda Trouvé / Christophe Fumeux.

Back Cover: In 1980, Cambodian boys carry fish traps down the processional
avenue of a largely deserted Angkor Wat. Photo by John Burgess.

Printed and bound in Thailand by Sirivatana Interprint Public Co., Ltd.

Contents

ANGKOR

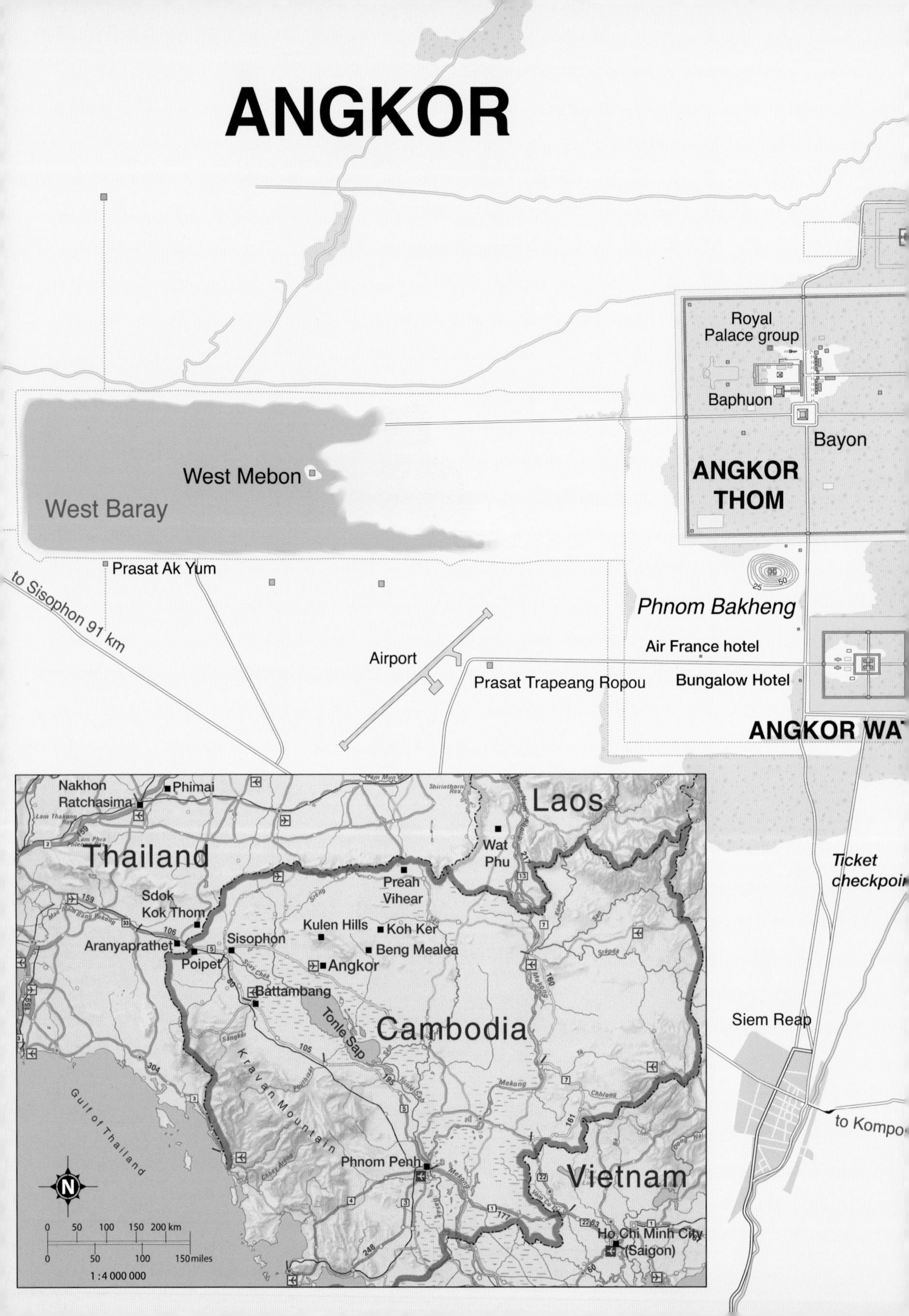

Royal Palace group

Baphuon

Bayon

ANGKOR THOM

West Mebon

West Baray

Prasat Ak Yum

to Sisophon 91 km

25 50

Phnom Bakheng

Air France hotel

Airport

Prasat Trapeang Ropou

Bungalow Hotel

ANGKOR WAT

Ticket checkpoint

Siem Reap

to Kompo

Nakhon Ratchasima

Phimai

Lam Mun

Shirinthorn Res.

Laos

Lam Thakong

Wat Phu

Thailand

Preah Vihear

Sdok Kok Thom

Kulen Hills

Koh Ker

Aranyaprathet

Sisophon

Beng Mealea

Poipet

Angkor

Battambang

Tonle Sap

Cambodia

Kravan Mountain

Gulf of Thailand

Phnom Penh

Vietnam

Ho Chi Minh City (Saigon)

N

0   50   100   150 200 km

0   50   100   150 miles

1 : 4 000 000

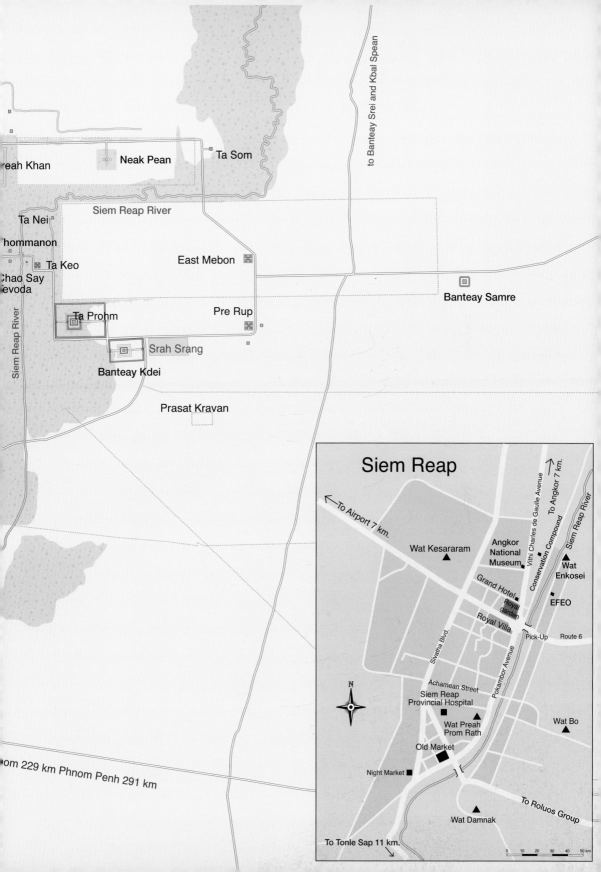

reah Khan

Neak Pean

Ta Som

Siem Reap River

Ta Nei

hommanon

Ta Keo

hao Say
evoda

East Mebon

Banteay Samre

Siem Reap River

Ta Prohm

Pre Rup

Srah Srang

Banteay Kdei

Prasat Kravan

to Banteay Srei and Kbal Spean

om 229 km Phnom Penh 291 km

Siem Reap

To Airport 7 km.

Wat Kesararam

Angkor
National
Museum

Vithi Charles de Gaulle Avenue

To Angkor 7 km.

Siem Reap River

Wat
Enkosei

Grand Hotel

Conservation Compound

Royal
garden

EFEO

Royal Villa

Pick-Up

Route 6

Sivatha Blvd

Pokambor Avenue

Achamean Street

Siem Reap
Provincial Hospital

Wat Preah
Prom Rath

Wat Bo

Old Market

Night Market

To Roluos Group

N

Wat Damnak

To Tonle Sap 11 km.

0 10 20 30 40 50 km

INTRODUCTION

At the centre of the eleventh century island-temple known as the West Mebon, there is a ruined stone platform. In 1936, a local farmer began telling people that he had had a dream. A Buddha image lay buried beneath rubble at the platform and was asking to be freed. Word reached a French archaeologist. He ordered an excavation, and soon there was a spectacular find – pieces of a huge image not of the Buddha, but the Hindu god Vishnu. Cast in bronze in the reclining pose, the god was carrying out one of his fundamental roles in Hindu cosmology, a slumber beneath the Sea of Creation to start the universe on a new cycle of existence.

* * * * *

Along a well trafficked road a few kilometres away runs a low brick wall, broken in places. Behind it once stood a wooden bungalow-style hotel, on whose veranda guests relaxed with aperitifs on rattan chairs and gazed out on a stupendous sight beyond the wall, the five towers of Angkor Wat temple. Among the people who checked in during the hotel's sixty one-year existence: a Titanic survivor who didn't give up traveling, a very determined art thief, and a Hollywood star who thought the place scandalously overpriced.

* * * * *

Inside Angkor Wat a short walk away are galleries that extend for close to five hundred metres, their walls covered with bas-reliefs that depict the Hindu epics and life in the ancient royal court. In 1970, thousands of fearful Cambodians arrived and turned the galleries into a makeshift shelter. Sleeping on reed mats, cooking on charcoal braziers, they were seeking protection from war that had just overrun their communities. International laws protecting cultural assets would keep soldiers from firing on the temple, they hoped. So would the powerful guardian deity who stood near its entrance, Ta Reach.

Most history books about Angkor, Cambodia's fabled city of stone temples, focus on ancient times, when it was capital of an empire that united much of mainland Southeast Asia, then took a centuries-long slumber in the forest. This book is about what came next. The stone platform, the vanished hotel, the galleries are just a few settings for events of a remarkable *modern* history.

At various times in the past century and a half, Angkor has been

Opposite page: A monk sets off down the processional avenue at Angkor Wat during the peaceful times of early Cambodian independence. Photo by Wim Swaan. Digital image courtesy of the Getty's Open Content Program.

a battleground, a course for a half marathon, a destination for early feminist travellers, a wedding photo backdrop, a prison camp, an inspiration for fanatics, an archaeological dig, a movie set, a launch pad for hot-air balloons, a magnet for Buddhist pilgrims, and a financial enabler of Lexus SUVs.

Its modern history veers between bright and whimsical, dark and violent to add up to what we see today. Some of the events are simply interesting to know. Others had profound outcomes: through them, an ancient civilisation was brought back to light and became the symbol of the modern Cambodian nation, indeed an inspiration to the entire world of what the human spirit can accomplish.

In one sense, it's no surprise that Angkor has had a rich modern history. It is so extraordinary a place that it keeps drawing people from all over the world, whether to enjoy it, possess it, understand it, or worship it. People simply won't leave it alone.

Angkor was founded as an imperial capital around 800 CE (and is not to be confused with Angkor Wat, its best-known temple). Over the next four centuries, it grew to be a pre-industrial metropolis of perhaps half a million people. Kings processed atop vested elephants, men cheered and jeered at cockfighting matches, women hawked fish and water spinach in outdoor markets. Soldiers marched off to defend a realm that at its peak covered not just present-day Cambodia but large parts of Thailand, Laos, and Vietnam.

But what really set the Khmers, as ancient Cambodians are known, apart from so many ancient cultures is that they were possessed of one of history's most tireless compulsions to build. In addition to the many temples, they left us bridges, highways, bathing pools, triumphal gates, a royal reviewing stand, and towering city walls that measure more than twelve kilometres around. With hoe, shovel, and harnessed elephants, they dug a vast network of reservoirs (one of them, a near perfect rectangle, measures eight kilometres long), canals, and moats that holds and channels water in ways that archaeologists are still working to understand. In hills to the north, they quarried blocks of sandstone by the tens of millions and floated them to the capital to take their allotted spots in monuments that were going up.

For reasons that remain debated, the kings and most of the people decamped from the city, likely in a gradual process beginning in the fourteenth century. Invasions from neighbouring Siam, drought, the breakdown of water infrastructure – these and other long-term factors likely caused this move. Tropical foliage and clouds of bats moved in. The temples lay still in the forest, most of them deserted, forgotten by the outside world though not by Cambodians. Starting in the mid-nineteenth century, Angkor re-emerged through the work of French colonial archaeologists. War largely sealed it off from 1970 to the early 1990s. Today it is a UNESCO World Heritage site. Close to 2.2 million foreigners visited in 2019; in early 2020, however, foreign arrivals dropped to almost zero in the face of the COVID-19 pandemic.

I first saw Angkor in 1969, as a teenager. I got up early one morning (my mother and I were staying at that now-vanished hotel) and made a solo exploration of a largely deserted Angkor Wat. You could do that in those days. The eighteen-year-old me strolled the silent arcades and passageways of a bygone people's gift to Vishnu and the Hindu cosmos. The scale, beauty, and accounts of ancient events made their impression, but over the course of repeated visits to Angkor in later years and the writing of books about it, I found myself taking a special interest in things that had transpired in recent times. I decided to write a modern history, starting with the first French visitors in the mid-nineteenth century and running to the very present.

There was plenty of research material to tap: books, films, government directives, archaeological logs, letters, scholarly journals, blogs, diplomatic cables, lectures, colonial newspapers, and court records. At the Paris headquarters of the École française d'Extrême-Orient, the institute that oversaw the old capital for almost seven decades, the staff kindly gave me access to box after box of old records (the EFEO archive is by far the world's largest trove of Angkor documentation). The National Archives of Cambodia, the Center for Khmer Studies Library in Siem Reap, the U.S. Library of Congress, the U.S. National Archives, the French National Archives, the French Overseas Territories Archives Department, the National Library of France, the library of the Société Asiatique, the Air France Museum, and the Musée de l'Hydraviation (a museum about seaplanes), all had their own material of interest. I also had interviews with people who by choice or fate had lived the recent history of Angkor, and my own memories and notes of things I had seen and heard during visits spread out over close to fifty years.

I was disappointed at how little I could learn about individual Cambodians who lived in Angkor in the nineteenth century and early twentieth. Most accounts from those times are by and about westerners. To them, local people were for the most part background figures, variously 'mandarins' who exercised royal authority and 'coolies' who toiled for a pittance. Yet it was Cambodians who did virtually all the heavy lifting at Angkor's countless projects of clearing and reconstruction, and much of the skilled planning and supervision as well. Sadly their names and stories go almost entirely unrecorded. Here and there I found such a name or an unfiltered expression of Cambodian thinking, such as doleful verse that a courtier wrote about the French removal of religious images from Angkor Wat. Still, it would be wonderful to find a detailed account, from the inside, of a single Cambodian life at Angkor in, say, 1885. Perhaps this book will shake the tree and bring such an account falling down.

But even without the ordinary Khmer, a common theme emerged in my research: an evolving but ever-present divide in outlook between the foreigners who have come to Angkor beginning in the 1850s and the Cambodians who were already there. The French for the most part treated Angkor as a mammoth archaeological site, its monuments and sometimes its people a subject for focused study to solve a 'scientific' puzzle. They measured, photographed, sampled, categorized, and analysed with a goal of understanding Angkor in rational terms and physically restoring a selection of its monuments. The Cambodians working alongside them treated Angkor as the realm of spirits, something better left to itself, whose origins could not and perhaps should not be known. The stripping away of vines, the rebuilding of tottering walls and towers offended their religious sensibilities. They often resisted the newcomers, but, given the imbalance of power in the almost century-long colonial relationship, they rarely prevailed.

This divide continues today, though manifested in different ways. Most foreigners today come not to study but to play. Strolls through the temples, dips in the hotel pool, dinner and drinks, elephant rides, souvenirs, and photos posted on social media – these are their purposes. The Cambodians they meet continue to see the temples as spirit havens, proof of bygone (and perhaps future) glories for their nation, and as gifts from forebears that generate money in the here and now, whether it's a tour guide's daily fee or a resort hotel's annual earnings. As in colonial days, Cambodians struggle to make the foreigners respect this heritage – there's today an official code of conduct for tourists – but they have the same mixed success.

The modern history of Angkor is so rich, diverse, and filled with captivating characters and events that there is no way to cover it all in a single book. In what follows I have had to choose from a mass of material and leave much to the side. For instance, in the nineteenth century the French sent multiple 'missions' to Angkor, but I recount only one in detail. I offer my apologies for this and other omissions, but hope that what remains is more than enough to tell this fascinating story well.

John Burgess
July 2020

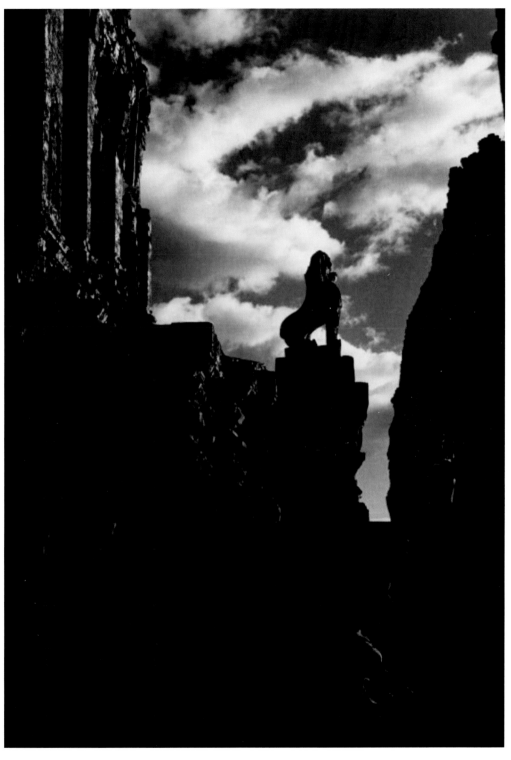

A stone lion offers protection on the heights of Angkor's Pre Rup temple, built in the tenth century.
Photo by Wim Swaan. Digital image courtesy of the Getty's Open Content Program.

1: FIRST FOREIGNERS

Led by local Cambodians, foreigners visit the largely overgrown Angkor again and again, but fail to get the world's attention. Then along comes Henri Mouhot.

If only he'd had a sketch pad and a bit more flair in his writing, Charles-Émile Bouillevaux might be remembered today as the man who woke the world up to Angkor.

He was a Roman Catholic priest, a Frenchman, sent in 1848 to spread the faith in Southeast Asia. A young man at the time, he began his stay with a lengthy study of language in Vietnam. Then one day came a letter from his bishop instructing him to go scout the interior of the Indochina peninsula. Soon he was on the first of many boats that would take him up the Mekong into Cambodia, and from there around to different parts of the kingdom.

Like many missionaries, Bouillevaux had a sharp eye for the traditions and history of the places he visited. So it was that, in December of 1850, finding himself near Cambodia's great lake, the Tonle Sap, he made a point of going to see something he'd heard about, located just north of the little town of Siem Reap.

I walked for more than a league across burning sand that put my poor naked feet in a sorry state. Finally, emerging from the forest, I arrived suddenly at a wide pavement of cut stone whose entrance was guarded by fantastical lions. In following this roadway, which runs across a pond where a herd of buffaloes was eating and soaking, I saw here and there several small pavilions, partly fallen down. The ruins still revealed the old elegance. I went further under two rather narrow quadrangular galleries, covered with sculptures, and found myself in front of the pagoda proper.

Father Bouillevaux was looking at Angkor Wat.

The pagoda of Angcor is quite well preserved and deserves to be ranked alongside our most beautiful monuments. It is the wonder of the Indochina peninsula. This Buddhist temple by no means looks like a European church. The main body of the building

Opposite page: Angkor Wat, as depicted in an image detail from the first publication of Henri Mouhot's journal, in *Le Tour du Monde* in 1863. (Bibliothèque nationale de France)

Father C. E. Bouillevaux, from *Les Explorateurs du Cambodge*, 1878. (Library of Congress collection)

is a perfect square and at each corner stands a beautiful tower which ends in a dome. In the middle is a fifth tower, higher than the others…Despite its peculiarity, I found this monument to be grandiose, magnificent.

After a while, he walked ahead and entered the temple itself. He climbed to its top tier, where he took note of images of the Buddha and other deities. He listened to Buddhist monks chant prayers in the Pali language. Later in the day, he entered the walled city of Angkor Thom. Elephants carved in bas-relief were doing battle there.

All that I saw at Angcor proved to me, based on the evidence, that Cambodia was once rich, civilized and much more populated than it is now, but all the riches have disappeared and the civilisation is extinguished. Today, a thick forest fills the enclosure of the ancient capital and gigantic trees grow among the ruined palaces. Few sensations are sadder than what one feels on seeing wastelands that were once the theater of scenes of glory and pleasure.

Contemplating these 'vanities of the world,' Bouillevaux met a Cambodian man, the local 'chief of the forest,' who invited him to stay the night in his nearby hut. The next day, the priest departed Angkor.

He returned to France in 1856. Two years later, he published a book called *Voyage dans l'Indo-Chine*, from which this account is taken. Write-ups of travel to faraway tropical countries were common enough in mid-nineteenth century France, when the country was assembling a colonial empire. This one got little attention, even with its message that an astounding ruined city lay in the forest. Perhaps that is understandable. The book was issued by a church publisher, not one that sold to the mass market. The priest gave Angkor only five of his book's three hundred seventy-six pages. There were no illustrations, and beyond his flight of fancy about the now silent wastelands, it was generally sober in tone.

In fact, accounts like his were overlooked time and again, as if spirits resident at Angkor were manipulating human affairs so as to be left in peace. As far back as 1585, a Portuguese friar called Antonio da Magdalena visited Angkor. 'One of the marvels of the world,' he later told a chronicler, giving a lengthy and insightful account of temples, city walls, moats, and sculpture. (One charming period-specific detail: the moats of Angkor Thom were 'the width of a blunderbuss shot.') But Europe barely noticed. In the 1630s there came Japanese pilgrim Kenryo Shimano, who drew a stylized bird's-eye-view diagram that despite its Japanese-style towers is recognizable as Angkor Wat. But Japan barely noticed – the drawing lay hidden in an archive there for almost two centuries. And not long after Father Bouillevaux's feet crossed those burning sands, those of other Europeans were doing the same. In 1859, Britain's Royal Geographical Society received a paper by James Campbell Esq., a surgeon at the British mission in Bangkok, 'compiled from manuscripts of the late E.F.J. Forrest, Esq. and from information derived from the Rev. Dr. House.' It is unclear which of these men actually went to Angkor and when, but whoever it was felt deeply moved, as the paper, presented at a London meeting of the society, made clear.

> *Enveloped as are these ruins in the most unfathomable mysteries, unpossessed of any tradition beyond mere conjecture and popular rumour which can throw light on their origin or foundation, and surpassing in splendour of design and beauty of architecture the most renowned remnants of bygone ages to be found in Hindostan, they offer to the student of Asiatic archaeology matter for the most profound research…*

Still more attention was coming from Siam, which was coming into greater contact with the world under the rule of King Mongkut, known also as Rama IV. Siam, in fact, *owned* Angkor. In the 1790s it had absorbed three provinces in western Cambodia, including the one in which Angkor stood. In the Siamese capital Bangkok, aristocrats and Buddhist scholars knew that extraordinary things could be found in the forests there. King Mongkut himself took a deep interest. According to accounts that feel apocryphal, in 1859 or 1860 he dispatched two thousand men with orders to dismantle Angkor Wat and bring it back, stone by stone, to Bangkok for reassembly. More plausible versions of the story say the group was much smaller with a less ambitious goal, the removal of only a small temple, or part of one, with its new home to be a Bangkok monastery that stands today by the lavish Siam Paragon shopping mall.

Whatever the mission's size, why would he have done this? Many explanations have been offered. Before ascending the throne, the king had spent many years as a Buddhist monk and had developed an interest in reaching beyond the legends about religious edifices to discover their verifiable history. Likely too, as a man of deep religious accomplishment, he was interested in spiritual energy believed to emanate from the temples. And Mongkut was, by necessity, much attuned to the geopolitics of his day. The French had already taken over southern Vietnam and were looking west to Cambodia and perhaps the Siamese-ruled lands where Angkor was to be found. The sovereign may have been looking to secure for his kingdom an at-risk relic of the mysterious ancient civilisation.

Henri Mouhot, from *Les Explorateurs du Cambodge*, 1878. (Library of Congress collection)

Any such mission that did take place was, of course, doomed to failure. Angkor's temples are far too big to be carried off; all of them remained in place. There may also have been resistance from local Cambodians. According to some accounts, they attacked the approaching Siamese party and drove it back. The abiding result of King Mongkut's interest was the building of a large model of Angkor Wat inside the walls of the Temple of the Emerald Buddha in Bangkok, where today it draws the occasional puzzled attention of tourists.

Looking back, it's hard to believe that Angkor remained unknown to the outside world for as long as it did. It was hiding in plain sight, situated not in some remote wasteland, but on a relatively fertile, forested plain not far from Siem Reap town, which was reachable from the Cambodian capital Phnom Penh by boat across the Tonle Sap or from Bangkok by land and water. Siem Reap in the mid-nineteenth century had marketplaces, inns, and about two hundred houses. It had Buddhist monks who processed in the morning to collect the daily alms. A Siamese-approved lord presided in a stone-walled, cannon-protected citadel built partly of stones taken from Angkor. He was ready to receive foreign visitors and provide a *laissez-passer* to the temples in return for polite conversation and gifts, which early on could be as small as a bar of soap and a few lithographs. Ox carts and elephants were for hire for transport; the lord sometimes assigned a relative to act as guide.

By heading north on primitive but passable roads, visitors could reach the former capital in an hour or so. There were many more people to be encountered there. Farmers tended rice fields alongside the temples; children fished the moats. People stayed out of most of the temples in respect for resident spirits, but Angkor Wat was an exception. It appears never to have been abandoned. In the mid-nineteenth century, a sizeable community of Buddhist monks was pursuing enlightenment at a monastery within its compound walls. In elaborate wooden buildings, monks prayed and chanted, studied the scriptures, and performed a special kind of merit-making labour, the clearing of vegetation from the ancient stones. Pilgrims came from far away, sleeping in close to a hundred rest houses built for them inside the temple's walls. Annual religious festivals drew families from neighbouring villages. Gatherings could be large, noisy and lengthy: when a prominent monk died, he might receive a three-day funeral at the temple, with local aristocrats arriving on elephant back to pay their respects and small cannons firing salutes.

* * * * *

In the end, Angkor surrendered its obscurity to Henri Mouhot.

He had the perfect set of talents and connections that would set world interest alight – literary flair, an eye for romantic detail, provocative comparisons, skill with a sketch pad, and, perhaps most important, the interest of European publishers who made their money selling to a broad audience.

His story is now well known. He came to Southeast Asia in 1858 as one of a new class of European visitors, the man of science. Study of flora and fauna was his objective. He was largely self-financed, though Britain's Royal Geographical Society was showing an interest in his travels (Mouhot was something of an Anglophile, and had married an Englishwoman). He based himself in Bangkok and made four extended trips in the region. The final one took him winding around Cambodia, then up into Laos. There, in a riverside camp near the city of Luang Prabang, he died of fever, likely malaria, on 10 November 1861. He had been keeping a detailed journal, with sketches and diagrams. These were published in 1863 in *Le Tour du Monde*, an illustrated weekly journal of adventure abroad, sold at rail stations and street corner kiosks to people who would never have such adventures themselves.

These created a sensation, because Mouhot had spent two weeks in Angkor and described it with lyrical intensity. Angkor Wat, he declared, was the work of a 'Michelangelo of the East.' It 'exceeds the grandiosity of all the art that the Greeks or Romans ever built.'

Henri Mouhot and his team break for the night during their travels, in this illustration from an English-language version of his journal. (Project Gutenberg)

Above: This image from Henri Mouhot's published journal appears to depict one of Angkor Wat's two 'libraries' located along its processional avenue. French archaeologists gave the structures that name in the belief that they once stored religious texts. (Project Gutenberg)

Top right: The western entrance of Angkor Wat proper, as depicted in Henri Mouhot's published journal. (Project Gutenberg)

[Angkor Wat is] the most beautiful and the best preserved of all these monuments; it is also the first that smiles on the traveler, makes him forget the fatigues of the journey when he arrives, transports him with admiration, and fills him with a joy much greater than coming upon a charming oasis in the middle of the desert. Suddenly, and as if by magic, one feels one is transported from barbarism to civilisation, from deep darkness to light…

From up close, the beauty, the finish and the grandeur of the details far outweigh the graceful effect of the image seen from a distance and that of its imposing lines.

Instead of a disappointment, as one approaches one experiences a deeper admiration and pleasure. There are, first of all, tall and beautiful columns, all of one piece, porticoes, capitals, rounded roofs, all composed of large, beautifully polished blocks, carved and sculpted.

At the sight of this temple, the mind feels crushed, the imagination surpassed. We look, we admire, and, with respect, we remain silent. For where to find words to praise a work which perhaps has no equivalent on the globe, and which could have had as its rival only the temple of Solomon!

On he went in that vein. Surveying Angkor from the hilltop temple Phnom Bakheng, he offered visions of ghosts wandering the ruins. He dwelt on the tragedy that the heroic deeds of warriors and kings of past ages were lost in the fog of time.[1] Accompanying the words were sketches that were evocative and remarkably accurate in architectural terms.

How easy it was in the cafés, drawing rooms, and rail station waiting rooms of France for people to become enchanted. And it didn't hurt that the man whose adventures they were sharing

From Laotian Campsite to Parisian Publishing House: A Journal's Journey

After Henri Mouhot died in the riverside camp, members of his team buried him there. But they brought out his baggage and personal effects, which were forwarded to Bangkok. There his journal, sketches, and collections were entrusted to James Campbell, the same man who had written the Angkor paper heard by the Royal Geographical Society in 1859.

In a letter of 7 April, 1862 to Annette Mouhot, wife of Henri, Campbell delivered news of the death and offered condolences. 'Your husband – my valued friend – is, alas! now no more.'

Campbell was soon to leave for England, and promised to deliver the material to her there the following month. Mouhot's account was first published in France, however, in an 1863 edition of the journal *Le Tour du Monde*. By some accounts, publication was intended in part to bring financial relief to Annette, who had been petitioning the geographical society for a pension, saying she was destitute because all the couple's resources had gone toward the travels.

Mouhot's published words are often described as a diary, but what the public read was not a word-for-word transcription. With help from Mouhot's brother Charles, the original hand-written journal entries and notes underwent editing to produce a comprehensive, readable narrative following the journalistic/literary conventions of the time. It was something of a challenge: Most of the journal was in pencil; some passages were illegible.

Editing continued as his work was published in book form. For example, an English-language version that came out in 1864 contains the following quote, which brings together ideas expressed separately in the

Henri Mouhot's grave, near Luang Prabang, Laos, draws visitors to this day. Photo by Boyloso/Shutterstock.com.

Tour du Monde article. 'One of these temples – a rival to that of Solomon and erected by an ancient Michael Angelo – might take an honourable place beside our most beautiful buildings.'

Likewise, illustrations published in the accounts were not by Mouhot's hand. They were drawn, 'based on' the late naturalist's own, by artists well established in 1860s Paris, Jacques Guiaud, Émile Thérond, and Marie Firmin Bocourt. Indeed, memorable pictures were part of *Le Tour du Monde*'s stock in trade. Its title pages proclaimed that articles were 'illustrated by our most famous artists.'

The original journal and sketches appear not to have survived. At least, the author was not able to locate them.

was speaking from beyond the grave. A glorious lost civilisation was out there, provenance unknown, waiting to be uncovered, and perhaps even possessed by the expanding French empire. In this way, Angkor's name became known in Europe and parts of the Americas as well.

* * * *

It wasn't long before more Europeans headed in its direction. Some left detailed accounts, others basically nothing. But each was armed, it seems, with a copy of Mouhot's account, which can also go down in history as Angkor's first guide book.

In February 1866, a Scottish photographer called John Thomson arrived to create the first photographic images. He had spent months in Siam photographing the court of King Mongkut and daily life beyond the palace walls; now, in the

1   Mouhot also briefly mentions Siamese interest in moving an Angkor temple. 'The deputy head of the province of Battambang was in Angkor at the time of our visit. He had just received an order from the Siamese government to remove one of the smallest but at the same time most attractive monuments of Angkor and transport it to Bangkok.'

Above: One of these elephants at the entry causeway of Angkor Wat was probably the transportation that brought photographer John Thomson to the temple in 1866. (Courtesy Wellcome Collection)

Opposite page: Members of the Mekong Commission posed for the camera of Émile Gsell on an Angkor Wat stairway in 1866. Louis Delaporte is second from right. Commission leader Ernest Doudart de Lagrée is on far left, and Francis Garnier on far right. Photo copyright Archives du Ministère de l'Europe et des Affaires étrangères – La Courneuve.

company of an acquaintance from the British consulate in Bangkok, he was training his bulky camera equipment on Angkor. Thanks to their two weeks at Angkor, we can see a pair of elephants, each with a large *howdah* atop its back, waiting at Angkor Wat's western entrance – the animals seem to have been among the transport rentals that the local lord was offering. We can see images of the temple proper, of various of the women who are carved there in bas-relief, and of some of the face towers of the Bayon temple.

Later that year it was the turn of a party of Frenchmen who'd been assigned to investigate the Mekong River as a possible water route to southern China, but first took a detour to Angkor. 'Science' was the purpose of their visit to the old capital, but politics were in play as well: The work of Thomson and the second man, an official British government agent, had seemed to some French as a possible laying of claim to the place. With their new control of Cambodia and their compatriot Mouhot being called the 'discoverer' of Angkor, the French were anxious to maintain leadership in its technical examination.

In their time at the monuments, these new visitors sketched a detailed floor plan of Angkor Wat, made some small plaster casts of sculpture and architectural elements, drew maps, and calculated Angkor Wat's cartographical coordinates. With them was the Saigon-based photographer Émile Gsell, who took a fascinating set of photographs.

Known formally as the *Commission d'Exploration du Mekong*, the group would be better remembered for what came next, the ascent up the river. Early on, they found that rapids and falls around what is now the Cambodia-Laos border made it impassable for boats. But they kept going, exploring, observing, taking detailed notes, despite chronic illness and exhaustion. In

John Thomson made the first photographs of Angkor, in 1866. Here a local man gives scale to stonework in Angkor Wat. (Courtesy Wellcome Collection)

A colonnade at a lower level of Angkor Wat caught the eye of photographer John Thomson in 1866. (Courtesy Wellcome Collection)

24

The Buddhist faithful had placed many images at Angkor Wat, including these photographed (in the stereoscopic format that was popular at the time) by John Thomson in 1866. (Courtesy Wellcome Collection)

northern Laos, they paused to pay tribute at Henri Mouhot's grave and arranged for a permanent monument to be built over it.[2]

Two years after they set out, they reached their journey's end, the town of Dongchuan in southern China's Yunnan province. There the group's leader, Ernest Doudart de Lagrée, succumbed to illness.

One of the commission members, Louis Delaporte, would turn out to be a key figure in Angkor's reintroduction to the

Early French visitors found a vibrant monastic community at Angkor, including these two monks photographed by Émile Gsell. Photo copyright Archives du Ministère de l'Europe et des Affaires étrangères – La Courneuve.

2 Today a statue of Mouhot, wearing a broad-brimmed hat and carrying a notebook, presumably his journal, stands near the grave.

world. He had gone away with the Angkor bug, and would make study of the old civilisation a passion for the rest of his life. 'We dream of a beautiful monument of the East,' he wrote. 'The reality even surpasses the dream.'

* * * * *

As for Father Bouillevaux, he came back to Southeast Asia in 1866 for a second term as a missionary, then returned to France for good. He settled into the life of a parish priest, serving his home town of Montier-en-Der. According to an Asia enthusiast who knew him, the Marquis de Croizier, the priest remained silent for years as Mouhot achieved international fame as 'first' to Angkor. Bouillevaux was not a man to care about temporal things, the marquis averred, and it was only at the insistence of family that a few words of dissent found their way into another book that the priest published, in 1874. 'Let us protest a certain pattern of exaggeration and charlatanism,' Bouillevaux wrote. 'There are claims of valuable discoveries being made in Cambodia and elsewhere. But most of these beautiful discoveries were already known for a very long time. For example, the temple of Angkor and the ruins of Angkor Thom were not rediscovered by Mouhot, as it is said, for the good reason that they were never forgotten or lost.' He went on to cite Chinese and Portuguese visitors of past centuries, as well as Christian missionaries. 'Mouhot saw Angkor after several others, in particular after me.'

In 1879, the priest was inducted into the newly formed *Société Académique Indo-Chinoise de France* (the marquis was its

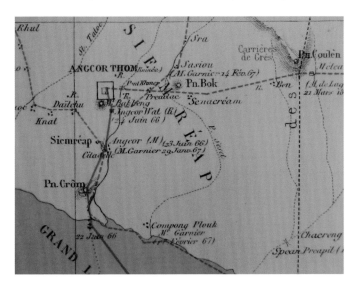

An atlas published by Mekong commission members in 1873 showed basic geographic features of the region and movements of commission members. This detail marks major sites including Angkor Thom, Angkor Wat, Phnom Krom, and Siem Reap. (Library of Congress collection)

This elevation of Angkor Wat's west side, included in the Mekong commission's atlas, was among detailed architectural studies that team members made of major temples. (Library of Congress collection)

president). Its first official report displayed a portrait of the new honorary member with the caption 'First explorer of the ruins of ancient Cambodia.'

The dispute sputtered on, but the priest's cause gained little ground. No doubt he was undermined by being a man not of science but of the church, which many French intellectuals despised or ridiculed. His death in 1913 at age eighty-nine did not bring the debate to a close.

In May 1926, when the centenary of Mouhot's birth arrived, the philosopher and human rights activist Félicien Challaye hailed Mouhot in the newspaper *L'Oeuvre*. He was 'the heroic naturalist-explorer' who had the 'rare fortune of discovering the ruins of Angkor,' Challaye wrote. Toward the end of his essay, he did note that Father Bouillevaux had visited earlier, but averred that the priest 'neither understood nor felt the unique magnificence' of Angkor. Bouillevaux stayed just a day, he pointed out, and, among other perceived transgressions, he dismissed sculpture he saw as 'grotesque.' In Challaye's view, the honor of discovery belonged firmly to Mouhot.

Two weeks later, the newspaper published a letter from one Gosselin Quertier, who identified himself as the priest's sole surviving relative. 'You do not dispute – and it is indisputable – that it is my uncle, the R.P. [Révérend Père] Charles-Emile Bouillevaux, who was the first white man to see the ruins of Angkor[3]...The fact that his judgment concerning these ruins was different from that of Mouhot is a separate issue and cannot negate the advantage of discovery.' Yes, Quertier said, the priest did use the word grotesque, but some of the sculpture fit the meaning of the word – and Quertier would be happy to share photos to prove it. He closed by saying that the priest had always maintained strong enthusiasm for Angkor. He

3 He seems to have forgotten or never read his uncle's words that a Portuguese had preceded him.

4 In what might be seen as a consolation prize, the priest is honoured today in Montier-en-Der by a road named after him.

'frequently told us stories which proved his great admiration, probably having no equal, for the monument.'

Challaye got the last word, at least in the newspaper, pointing out that Angkor experts shared his view. 'Only the family of Father Bouillevaux supports a contrary opinion,' he wrote. 'I pay respectful homage to the power of this family feeling.'[4]

Missing in this back and forth was the broader point that Angkor was never forgotten by Cambodians. It was Cambodians who told the foreign 'explorers' about it and who greeted them on arrival. It was Cambodians who fed and showed them around, who shared local lore and temple names, and put them up for the night. Among Europeans, however, what mattered was when the first European had come. This often dismissive view of the many residents of Angkor – of their very presence, even – would colour the relationship for decades to come.

Angkor Wat as photographed by Émile Gsell in 1866 or during a subsequent visit in 1873. Barely visible to the left of the steps is the photographer's portable darkroom (detail), with a man standing in front of it. Digital images courtesy of the Getty's Open Content Program.

2: The Delaporte Mission

A French naval officer-turned-archaeologist conducts the first detailed survey of Angkor – and brings home many tons of sculpture.

Following the Mekong expedition, Louis Delaporte went home to France. There he received the Legion of Honour for his role in what had become a much-celebrated undertaking. He devoted extensive time to writing up Mekong findings and editing an atlas. Then in July 1870 came something unforeseen: war with Prussia. As a career naval officer, Delaporte was dispatched to assist with coastal defences. Prussian troops' quick defeat of France and occupation of Paris were a special humiliation for his generation of young military men. Some responded by leaving for the colonies. For Delaporte, the escape was back to Indochina, where he was to have a dual assignment: continue the study of Angkor, and survey the Red River of northern Vietnam as the possible water route to China that the Mekong had turned out not to be.

By now a decade had passed since publication of Mouhot's diary. The European public's appetite was whetted by successive visitors' collections of writings, photos, diagrams, and etchings. But there remained something lacking in what had been brought home: artefacts larger than what could fit in a carpet bag. The travellers spun tales of giant sculpted deities, bas-reliefs that ran hundreds of metres long, and gigantic gates and towers. Delaporte and his team laid plans to take high-quality photographs, make precise surveys, and advance the general state of knowledge of the Angkor civilisation. And they would try to give people at home some large-scale sculpture and sections of sacred buildings. This would also help France keep abreast in a sort of antiquities arms race that was developing with the British. In London, the British Museum was displaying such treasures as the Elgin marbles and Rosetta Stone. France would now get something comparable.

With financing from the *Société de Géographie*, Delaporte assembled in Saigon a team of five Frenchmen and forty Indochinese. The men departed on the morning of 23 July 1873 on the gunboat *La Javeline* and a small steamer. They stopped in Phnom Penh, where the Cambodian King Norodom

Louis Delaporte, as depicted in *Les Explorateurs du Cambodge*, 1878. (Library of Congress collection)

Opposite page: On a fast-running river, Cambodian men steer a raft carrying a statue that is destined for France. The image was in Louis Delaporte's 1880 book *Voyage au Cambodge, l'Architecture Khmer.*

King Norodom, captured here by the camera of John Thomson, was on the Cambodian throne during Delaporte's visit to Angkor. (Courtesy Wellcome Collection)

Prea Tomey, the holy elephant, originally stood on a pyramid in Preah Khan-Kompong Svay temple. It is now part of the Musée Guimet collection in Paris. (Photo Karen Buck Burgess)

received them. He pledged support for their work. That was no surprise. A decade earlier, the French had made his kingdom a protectorate.

From Phnom Penh, the team did not go directly to the Siamese-controlled Angkor. Rather, it went to the temple known today as Preah Khan-Kompong Svay, about one hundred kilometres to the east of the ancient capital. This enormous complex, little visited by foreigners even today, was well within Norodom's recognized realm and had large quantities of free-standing sculpture, available for the taking under the king's authority.

Delaporte first caught sight of the temple from across a moat. He spied a causeway supported by stone images that he called, in the style of classical European sculpture, 'caryatids.' Moving closer, he and the team came upon a grand temple building with stone columns and 'lion bodies buried in the grass.' They found statues 'still beautiful in their dreadful state of mutilation.' With Angkor in his memory from seven years earlier, Delaporte took pleasure in seeing such a place again, and in hearing the cries of wonder that first sight evoked in his fellow Frenchmen.

Cambodians living in the area were horrified when they learned what the foreigners intended for the temple's sculpture. They bedevilled the French with tales of hauntings and supernatural vengeance. But these visitors had to be obeyed. Local men took them, reluctantly, to various sites in and around the temple, throwing grains of rice as apologetic offerings to the spirits. There were temporal-world obstacles to the French plans too, such as flights of bats, snakes that slithered from rubble crannies, and heavy overgrowth that made it difficult to get even a good look at the temple. The men took photographs. They recorded technical observations, such as a counter-intuitive building technique by which the Khmers sometimes used wooden beams to reinforce stone elements of construction. Delaporte noted a hollowed-out lintel in which there remained rotten remnants of wood.

On an excursion away from the main temple, the men came to a ruined pyramidal structure that had once had four large stone elephants, eight guardian divinities, and eight lions. Most of the images now lay in pieces, destroyed, Delaporte surmised, by Siamese invaders in the past. Just one elephant was still standing, a handsome beast wearing finely carved vestments and neckpiece, with even its floppy ears well preserved. The local people knew it as *Prea Tomey*, the Holy Elephant. Such veneration was of no great concern to the Frenchmen; they

Superhuman Transport

It is a wonder that Delaporte's team brought out as many statues as it did, given their weight and the enormous challenges of floral overgrowth, lack of roads, and primitive handling technology. The heavy labour was carried out by Cambodians; the French mostly supervised.

Typically the job began with the rigging up of a rope-and-pulley lifting contraption over a selected statue. Men pulled hard to winch it up from its original place and lower it onto platforms made on the spot from cross-ties of tree trunks and branches, secured with vines. Each of these platforms, heavy with its sacred cargo, was placed on top of an ox cart or on the shoulders of squads of men, then moved slowly toward the nearest river, which might be several kilometres away.

Woodcutters went in front to clear the way with machetes and axes. Accidents were frequent, as when horseflies bit the oxen and sent them off on panicked sprints. The stone cargo sometimes suffered damage in the process, but was fixed as best possible, and secured again so that the procession could resume.

At water's edge, the men placed the statues on rafts built from bamboo cut in the forest, and then floated them downstream. In places, the rivers ran rapid, and the men struggled to prevent the rafts from capsizing. If all went well, the artwork ultimately reached a steamboat in deeper, calmer waters downstream. Then it was on to Phnom Penh and Paris.

Cambodian workmen transport a Khmer guardian statue across a stream. Image from *Voyage au Cambodge*.

A sitting image is brought to a stream bank for onward transport by raft. Image from *Voyage au Cambodge*.

The Shiva head that Delaporte's team unearthed at Phnom Bok temple is now in the Musée Guimet in Paris. (Photo Minja Yang)

made preparations to haul off the elephant, along with other large statues that stood elsewhere in the complex. These included a sitting Buddha, a standing guardian deity, and two lions from the main temple itself. All were in very good condition.

For other things that struck their fancy, variously statues, bas-reliefs, or entire walls decoratively carved, Delaporte's men employed a nineteenth century copy technology, moulding. The team had brought supplies of a gelatine mixture with which they coated the desired object. The covering quickly hardened, then was removed in large, rigid pieces. These became casts that, back in France, allowed the creation of remarkably accurate replicas in plaster. Even the complex bas-reliefs in which the Khmers specialized, with figures and foliage creating veritable forests of mythological action, could be replicated in detail. The gelatine mixture filled in even the 'undercuts' and then came free.

From Preah Khan-Kompong Svay, the group moved on to the huge Beng Mealea temple, located roughly half way to Angkor. There was little sculpture to be found there, so team members gave extra attention to a secondary goal of their mission, the collection of natural specimens. They also examined ancient quarries to the northwest of the temple. One Frenchman surveyed nearby villages for some clue to the tools of stone extraction, but reported finding nothing. This man also climbed the Kulen hills where he saw a large reclining Buddha that in the post-Angkor period was carved from the top of an enormous boulder. The foreigners mixed with local people, taking part in a rite in which a lengthy recitation recounted the legend of a young monk who wanted to quit his order to marry.

From Beng Mealea, they proceeded to the small three-towered temple which bears the same name as the hill atop which it stands just east of Angkor, Phnom Bok. Entering a dark chamber with torches, they made an exciting find. Their eyes drawn by candle debris on the floor, they saw, barely showing above the surface, Delaporte later recounted, 'a cylinder of very fine grained sandstone, covered with sculpted hair curls.' They dug and uncovered a large and beautifully crafted, well-preserved head. Nearby they unearthed a large four-faced head of equal workmanship, and a third head in pieces. Despite the candle debris in the chamber, which suggests worship by local people, Delaporte wrote that the Cambodians on the team viewed the heads as representing only insignificant spirits and so had no compunction about hefting them out. The French soon identified the statues as the Hindu trinity, Brahma, Vishnu, and Shiva, and speculated that each had held a place of honour in one of the temple's three towers, before being deliberately buried, perhaps during a time of war or religious desecration.

* * * *

Then it was on to Siem Reap, and Siamese authority. In this period, Siam was attempting to adapt some western ways. Greeting the Delaporte party was the provincial lord's brother, a young man whose dress (western-style white tunic, navy hat, bare legs) the Frenchmen privately ridiculed. They nonetheless had to deal with him. They were less than honest about what they intended to do. Delaporte later recounted that a mission member called Bouillet had handled the audience with the lord, who told him that the king of Siam forbade the removal of sculpture. Bouillet responded with assurances that the team intended only to study the ruins, copy inscriptions, and make mouldings. This pledge was followed by the handing over of numerous gifts. Reading between the lines, one senses an unspoken understanding: the lord had delivered his pro forma warning; he would now look the other way as piece after piece of sculpture disappeared.

For that privilege, Delaporte had paid a bribe, a large one. He would later complain that while Mouhot had bought his way into Angkor with just a bar of soap and two tinted lithographs, the man now in charge (the son of the lord Mouhot had dealt with) required much more. In fact, gifts handed out to Siamese and Cambodian 'mandarins,' such things as music boxes, lengths of fabric, and glassware, depending on the recipient's rank, consumed roughly a quarter of the mission's entire budget. And the Siem Reap lord was not satisfied with gifts alone. He directed that the visitors would buy all their supplies through him, at prices the Frenchmen believed were triple the going rate. Likewise, local labourers had to be engaged and paid through him, at no-doubt inflated rates from which he skimmed a portion for himself.

The team camped near the Bayon temple and began the first systematic clearing under French supervision of a Khmer temple. For twelve days, sixty Cambodian labourers toiled to remove trees and brush and open trails inside the Bayon's perimeter so as to allow a clear view and the drafting of a diagram of perhaps the most architecturally complex structure in the Angkor domain. Frenchmen and Cambodians alike

The *naga* with deities ensemble, on display at Musée Guimet, was originally at Preah Khan temple in Angkor. The sculpture almost didn't make it to France – a small boat carrying the load capsized, but the sculpture was later recovered. (Photo Minja Yang)

were amateurs in the business of clearing. They may not have realized that roots of trees could be removed only with great care, because they had often become a new framework of structural support, holding up that which they did not knock down. Inexpert removal may help explain an event that Delaporte later reported: 'One night, during a terrible storm, we heard a terrific noise. The next day, there was just a pile of rubble in the place of a tower that we had admired.' The tower's loss, he said, made him double down on the task of documenting temples through photography, drawings, and measurements.

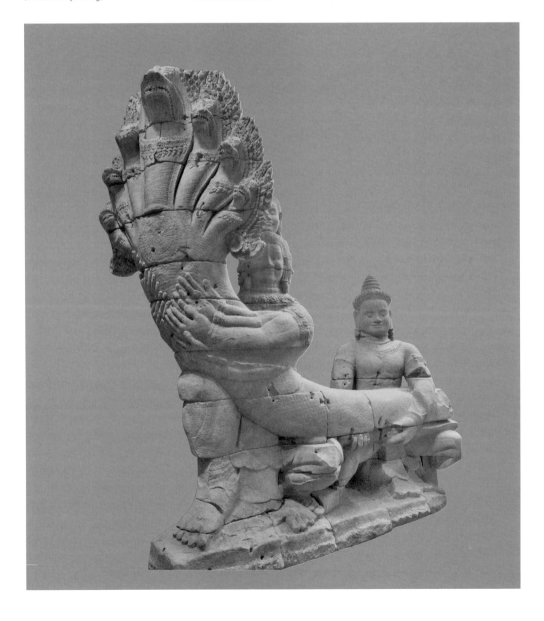

From the Bayon, they went to Preah Khan, a twelfth-century Angkor temple that bears the same name as the Kompong Svay monument that they had surveyed earlier. They came upon an entrance balustrade depicting a great event in Hindu mythology, the Churning of the Sea of Milk, in which deities and demons tug on the body of a *naga* serpent to produce the elixir of immortality. There it was in stone – a seven-headed *naga* standing more than four metres tall, with deities clutching the serpent god's body. His crew got to work, taking the *naga*'s multiple heads and two of the gods.

The Leper King, as depicted in *Voyage au Cambodge*.

In front of the palace compound the men examined the already famous sitting statue that locals called the Leper King. This the Frenchmen left in place, though they did take a cast of its head.[1] The men later struck camp and moved to Angkor Wat. They lived among the monks there and gave the temple's bas-reliefs serious study to identify scenes and characters from the Hindu epics.

By now, several of the men had fallen ill, as happened so often to the French in Indochina. Delaporte believed he was suffering from liver disease. Most commonly the problem was dysentery and malaria. That last illness was treated with limited effect by quinine, which the French often gulped down mixed with wine.

It came time to leave. The men packed their equipment and sculpture booty aboard twenty-seven oxcarts and set off for Siem Reap. There the local lord balked at letting so much be taken out. But somehow he relented. The sculpture was divided among a gunboat and several locally-obtained boats that it would tow. There was more trouble: on the Tonle Sap, a towed boat carrying the disassembled Preah Khan *naga* sank in rough waters. The stones settled into the muddy floor. The gunboat went on, but at some later point the stones were recovered.

Various other pieces had been left 'along the way' in the previous months. Among them were the statues sent downstream from Preah Khan-Kompong Svay on rafts (Cambodians labourers had abandoned some of the statues mid-way, apparently fearful of giving offense to spirits). But most of these pieces eventually reached a riverside town from which a steamboat took them to Phnom Penh for forwarding

1 This statue, which experts identify as the god Yama, today sits at the centre of the courtyard of the National Museum of Cambodia, sheltered by a red and black pavilion. A reproduction occupies the original spot in Angkor Thom.

The Delaporte team pauses at a Khmer temple. With their jackets and cravats, early French visitors often dressed as if they hadn't left home. Image from *Voyage au Cambodge*.

with the others to Saigon and on to France. The mission's full tally was seventy pieces of sculpture and architectural fragments (such as window frames and pilasters), more than eighty mouldings, and numerous diagrams, rubbings, and technical measurements.

As it happened, Delaporte did not carry out the second part of his Indochina assignment, the Red River survey. That trip was cancelled due to tensions in northern Vietnam (it had not yet been taken as a French colony). In any case, he would have been too ill to take part. He arrived home in such a state that friends barely recognized him.

* * * *

Though he had bought the cooperation of the Siem Reap lord, Delaporte left behind bad feelings among other people he met. A French officer called Auguste Filoz would learn that first hand. Tasked with making more mouldings, he arrived at Angkor as Delaporte's group was leaving. He settled in at Angkor Wat, where he soon sensed hostility from the monks. They hovered around him, watching closely, snatching away shards of sculpture from him. Filoz decided to go see their abbot.

Speaking with agitation, the senior monk delivered a round condemnation of Delaporte. He had 'taken away idols and plundered the country.' And he did not even come to see me, the man complained. Filoz was told he would do well to leave quickly himself. But he stayed where he was, trying to calm the abbot's anger by pledging that he would not take anything, but would only make mouldings. He courted support by, right then and there, making a gift of his own boots. By Filoz's later account the old monk's mood changed, and he tried them on with delight. Filoz, it seems, chose to conclude that the real source of the abbot's ire was the insult of being ignored.

Delaporte gave his readers an imagined aerial view of Angkor Wat. Image from *Voyage au Cambodge.*

Filoz would commit his own offenses against local sensibilities, including killing two scavenging dogs with his revolver inside Angkor Wat. Blood was not supposed to be spilled within the temple walls. Yet, by his account, the monks forgave him (dogs were not spiritually protected creatures) and came to accept his presence and work.

In a book published in 1876, he described winning them over in part by explaining that Delaporte had taken Cambodian art for display in 'splendid palaces' in France. ' "Are there other monuments as beautiful as ours?" one of the monks asks me. I answer him sincerely that I do not know of any. "That is because," he continues, "our monuments are the work not of men, but of angels!" '

3: LA MISSION CIVILISATRICE

Angkor takes centre stage in France's official rationale for its colonisation of Cambodia, a need to 'civilize' the kingdom, bring it into the modern era – and glorify its past.

Economic exploitation, geopolitical gamesmanship with the British, adventurism, theories of racial supremacy, religious proselytization – all of these figured in France's gradual assumption of colonial control over Cambodia, starting with a document that Norodom, then crown prince, signed in 1863 making the kingdom a protectorate. But the official reason came to be known as *la Mission Civilisatrice*, the civilizing – mission.

Early French visitors, Henri Mouhot among them, were quick to lament what they saw as the 'decadence' of nineteenth-century Cambodia. In their view, the kingdom was beset with immorality, corruption, and lethargy. We will fix Cambodia, the colonisers told themselves. We will take it under our wing and civilize it, raising it back up to a place of pride and admiration in the world. Looking to the future, they saw themselves establishing modern institutions such as railroads, banks, and post offices. But they also felt the job required looking to the past. They would need to salvage the Khmer glory of centuries gone and make the current king its deserving heir.

That would mean, among other things, giving that king a proper palace. Tourists who pass through the gates of the royal palace in Phnom Penh today can be forgiven for thinking they're stepping into an historical relic. The spires, the orange-tiled roofs, the throne room brightened with gilding and stylized parasols evoke times in the distant past. In fact, the palace was built starting in the 1860s through the financing, design, and direction of French *functionaires.* Composed largely of fireproof brick and cement, it replaced a smaller wooden and blaze-prone royal compound in the city of Oudong about thirty kilometres to the north, which had been the kingdom's capital for the previous two centuries. In 1866, King Norodom formally moved to the new palace; Phnom Penh became the

Construction of royal palace buildings in Phnom Penh was carried out under French supervision starting in the 1860s. (John Burgess)

Opposite page: The French painter Vincent Lorant-Heilbronn created this idealized watercolour of King Sisowath viewing a classical dance performance at Angkor Wat in 1909, with colonial officers at his side. (National Archives of Cambodia)

capital. Construction of grand new buildings in the palace compound would continue into the 1920s.

The palace was meant to cause pride in the hearts of Cambodians, which would filter upward as reverence for the king and his colonial overlords. The paradox was that with each French-inspired rise in pomp and fittings, the king experienced a decline in actual power, another nudge in the direction of figurehead status.

* * * * *

The Angkor side of the civilizing mission would entail archaeological study, protection of the monuments, and their display to the world. But for the first four decades of French rule, a basic obstacle stood in the way: Angkor wasn't in Cambodia. It was in Siam. Getting access was costly, as Delaporte had found, and as the years progressed the price only rose. Lucien Fournereau, a Delaporte subordinate who visited in 1887 to make more mouldings, complained of the 'formidable guard dog of the Khmer ruins,' that is, Siam's lord in Siem Reap. 'His avidity, excited by the largesse of rich visitors, knows no bounds,' Fournereau complained in a report to the French government. Despite the inconvenience, the French kept up with Angkor projects intended to lay a moral, if not a legal claim to Angkor, all the time contrasting their work with Siam's generally passive attitude toward the old capital. They cleared temples, they sent more research missions. They sketched and photographed. They commissioned a full archaeological survey of Khmer monuments, regardless of which country they lay in. *Inventaire descriptif des monuments du Cambodge* became a massive work penned over the course of many years by a French military officer turned archaeologist called Étienne Lunet de Lajonquière.

Late in the century, history began to churn in ways that would deliver up Angkor: France employed the force of

Colonial soldiers march in this mural from Siem Reap's Wat Bo. (John Burgess)

arms that Siam had feared for decades. On 13 July 1893, a pair of French gunboats moved up the Chao Phraya River toward Bangkok and exchanged fire with a waterside battery and boats, killing about thirty Siamese soldiers. The warships proceeded further upriver and anchored near the royal palace, daring the Siamese to strike back. They did not. As military operations go, the gunboat attack was small, but it served as a deadly demonstration of France's capabilities and the weakness of Siam's defences. The stage was set for years of one-sided negotiations and Siamese surrender of vast tracts of land.

The process climaxed in 1907, when Siam gave up the three western Cambodian provinces it had absorbed in the 1790s, as well as parts of what now constitutes Laos. Angkor reverted to Cambodian hands –

Major build-ups of soil and vegetation show in this photo of Angkor Wat taken by Émile Gsell in 1866 or 1873. Work teams mobilized by the French cleared away these coverings roughly four decades later. Photo copyright Archives du Ministère de l'Europe et des Affaires étrangères – La Courneuve.

though only in a sense, because Cambodia was now not its own master. Still, this was cause for huge celebration among the kingdom's people, both high and humble. They had long dreamed of recovering the provinces, but knew they lacked the military might. Here was an undeniable benefit of rule by the French, who had their own reason to celebrate, an expansion of their country's overseas empire.

Siam's man in Siem Reap bowed out. His stone citadel became barracks for colonial militiamen. Angkor was placed under the control of the *École française d'Extrême-Orient (EFEO)*, a research institute founded a decade earlier in Saigon. A senior EFEO official called Jean Commaille, who in his spare time would paint watercolors of the temples, was named the first conservator and took up residence in a large Cambodian-style house near Angkor Wat. With teams of Cambodian laborers and artisans, he began turning the old capital into an enormous outdoor museum.

His initial focus was Angkor Wat. Despite centuries of merit-building effort by resident monks, grass and bushes were flourishing on the grounds and in the cracks of temple stones. Moving through darkened corridors could mean walking on carpets of bat dung. Thigh-deep soil had built up in the stone-paved courtyards of the temple's second and third tiers.

Commaille's men use a primitive crane to repair Angkor Wat's processional avenue, as depicted in the guidebook that Commaille published in 1912.

So clearing was the first big job. Soil was laboriously shoveled from those courtyards and thrown down to lower levels. Vegetation was cut. Two courageous men climbed each of the five towers to pluck out plants that had taken root high up. Down below, modern steam power was applied: a small locomotive known as a Decauville hauled away vegetation and other debris on temporarily laid tracks. By the time the job neared its end, things were looking different: 'This great temple might have been believed to be in a good-enough condition,' the scholar Louis Finot later wrote. 'But as soon as it was denuded, it revealed itself to be full of deformities and wounds.'

Commaille's teams salved some of those wounds. On the western processional avenue, for example, they recovered half-buried *naga* serpents – their long bodies again formed the avenue's railings – and put them back in place. Where stones, such as paving slabs, were missing, they sometimes substituted concrete ones. They dug out and restored the two large ponds that lay on either side of the avenue.

The goal was not only to clear and repair but to *re-Hinduize*. The French believed that the temple's conversion into a Buddhist edifice in more recent centuries had made it somehow inauthentic – its altered form distorted history. So, many of the Buddha images that Cambodians had set up with reverence in chambers and corridors were removed. Perhaps the most radical step in this turning back of the clock came in June 1909, when Commaille's men broke into the sealed chamber at the third-tier base of the central tower. The chamber had originally been almost open-air, with large doorways facing the four cardinal directions, and had apparently housed a large statue of Vishnu, to whom the temple was originally dedicated. Buddhist retrofitters had walled off the doorways, perhaps as

Wooden monastery buildings and pilgrim huts on the west side of Angkor Wat were removed by the French after 1907. This postcard image by Hanoi photographer Pierre Dieulefis shows some of the larger structures before their dismantlement. (John Burgess collection)

an architectural statement of the new faith's supremacy. Each sealed doorway became a niche for a Buddha image. But had Vishnu's image been left inside? Commaille wanted to find out.

First his men removed a Buddha that graced the chamber's south walled-up doorway. Then they breached the wall itself, which turned out to be of substantial construction including iron bars. Inside – disappointment. No Vishnu image, no inscriptions. Instead a few Buddha image fragments, bats, and a deep hole clogged with dung. Workers used torches to drive out squealing winged residents from one more place in the temple.[1]

Down below, on the western part of the temple grounds, the French set about removing structures that local people had erected over the years as part of the Buddhist monastery. Some were simple pilgrim shelters of straw and bamboo. Others were large, elaborate wooden buildings with eaves and tile roofs that appear to have sheltered images and Buddhist texts. Large or small, they came down on grounds that they blocked the view and were not part of the ancient Khmers' design. Monks and pilgrims regrouped in what are today two clusters of monastery buildings south and northwest of the main temple. Though they were inside the temple's walls, they stood off to the side and were largely hidden by trees.

There was also the question of the people who inhabited the many villages of Angkor – the farmers, sap tappers, fishers, and market vendors. Conflicts between them and Angkor's new overlords were inevitable. A French conservator who wanted to return water to a dry moat bed, for instance, would naturally find himself at odds with a farmer who had been planting vegetables in it. There were also issues, the French felt, of order and hygiene. The releasing of water buffalo to graze at the temples, a common practice (Father Bouillevaux had seen it

Femmes Cambodgiennes en pèlerinage dans le sanctuaire

Angkor Wat was continuing to draw large numbers of pilgrims when the French took formal control in 1907. This postcard image by Pierre Dieulefis shows women who made the holy journey in this period. (John Burgess)

1 Many of today's archaeologists believe that the image Commaille sought was there for him to see in Angkor Wat's western entrance complex – Ta Reach, literally "Royal Ancestor," honored today as the temple's prime guardian deity. By this theory, the image was moved there from the central tower at some point after the temple was converted into a Buddhist sanctuary.

Local men drove oxcarts on Angkor Wat's main avenue around the turn of the century, in this postcard by Hanoi photographer Pierre Dieulefis. (John Burgess collection)

44

Fournereau's team encountered
this Cambodian family and ox carts
along the processional avenue of
Angkor Wat. (*Les Ruines d'Angkor*)

at Angkor Wat in 1850), meant unsightly
dung on walkways. Among themselves,
the French debated the proper level of
regulation. Would foreign visitors be put
off by local life proceeding in their midst,
or would they go away with a better grasp
of Cambodian culture? Questions of the
welfare of local people could get lost in
these discussions. They were finding that
through no fault of their own they had
become part of something larger than
themselves.

This debate would continue for
decades, with policy shifting as one French
official was replaced by another. Many of
Angkor's people stayed put, but many were cruelly uprooted.
Families living inside Angkor Wat, for instance. Twenty were
said to have had houses on the inner banks of the southern
moat's western segment. They were told to leave. People had
cultivated a few rice fields inside Angkor Wat. That was now
forbidden. Smaller monasteries in Angkor Thom were closed,
or gradually slipped into a deserted state.[2] Cambodians seem
to have variously obeyed the edicts and passively resisted. One
can imagine that enforcement was no easy task – there was only
a handful of Frenchmen on the scene, and their Cambodian
subordinates may have had little enthusiasm for the task, or
been willing to take gifts to look the other way.

Commaille also put in place the basic physical infrastructure
of an early twentieth-century public attraction. Construction
crews laid out a road from the shores of the Tonle Sap, where
steamboats arrived, to Siem Reap, and from there on north
to Angkor. Inside Angkor Thom, they built roads to replace
simple tracks through the forest, sometimes repurposing
causeways and levies left by the ancients. The roads were
simple and unpaved, but passable, at least in the dry season.
And right by the causeway that was the main entrance of
Angkor Wat, a guesthouse with basic western comforts opened
in 1909. For anyone who might take a room there, Commaille
penned a book called *Guide aux Ruines d'Angkor*.

Step by step, the 'Angkor Archaeological Park' would
become in effect a mini-state within Siem Reap province. It
acquired specific borders, a complex set of laws and regulations,
its own administrative, maintenance, and guard staff, a
citizenry, and its own budget and revenue streams. In addition
to official funds from the colonial administration, money

2 These details are from the
writing of the anthropologist
Keiko Miura, who found in
interviews between 1999 and
2003 that memories of the
French relocation, passed
from generation to generation,
remained very much alive
among Angkor's residents.

sources that the park tapped included the royal treasury in Phnom Penh (by some accounts close to half of the park's total came from here) and donations by private Cambodians, wealthy and otherwise. In France, interested people helped by joining *La Société d'Angkor*. French people in Indochina joined in as a subcommittee of that group. Foreigners who visited were charged to enter. And any donations that they felt inspired to make were gladly accepted.

But even with these many streams of revenue, the park seems never to have achieved financial comfort. Funds available would be chronically mismatched with the ambition of plans. During a ten-day visit in 1913, the American archaeologist and art historian Langdon Warner found that Commaille was still the only Frenchman on site. Commaille felt he needed a European assistant, but could not get funding even for a single individual. Warner's descriptions give further evidence of money problems. 'Thousands of sculptures, in more or less fragmentary condition, but still invaluable to the student of art…are piled in heaps over which the visitor must scramble in his rounds, scraping, chipping, and destroying the delicate details of statues and ornament as he does so.'

Late nineteenth century Angkor had many villages, like this one, Lahal, located just north of Ta Prohm temple, depicted in an 1890 book by Lucien Fournereau and Jacques Porcher, *Ruines d'Angkor*.

* * * * *

Commaille had barely begun his work when in 1908 Indochina Governor General Antony Klobukowski put his weight behind an idea: a grand ceremony at Angkor. It would mark *pchum ben*, the festival in which Cambodians honor their ancestors, but would also be a political celebration of the western provinces' reversion. A new king, brother of Norodom, was on the throne in Phnom Penh. 'His Majesty King Sisowath has welcomed this idea with joy,' Klobukowski reported to EFEO. The royal court generally went along with French recommendations, but in this case the king was no doubt as excited as the French were concerning the return of Angkor. 'The Angkor festivals will be as close as possible to those of the past,' Klobukowski wrote. 'They will bring to light all that Cambodian civilisation has preserved in ancient traditions and rites.' In fact, no one really knew what form the ancient rites had taken.

46. - Ruines d'ANGKOR-VAT (Cambodge)
Procession de plus de 90 Éléphants et 5.000 figurants
en l'honneur de M. le Maréchal Joffre

Elephants process down Angkor
Wat's main avenue in 1921 in this
postcard image of festivities staged
for Marshal Joseph Joffre. Postcard
image courtesy of Joel Montague.

It was a scramble (among other tasks, one hundred
labourers worked for twelve days to clear vegetation in Angkor
Thom), but in September 1909 things were ready.

King Sisowath arrived on the 25th of the month and took up
residence in a temporary bamboo palace that had been erected
outside Angkor Wat for him and his entourage. On the 26th,
in a solemn rite conducted inside the temple by torchlight, the
monarch offered gifts and foods to the spirits. Royal dancers
performed. The next day the governor general and various
senior French officials toured the temple and inspected the
restoration work. As the ceremonies progressed, the religious
and political, the past and present, intermingled repeatedly.
A rite honoured the spirits of the ancient kings of Angkor;
Cambodian officials from the recovered provinces swore oaths
of allegiance. A new school for the study of Pali, the language
of Buddhism, was inaugurated within the temple's walls. The
King entertained the French at a dinner, and they hosted him
at one of their own.

Who can say how true to life it is, but a watercolor by
the French painter (and silent-film maker) Vincent Lorant-
Heilbronn records a tableau of colonial order and contentment
(see p.38). The enthroned king watches approvingly as a corps
of Khmer dancers performs in the second tier of a somewhat
romanticized Angkor Wat, sun-bathed towers looming high
above. Two Frenchmen in formal whites stand in dignified
support at his side. Monks and a woman and child, perhaps
meant to represent the Cambodian people as a whole, take in
the spectacle as well. The symbolic message was clear: today's
king was the latest in a line stretching back to the ancient glories,
his position confirmed in the present day by Cambodia's new
friends from afar.

26. - Ruines d'ANGKOR-VAT (Cambodge). - Ruines de la Bibliothèque
Procession de 90 éléphants et de 5.000 figurants (Prince, Princesses, Danseuses,
Musiciens, etc.) en l'honneur de M. le Maréchal Joffre

Colonial officials wearing the white dress uniforms of the time watch the Joffre festivities from a structure at Angkor Wat known as a library. Postcard image courtesy of Joel Montague.

King Sisowath made frequent pilgrimages to Angkor in subsequent years. A Cambodian translation of the *Tripitaka*, the 'Triple Basket' of Buddhist wisdom, had been deposited at the monastery in Angkor Wat, creating a formal spiritual connection with the palace in Phnom Penh. In 1921, the king was present for grand ceremonies staged at Angkor Wat for the visiting Marshal Joseph Joffre, known at home as the Victor of the Marne for his role in that pivotal battle of World War I.

* * * * *

When the French looked for visual icons for the new Cambodian kingdom and nation, they often settled on Angkor. As the centrepiece of the protectorate's flag they placed a stylized silhouette of Angkor Wat. Angkor temples graced postage stamps and banknotes. When French city planners renovated Wat Phnom, the hilltop Buddhist temple that is the spiritual core of the capital, they gave it a long staircase with giant Angkor-style heads of mythical *naga* serpents at the bottom, though the temple is of a much later period and style.

Just as the monuments came under French tutelage, so did certain cultural institutions. Classical dance at the palace in Phnom Penh was one. Many of the French *savants* believed it was the direct descendant of dance depicted in stone at Angkor. Body positions and hand gestures of the ancient *apsara*, after all, seemed to match those of modern dancers. It was a politically convenient connection in support of the French narrative that the king in Phnom Penh was the successor to the Angkor monarchs.

Colonial Curator of the Khmer Heritage

George Groslier. Photo courtesy of Groslier Family Archive and DatAsia Press.

Artist, author, ethnographer, and all-around Khmerophile, George Groslier had a special connection to Cambodia from the moment he was born in 1887 – his was the first French birth recorded at Phnom Penh city hall.

As a young man, he was as pessimistic as any of his compatriots concerning Cambodia's decline. But later in life he made a personal mission of trying to preserve a culture that was under threat from the outside world. 'They're dying! The charming traditions and poetry of yesteryear are dying!' he wrote, in his often impassioned style. 'Our steamships and automobiles generate a smoke in which champa flowers wither.'

His 1913 book *Danseuses Cambodgiennes, Anciennes et Modernes* revealed love and technical understanding of classical dance (it is filled with his own sketches of dancers). After colonial administrators diagnosed the social illness of 'decadence' in the palace dance troupe, Groslier actually ran the school for a time.

When French authorities looked to create a national museum, they turned to Groslier, both to assemble a collection and design the building. Opened in 1920, it combined Khmer architectural motifs in the roofs with western-style display halls below. Today it is the National Museum of Cambodia.

Colonial rule exposed Cambodia's economy to foreign competition. As imports began replacing traditional goods, Groslier helped create workshops where Cambodian artisans sustained old skills and crafted new products for sale to foreigners and Cambodians alike. He established a school of arts near the palace, with Cambodian instructors. Concerned that artefacts were being lost to the illicit antiquities trade, he set up programs that encouraged farmers to turn over objects unearthed in the fields for study and preservation.

In 1946, the street that passes in front of the museum was named rue Groslier in his honour. After independence, it became Preah Ang Eng Street as many French names were dropped for reasons of national pride. Now there is talk of putting his back.

George Groslier's celebration of Khmer heritage opened in April 1920 as the Albert Sarraut Museum, named in honour of a former governor general of Indochina. Photo courtesy of Groslier Family Archive and DatAsia Press.

* * * *

It would become one of the paradoxes of colonial rule that not a few French officials saw the kingdom's past decline as a parable for their own country, proof of the dangers that face a great nation when discipline and unity erode. As socialist political movements gained sway back home, conservatives worried that France's literature and art were being corrupted; the working class was gaining too much power. Paul Doumer, who served as Indochina governor general from 1897 to 1902 and as president of the republic from 1931 to 1932, went as far as to suggest that Cambodia's history should be taught in the classrooms of France as part of efforts to do 'everything possible in our power to prevent [France]…from slithering down the slope of decadence, which ends only in ruin.' He pressed, unsuccessfully as it turned out, for young French people to be brought to Cambodia to witness the menace first hand.

It would be fascinating to get inside the heads of French officials like Doumer to plumb what they truly thought of Angkor's architecture and sculpture. Certainly the writing of Europeans who had just got their first look often betrays a certain cultural anxiety.

In June 1866, Mekong commission member Francis Garnier was among a group that climbed Phnom Krom, the rocky hill near the great lake. At the top he came face to face with a tenth-century temple. 'This architecture, scholarly and original in its conception, severe in its general forms, elegant in its details, moved me with admiration,' Garnier later wrote. 'My thoughts went back to the great age which had produced a relatively perfect art, and at that moment I would hardly have hesitated to add a fourth age, the Khmer Age, to the three centuries of Pericles, Caesar Augustus, and Louis XIV.' But Garnier quickly decided that, on balance, the ancient Khmers did not really measure up. 'The sight of a group of mutilated statues lying not far from the main monument calmed down my first enthusiasm. Some of the heads there were quite interesting, [but] they were far from the masterpieces of the Greek chisel.'

Many of the French in Cambodia seem to have made similar rationalizations to maintain a sense of cultural superiority. There is a hint of that in an editing change in the book written by Auguste Filoz, the officer who came to Angkor in 1873 as the Delaporte party was leaving. The book's original 1876 edition has him telling a monk that he knows of

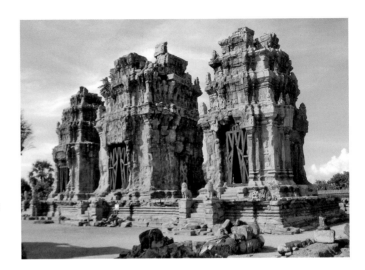

Phnom Krom temple, which Mekong Commission members climbed in 1866, stands atop a hill of the same name south of Angkor, overlooking the Tonle Sap. (John Burgess)

no monument as beautiful as Cambodia's. In an 1889 re-issue of the book, Filoz states that 'there are few' as beautiful.

Other French made no pretence of admiration. One was the poet, playwright, and diplomat Paul Claudel. En route to a posting as ambassador to Japan, he stopped over in Angkor in 1921. Diary entries from his visit record what can only be called outright horror: everywhere he turned, he sensed an affront to the Roman Catholic convictions for which his writing was known at home. Angkor Wat, he suggested, was 'the Devil's temple.' Most everything seemed to him to have disturbing supernatural overtones. The swarms of bats that flapped through the corridors, spreading foul odour, colliding with religious images, seemed to be trying without success to destroy those images. The *apsara* were dancing some kind of sinister can-can. Claudel spent an afternoon alone 'at the top of this cursed temple, not having yet understood the strange feeling of oppression and disgust.' The sights and sounds there – far-off virgin forest, the peal of thunder, the cries of monkeys – were all things that would enchant many other visitors, but him they put on edge. There were also 'the yellow priests wandering and chanting, one of them behind me with a big knife.'

* * * * *

Still, there was no denying that Angkor was extraordinary by any standard. This fact would be used over the years to sell the *mission civilisatrice* back in France and to the world. But the task was not always easy, even in France, as Delaporte himself discovered on returning home from his 1873 mission.

He was dismayed to find that his trove of sculpture, brought to Paris at such cost and sacrifice, prompted indifference in French officialdom. For weeks, crates containing the artwork waited stacked in a courtyard of the Louvre. Delaporte of course wanted it displayed in the nation's premier museum. But the best he could get was a chateau-turned-exhibit hall in Compiègne, 60 kilometres northeast of Paris. Not about to give up, he took the collection there, then set about to win it the fame he was convinced it deserved. Artists, geographers, and many members of the public came to see the artwork in Compiègne. So did journalists, who sometimes wrote with emotion about the man who had fathered the exhibit. 'There is great honour for France and for the intrepid officer in this work,' declared one commentator, 'who, we shall add, has managed despite meager means to extract from the destructive forests these unknown treasures and to reveal them to the world of scientists and artists.'

It took four years, but in 1878, the exhibition moved to Paris, to be part of the world's fair known as the *Exposition Universelle*. It remained in the capital after the fair's closure and became a permanent part of the collection of the city's newly founded Musée de Trocadéro.

Delaporte was proud of what he'd achieved in the 1873 trip, but he wanted more. He went back to Cambodia in 1881. This visit produced even higher-quality mouldings, the work of an Italian artisan he'd brought along for the purpose, Joseph Ghilardi. Delaporte came home the following year with another life-threatening illness. Again he survived, but his days in the field were over. He became director of the Trocadéro's Indochina collection and home-office planner and overseer of subsequent missions to Angkor. Delaporte's minutely specific instructions, complete with colour sketches, to Lucien Fournereau on what to look for during his 1887 visit, what to cast, have happily survived. Moulding that Delaporte was ordering up was almost an industrial-scale operation. At the upper level of Angkor Wat, Fournereau's team constructed bamboo and wooden plank scaffolding in front of a great pediment whose bas relief depicted the triumph of the Hindu hero Rama over the Rakshasa demons. The resulting 214 casts made possible the recreation in France of a structure measuring more than eight by eleven metres.

Thanks in part to Delaporte's efforts, France's enthusiasm for Khmer heritage began to grow. Over the years, many more expos were staged, treatises penned, lectures delivered, magazine articles perused in rail station waiting rooms.

The full-scale reproduction of Angkor Wat's upper tiers at the 1931 expo in Paris dazzles in the rays of spotlights. (Bibliothèque nationale de France)

The sculptor Auguste Rodin took an interest in Khmer dancing after witnessing a performance by a troupe that accompanied King Sisowath to France in 1906. Angkor postcards, penholders, and trinket bowls proliferated in the bric-a-brac of turn-of-the-century French households.

Delaporte died in 1925, but French interest in Angkor continued to grow. In 1931, France's Cambodia fixation reached a new height, literally, with the inauguration of a full-scale replica of Angkor Wat's upper tier at the *Exposition Coloniale* in Paris.

Standing fifty-five metres tall and seventy square, it formed the centrepiece of a fair that drew close to thirty million people. Of course the temple was not built using the ancients' methods or materials. It consisted of an enormous wooden skeleton faced with plaster panels that were mass-cast from moulds brought home starting with the mission of 1873. In addition, lay-out was reinterpreted to make space for displays of artefacts on the upper level and underneath the structure itself. Photographs, viewed today, reveal that it didn't quite catch the distinctive look of the real thing. Yet it was close enough to offer a haunting experience for the countless people who climbed its alpine-steep stairways, watched over by guardian lions and serpents.

Many people in France took great pride that Cambodia was French, but there were others who bemoaned the hypocrisy of the often harsh colonial rule in the kingdom that had produced the wonders. 'Here we reconstitute the marvelous staircase of Angkor and we twirl the sacred dancers,' wrote the politician and later-to-be socialist prime minister Léon Blum. 'But in Indochina we shoot, we deport, we imprison.'

With the expo's closure, the giant model was dismantled, with many of its plaster panels sold at auction. Dispersed around the country, they continued the job of proselytizing the bygone civilisation and France's role in reviving it. Casts continue to turn up today, pulled from musty storage spaces where they had been forgotten. Sometimes they are restored and treated as works of art in their own right. A choice few became part of a 2013-2014 exhibit at the Musée Guimet in Paris called 'Angkor: Birth of a Myth – Louis Delaporte and Cambodia.'

As for genuine Khmer sculpture, the stone marvels that were perilously moved across the Tonle Sap and down Cambodian rivers, most were relocated from the Trocadéro to the Guimet, which is among the world's premier museums of Asian art. They continue to enchant untold numbers of visitors today.

* * * * *

Back in Cambodia, the idealized *mission civilisatrice* remained at the core of colonial rule, despite the illogic of its underlying premise. Cambodians were supposed to be proud of their nation and history, of living free of Siamese and Vietnamese control. Yet somehow they were also to be proud subjects of France. Colonial officials continued to promote Angkor as the supreme symbol of this love of country and its potential. At some of the temples, officials organized special patriotism camps to which young Cambodians were sent to apply their hands and muscles to stones in reconstruction projects, thereby absorbing, the French hoped in their patronizing way, some of the discipline and self-assurance of the ancients.

But through programs like this, the French were helping set loose a force that in the long run they would be unable to control. True nationalism, the notion of a Cambodia free of all foreign control, French included, had begun a tentative bloom in the early twentieth century. It evolved in differing, competing strains, variously royalist, religious, and revolutionary, but in all versions Angkor played a central symbolic role. As the scholar Penny Edwards put it, 'Was Angkor a royal symbol, embodying the greatness of past emperors and the potential of royal regeneration…Or was it a public symbol and sign of *national* potential, evidence of the great skills and labours of those common people, enslaved to royalty, who built it?'

The year 1936 saw the inaugural issue of a publication that is remembered today as the first voice of modern Cambodian nationalism. Its name: *Nagaravatta*, Angkor Wat.

The Sdok Kok Thom
inscription, three
hundred forty lines
long, is the most
important written
record left by the
Khmer Empire.
Photo courtesy of
M.L. Pattaratorn
Chirapravati.

4: THE SEARCH FOR LOST HISTORY

By deciphering inscription stones, excavating temples, and gazing down at ancient outlines from airplanes, the French begin to recover Angkor's forgotten history. But they get some important facts wrong.

Some of the early European visitors to Angkor noticed that the temples contained mysterious messages chiselled into stone. The place might be a door frame, a column, a wall, or a free-standing *stele*, placed in isolation in a chamber so as to emphasize the importance of the words it preserved. Often whole sections of these missives had eroded away, or vanished beneath covers of lichen. But enough remained in legible condition to create the potential for blowing off the fog that shrouded the history of Angkor. If only they could be read. Local people who showed the Europeans around were at a loss to say more than that these were the words of gods. Henri Mouhot had a different description: 'A sealed book, for want of an interpreter.'

Foreign visitors began making paper rubbings of the inscriptions to take away, both as souvenirs, it seems, and for serious examination. In this way, work got underway on a crucial aspect of the *mission civilisatrice*, the recovery of lost history.

Before long, some of the messages were being read, by experts in Indian language. These inscriptions were in Sanskrit. Though no longer spoken, Sanskrit remained alive in India as the language of Hindu theology, rather like Latin's role in the Roman Catholic Church. Sanskrit was known among a corps of priests and temple scribes in India and scholars in Europe. But other of the Angkor inscriptions, though written in an Indian-style script, made no sense.

The cracking of the code had to await the arrival of a remarkable Frenchman called Étienne Aymonier. He stepped off a ship in Saigon in 1869, seemingly just another young military officer pursuing career advancement in one of his country's overseas possessions. But in subsequent years, he

Khmer history was preserved in sparse and enigmatic form in stone inscriptions, such as this one at a temple in the Koh Ker complex, which was briefly the Khmer capital in the tenth century. (John Burgess)

proved himself a genius at languages. He learned to speak, read, and write Cambodian and the separate language of the country's Cham minority. He composed dictionaries and taught Khmer to other Frenchmen.

After a decade in Indochina, he was appointed representative in Phnom Penh, the top French official in the kingdom. During his duty hours, he dealt with King Norodom and with petitioners seeking French help on various complaints; in his off hours, he puzzled over inscriptions found at the temples. He encountered the same obstacles that everyone had – some passages were a cipher. But one day in March 1879, he achieved a breakthrough as he pored over one of those texts. He had been trying to figure out a word that phonetically seemed to spell out as *kamraten*. Suddenly it came to him that he was looking at a sort of linguistic ancestor, a word that, altered by centuries of subsequent utterings, had emerged in the Cambodian language he spoke as *gamaten*, which meant something like 'high lord.' This epiphany allowed him to begin sweeping centuries of mystery away. The ancient Khmers, he realized, had adapted the Sanskrit writing system to phonetically depict their own entirely different everyday language. Using his knowledge of modern Cambodian, Aymonier was able to carry out a backwards reconstruction of what is now called Old Khmer. Many words were still in use, often with consonants and vowels that had morphed into different but still recognizable pronunciations (like with Middle English's evolution toward modern English). Other words had died out but could be guessed in meaning based on context. Before long, Aymonier was producing the first tentative read-

A Frenchman and Indochinese man make a copy of an inscription at the Khmer temple Wat Phou in present-day southern Laos, as depicted in *Le Tour du Monde*. ©Archimages @ AngkorDatabase

outs of passages that for years had held out as Mouhot's 'sealed book.'

In addition to his own study of inscriptions, Aymonier became a sort of leg man for scholars back home, going to temples to make rubbings for their examination. In 1881, he arrived back in France for an extended visit, bearing a gift to academia of fifty-four rubbings that he'd made. During his stay, he received an offer: would he like to devote full time to collecting inscriptions? He answered yes. In 1882, after receiving training in how to make *estampages* ('stampings'), a higher-quality kind of reproduction, he returned to Cambodia. There he was assigned a team of assistants. He spent the next three years traveling by foot, cart, boat, and elephant around not only Cambodia but areas of Thailand, Laos, and Vietnam that had once been part of the Khmer Empire. He visited countless ancient temples and structures, often led there by local people. He made diagrams and took notes about architecture and culture, but the core purpose of his mission was the collecting of the ancient messages. Each time his team encountered one, it made a stamping, sometimes multiple copies. It was Aymonier's habit to immediately copy readable sections into his notebooks, then study them at his leisure as his party moved on to the next place.

Early in 1883, he arrived at Sdok Kok Thom, a comparatively small eleventh-century temple in what is now the eastern Thai province of Sakaew. We don't know if local people had told him what a treasure awaited him there, or had left him to get the surprise of his life. But at the largely overgrown temple was a stele standing about a metre and a half tall and covered in text in the two languages, Sanskrit and Old Khmer, three hundred forty lines in all. The stone was miraculously in excellent condition; almost every word was legible. There was an odd pattern, however: toward the end of the text the letters became smaller and smaller. Either the engraver had not planned out the lines well, or had been given extra material to include at the last minute. Whatever the explanation, the Sdok Kok Thom stele was a priceless trove of information. It would become known as the most important written record left behind by the civilisation that built Angkor, confirming some theories, discrediting others, and opening the door to entirely new ones.

In February, Aymonier's group arrived in Khorat, a town in northeastern Thailand, and there a dog put at risk the future of Khmer epigraphy, as the study of inscriptions is known. In a letter preserved in the archives of the *Société Asiatique* in Paris,

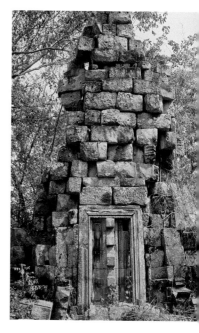

Sdok Kok Thom temple, where the most important Khmer inscription was found, was dedicated to the god Shiva. This is its central tower, in ruined condition in 1979. (John Burgess)

Aymonier recounted that he'd suffered a bite. 'So if I happen to get rabies [*la rage*], (the gossips and dishonourable rumour spreaders will say that I always had a predisposition towards it), you can say: it is the fault of the black dog of Ban Deng district of Pantaisong, province of Korat... It goes without saying that a few minutes later the animal was lying with a cartridge of lead in its stomach. As for me, I was washing the wound in carbolic water for lack of any carbolic acid handy. I was a good distance away from my pharmacy. I would have preferred a scorpion. At least with them you know what you're dealing with.'[1]

The letter, to his close collaborator Abel Bergaigne, a scholar of Sanskrit in France, was mostly about the Sdok Kok Thom inscription. Its 'content is not exactly what I thought it would be,' Aymonier wrote in his precise hand. 'Though it is not dated, it is from the reign of Udayadityavarman, whose date of succession to the throne it gives as 971 *saka* [a year from the Hindu calendar] and the date of the advent of his predecessor, Suryavarman, 965 *saka*. This inscription is very important. I am able to read it well enough to give right away a rough translation whose accuracy I can guarantee.'

The inscription relates the history of a Brahmin family that presided at the temple and its surrounding estate. Beginning around the year 800 CE, the narrative covers two and a half centuries. Each generation's patriarch is recorded as having served in the capital as a chaplain to the king of the time, carrying out important religious rituals. Sections in the two languages recount many of the same events, but are not word-for-word translations of each other. The Sanskrit is in verse, other-worldly, and delves heavily into religion; the Old Khmer part is all business, conveying practical information in a matter-of-fact tone.

The inscription's magic is that, by telling the family's story, it tells the story of the empire at large, because various members of the priestly line are recounted as having taken part in key imperial events in those two and a half centuries. It also gives glimpses of religious practice, royal gift-giving, the barter purchase of land, war that reduced settlements to ruins, and the assigning of villages to support the temple. It includes a paean to Sdok Kok Thom itself:

Who so views this ideal abode, foremost on earth,
Or merely hears it spoken of,
His mind is at rest, his soul is sanctified.

---

1   Thankfully, Aymonier did not get rabies. He lived until 1929.

Based on his early work with Old Khmer inscriptions when he was representative in Phnom Penh, Aymonier had already written a number of journal articles taking a first crack at the empire's history, notably the reign order of kings whose names were showing up on inscriptions. In his letter from Korat, Aymonier asked Bergaigne to look at the Sanskrit parts of the text and send him back an initial translation. Aymonier was at the time closing in on the solution to one of the key riddles facing inscription readers at that point – what to make of two lists of kings that had been pieced together from scattered stones? Was there perhaps a system of co-kings reigning simultaneously? The Sdok Kok Thom inscription made it clear that there were no co-kings. Rather, each king had one name while on the throne, alluding to his real-world glory, and another after death, alluding to his honoured place in the afterworld. Jayavarman ('victory-protector'), founder of the empire, became Paramesvara ('supreme lord of Shiva') on his death. This conclusion was possible because the Sanskrit and Old Khmer sections of the inscription described essentially the same events and successions. What emerged was a royal genealogy covering two and a half centuries.

Aymonier's mission ended abruptly in 1885 in Vietnam, when one of the first uprisings by nationalists against colonial rule made it too dangerous for a Frenchman to move around rural areas. Later he retired to France, ailing, and spent the remaining years of his life researching and writing scholarly studies. It took him until 1901 to publish his final translation of the Sdok Kok Thom inscription, with extensive commentary.

But there was more to epigraphy than finding and translating the stones. Grasping their *meaning* could be another thing entirely. Their authors assume a full cultural literacy of the time, in ritual, theology, personalities, and historical events. The identity of characters in narratives, clear enough to readers in ancient times, must often be guessed at today. Place names mentioned in inscriptions had often fallen out of use, creating uncertainty about location. Then there is the question of factual accuracy. Kings were depicted as fonts of royal virtue – schooled in the sacred texts, filled with compassion for their subjects, and courageous in battle, emerging victorious with sword stained red with the enemy's blood. While these traits may not reflect the reality of particular kings, they do tell us what society expected of them. At the other end of the factual continuum is land ownership, a common subject in Khmer inscriptions. Here we can sense painstaking accuracy in descriptions of precise boundaries of an estate's land, for instance, or the exact number of golden bowls and priests' garments that were paid for it in a barter transaction (Angkor had no currency).

* * * * *

Solving the puzzle of Angkor's lost history also involved integrating what had been read in inscriptions with evidence gathered through field archaeology. Surveys of temples and earthworks, for instance, could provide an understanding of the sequence of construction. If a dig revealed that Structure A cut through Structure B, then A was likely built after B. This type of analysis also revealed that in some temples, such as the Bayon, the Khmers could be dissatisfied with what they first created and go back in to modify. Passages at the Bayon that are too narrow to pass through, and walls that appear where logically they shouldn't, give evidence of alterations made after the initial dedication.

Art and its evolving styles served as another form of historical evidence. The temples' basic architectural form pointed to inspiration from southern India, implying close contact with that region. Statues and bas-reliefs of Hindu deities, meanwhile, gave proof of that religion's dominance, at least in court life. Plus, in some of the temples, Khmer sculptors began in the twelfth century to depict not just the supernatural but the real. Angkor Wat's bas-reliefs show a king conducting court, with priests, ladies, fan bearers, and various functionaries on hand. A military parade conveys the empire's great armed power in the form of war elephants, cavalry, and ranks of foot soldiers. In the Bayon and Banteay Chhmar temples, the artists went a step further, giving us a view of ordinary folk in daily life. Men gather around a pair of fighting boars, waiting for a match to begin; a woman gives birth with midwives assisting; kitchen helpers bend down to blow on

War and peace are depicted in these twelfth-century bas reliefs at the Bayon. On the left are Cham soldiers, foes of the Khmer Empire. On the right, Khmer men gather around a cock fight. Photos by Wim Swaan. Digital image courtesy of the Getty's Open Content Program.

the coals of braziers; thieves steal fruit from a dozing market vendor. There is depiction of real war, not just military pomp, as boats crammed with fighters clash in a naval battle, the dead falling overboard to be devoured by crocodiles. Military families carrying basic belongings trudge with their soldier husbands and fathers through a forest on campaign.

Interpreting the bas-reliefs became a subset of Khmer history scholarship. The presence of Hindu priests (their beards identify them) near the king at Angkor Wat indicate that they played a major role in palace life. The many parasols floating over the king show that these were symbols of rank.

In 1927, Sappho Marchal, who as daughter of conservator Henri Marchal had grown up around the temples, published a fascinating book analysing the headdresses, ornaments, and garments of Angkor Wat's approximately 1,700 *devata*. Among many other findings, she offered a theory on the design of their garments – that many were a long strip of fabric with a hole through which one end was threaded. Other specialists studied the weaponry on display in the reliefs to understand battlefield tactics. Surprisingly, the artists gave us barely a glimpse of the work that consumed the lives and wealth of millions of people, construction. A scene at the Bayon of masons using chisel and hammer to work stone underfoot is a rare exception.

Another crucial source for history reconstruction was Chinese accounts, which survived the centuries in archives in China. Some describe visits that Chinese mariners made to the states that existed in the region before Angkor. But the most fascinating one dates to much later, the late twelve hundreds. A Chinese envoy called Zhou Daguan spent close to a year in Angkor and left a remarkably detailed account. It is almost like he was a modern travel writer, walking around markets, settlements, and temples with a notebook open. From him, we learn such details as that communal bathing was common at Angkor, with people entering the water naked in groups that could number in the thousands; that the king emerged from the palace in a procession of soldiers, musicians and banner-bearers, and sometimes court ladies who held lit candles even in daylight; that strict rules governed how many parasols officials of various ranks could have; that transgender prostitutes worked the markets; that one to three families shared a pond for bathing and other uses; that people sometimes rose in the middle of the night to cool off with baths.

Starting in 1920, the French began getting a flood of insight through a new technology – aerial photography. In

Sappho Marchal studied carved *devata* like these to draw conclusions on ancient fashions and hair styles. (John Burgess)

coordination with the EFEO, the French military sent biplanes aloft to take pictures of areas of ancient settlement. At the heavily overgrown Preah Khan-Kompong Svay, Delaporte and his team had spent days walking about trying to grasp lay-out and had only partly succeeded. Fly-overs brought back black-and-white images that made the size and proportions of the temple and its moat system eminently clear and identified promising spots for investigation on the ground. The flights were frequent enough that there occurred a fatality. Much mourned by the EFEO, the victim was a Lieutenant de Reversat-Marsac, who died in 1928 in an accident during a photographic mission over Vietnam.

Initial images were primitive, but slowly they improved. Technicians learned how to reduce fuzziness caused by vibration aboard these early aircraft. Introduction of stereoscopic cameras that shot two slightly different views of a scene helped discern variations on the ground. The French were also using the eye-in-the-sky to advance archaeology in the vacant desert terrain of Syria. There the long shadows of early morning and late afternoon could reveal the low outlines of ruins. Cambodia's cover of forest and rice fields made this task more difficult. But the EFEO's specialists learned that ancient structures could show themselves through such clues as variations in the appearance of vegetation. For instance, it was tell-tale hues that in 1931 brought to light an ancient network of canals around Angkor Borei, a site in southeastern Cambodia. By piecing together overlapping black-and-white images, archaeologists were able to diagram many miles of disused waterways, the old silt of their beds nurturing a slightly different grade of vegetation than the land along them.

* * * *

Through long debates, played out in journals, books, lecture halls, and homes in Siem Reap, the basic history of Angkor was recovered in fits and starts. The body of knowledge that eventually emerged was much thinner than what we have for, say, Rome or Imperial China, but it was a history nonetheless. In subsequent decades, some of the theories would be refined or discarded as reflecting old-school research methods or the Eurocentric thinking of the times. But by the 1930s scholars had settled on the following basic narrative.

The empire was founded around 800 CE with a Hindu rite atop Phnom Kulen, a range of mountains north of Angkor, by a king who would become known to historians as Jayavarman

II. He later set up a capital at a place he knew as Hariharalaya, present-day Roluos east of today's Siem Reap town. The fourth king of the line, Yasovarman, moved the capital to the present-day Angkor around 900 with construction of Phnom Bakheng. Around 925, a new king moved the capital again, to Koh Ker, about one hundred kilometres to the northeast. But Angkor regained its status as capital after just two reigns. Early in the 1000s, the empire was riven by an extended war that brought to the throne King Suryavarman I. Construction of Angkor Wat began around 1120 under the dynamic monarch Suryavarman II, the king in the temple's bas-reliefs. The empire by now had expanded greatly, taking in what is now central and northeast Thailand, southern Laos, and southern Vietnam.

The empire evolved a unique economic and political system. All land belonged in theory to the king, who assigned lands to trusted lords. The rural estate was the basic economic unit, sending rice, soldiers and labourers to the capital and typically supporting a temple of its own. In its early centuries, the elite practiced Hinduism, usually with the god Shiva as first among equals in the Hindu Trinity. Priests tended *linga* shafts symbolizing his power, pouring water or milk over them. Worship of the god Vishnu prevailed during other reigns, notably that of Suryavarman II. Buddhism was tolerated as a secondary faith. Slavery was common, but the Hindu caste system was not adopted.

The Khmers fought many wars with their neighbours. These included the Chams, who had founded a Hindu-influenced state in what is now central Vietnam, and, to the northeast, the Vietnamese, and to the northwest, the Siamese. At the same time, the empire had peaceful diplomatic and trade relations with China. There was religious travel to India, homeland of the royal faith, and to other Hindu-influenced states in what is now Indonesia.

The late twelfth century brought disaster. The Chams invaded and in 1177 captured Angkor. A new Khmer military leader rallied forces and drove the Chams out in a war that included major battles on land and on the great lake. With peace restored, he was crowned Jayavarman VII and embarked on an enormous building campaign. Among its creations was the walled city Angkor Thom, which enclosed and protected the old royal palace area and many temples from previous reigns. The Bayon and the other face-tower temples of its style went up in this period. Jayavarman changed the state religion to Mahayana Buddhism. Following his death early in

Getting It Wrong for Half a Century

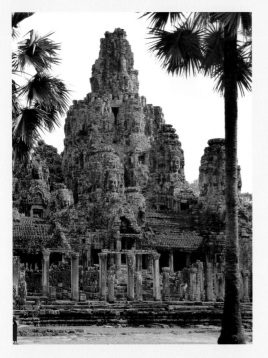

For decades, archaeologists believed that the Bayon was the 'central mountain' mentioned in the Sdok Kok Thom inscription. This led them to date it and other major temples of its style as having been built around 900 CE. (John Burgess)

The greatest minds of French archaeology could occasionally misfire. There is no better example than their initial answer to one of the core questions about Angkor, the timing and sequence of the temples' construction. The false conclusion was defended stubbornly for close to fifty years before error was admitted.

The story starts with the early read-outs of the Sdok Kok Thom inscription. It states that the Khmer capital was moved from Hariharalaya (today's Roluos area, located just east of Siem Reap town) to the area of the main Angkor group around the year 900, and that the king of the time, Yashovarman, built a 'central mountain' in the new location.

The word 'mountain' was clearly a reference to a temple, because many temples represented the greatest mountain of all, Mount Meru, abode of the Hindu gods. The word 'central' led the experts to look to the Bayon temple, because it sits at the very centre of the walled city Angkor Thom. Now, if the Bayon dated to 900, so too would the many other temples built in a similar style—Ta Prohm, Preah Khan, Banteay Kdei, and the far-away Banteay Chhmar among them. And so would the five face-gates of Angkor Thom. The extreme

fallen-down condition of some of those temples seemed to confirm that they were among Angkor's oldest. The theory also fit with romantic notions that a new capital could only have the civilisation's grandest creations.

For decades, this dating was taken as fact, showing up in monologues of tour guides and tomes of scholars alike. Its impact spread to work on other subjects. In 1925, for instance, George Groslier published a book on Khmer sculpture in which he labelled carvings at Banteay Chhmar as early Khmer art, based on the then-accepted understanding of the construction sequence. His analysis went on to discuss how these carvings had influenced other art that the chronology said must be from a later era.

But by the '20s the dogma was not sitting well with a few Angkor scholars. The tipping point came with a 1927 book by an art historian in France called Philippe Stern. He had never been to Angkor, only examined photos and diagrams of the monuments. But he made a point that was hard to dismiss: If the Bayon group temples had immediately followed those at Hariharalaya, how could their styles — elegant curved face towers versus straight-edged tiered pyramids — be so radically different? Didn't art need time to evolve?

In the following years, the cause was taken up by a larger-than-life personality who had joined the team at Angkor, Victor Goloubew, a French-Russian aristocrat-émigré, First World War veteran, violinist, and bon vivant. He became convinced that the 'central mountain' was in fact a place that today's Angkor visitors know mainly as an elevated stand for viewing Angkor Wat at sunset, the hilltop temple Phnom Bakheng.

In August 1932, Goloubew went aloft twice in French military airplanes that had come to Angkor. Looking down in fair weather, he believed he saw the outlines of a mammoth square moat system, measuring five kilometres across, with Phnom Bakheng at the centre. It enclosed what he would come to call La Ville de Yaçovarman, the city of Yasovarman, the king who had moved the capital from Hariharalaya at the start of the tenth century. In articles in the EFEO Bulletin, published after extensive investigation and digs, he laid out in detail the case for the huge city's existence. In doing so, he acknowledged having become a bit obsessed as a man on a mission. But, he promised, 'I am trying, as best I can, not to give in to the temptation to consider each vestige unearthed by my coolies as irrefutable testimony in favour of my thesis.'

Perhaps his key piece of evidence was a black-and-white aerial photograph, published by the Bulletin at full-page size, that captured ground features hinting at an ancient urban layout. Of special interest was a huge L-shaped berm structure that showed clearly from the sky. In Goloubew's view, it was the southwest corner of the moat system. A straight segment of the Siem Reap River formed the eastern moat. Various other parts of the system, the archaeologist surmised, had been obliterated by construction in later centuries. But still visible, in part, were what seemed to have been grand avenues radiating out from the temple in the four cardinal directions.

Goloubew argued that his work essentially settled the question of which temple the Sdok Kok Thom inscription had mentioned: 'In summary, all of these data, together with a number of other facts observed during our work, favour identifying Phnom Bakheng as the central mountain.' His work helped bring on eventual general acceptance of that conclusion. Certainly the temple's pyramidal design resembles that of the last great temple at Hariharalaya, the Bakong, addressing Philippe Stern's contention that style cannot evolve at hyper speed.

Later work established that the Bayon, other temples in similar style and the Angkor Thom gates in fact date to almost three hundred years later than the initial theories said – the late twelfth century. In other words, they were among the *last* great constructions of the Angkor civilisation, not some of the first. They were in tumbled-down condition in part because their architects skimped on foundations in the struggle to complete the biggest building program in the empire's history.

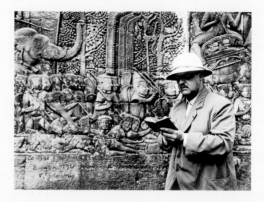

Victor Goloubew checks a notebook at the Bayon temple bas-reliefs. He often gave visitors signed copies of his portraits as mementoes of their stays at Angkor. This one dates to 1921. From the Aschwin Lippe Collection, Freer Gallery of Art and Arthur M. Sackler Gallery Archives. Smithsonian Institution, Washington, D.C., FSA.A2012.01

As for the other part of Goloubew's theory, that Phnom Bakheng was the eye of an enormous enclosed city, subsequent work did not bear it out. Digs in the L-shaped structure, for instance, found that it was in fact built centuries after Phnom Bakheng—though for what reason remains uncertain. Angkor still has many secrets to surrender.

Later analysis confirmed that the 'central mountain' was in fact this temple, Phnom Bakheng. (John Burgess)

the thirteenth century, the empire went into decline. Building largely stopped. Two reigns later, the king shifted the state religion back to Hinduism, sparking turmoil, but Buddhism soon returned and this time endured.

Historians had filled in the basics of the empire's glory days, but they had not made much progress on answering questions about beginning and end: how did Hindu civilisation come to Southeast Asia in the first place, and how did Angkor end up largely abandoned and overgrown?

On the first question, it was clear that the Khmer Empire's ninth-century founding was not the start of Hindu culture in the region. The Sambor Prei Kuk area 140 kilometres southeast of Angkor has brick temples dating to the sixth century. But what of before that? There was little in the way of historical evidence, so speculation, much of it Eurocentric, filled the gap. One of the theories went like this: Khmer civilisation was the work of an army of 'Brahmin warriors,' Aryans who early in the first millennium came from India, subjugated a savage local population, and used them as slaves to build the temples. This explanation sat well with many Europeans, who could thus picture the founders as light-skinned distant cousins, Aryans like themselves. Other theorizing, again based mostly on guesswork, albeit more plausible, ruled out military conquest and had the faith arriving through trade or proselytization. Priest-missionaries from India were said to have married into the local elite, which established the foreigners' faith in new lands. Indeed, this explanation fit with the foundation myth of the Khmer race, which holds that it descends from the union of a Brahmin priest and the human-form daughter of the king of the *naga* serpents.

All told, French historians saw the incoming Indian culture as an overwhelming influence, and the local people receiving it being small in number and largely uncivilized, living in small villages with little political structure tying them together. Their ways were said to have been largely eradicated by Hinduism, mighty kings, and temple building.

Theorizing about the empire's demise was equally shaky and unrestrained, there again being almost no forensic or textual evidence to work with – construction of temples and carving of inscriptions largely stopped after the twelfth century. But it was clear that the Cambodian court had moved out of Angkor. How to explain it? The Brahmin warrior line of thinking had it that late in the empire's history the slave people rose up and killed off or drove away their overseers. Thus the people in the villages around Angkor in modern times were not the heirs of its creators, just of its labouring class. This theory gave support to belief among the Siamese, who until 1907 controlled Angkor, that modern Cambodians had no legitimate claim to it.

Aymonier theorized that war brought the civilisation down, starting in the thirteenth century. 'The creative power suddenly collapsed in the deep night of an era that was undoubtedly marked by troubles, civil wars, and foreign invasions,' he wrote in his seminal three-volume work, *Le Cambodge*, whose publication began in 1900. Fratricidal conflict between two Indian-influenced peoples, the Khmers and the Chams, opened the door to gains by the Siamese and Vietnamese. One of the casualties, he wrote, was 'the powerful priestly aristocracy, from which the lords and the sovereigns had emerged. Perhaps it was destroyed partly in the wars and troubles of the thirteenth century, or melted into the mass of the people, or simply became the insignificant and shrunken caste of modern Baku,' the Brahmins who retain a ceremonial role today in the royal palace in Phnom Penh.

Other war theorizing focused on the Siamese, whose Ayutthaya state was rising as a regional power. Siamese troops seemed to have captured Angkor in 1431 following a siege. Perhaps the Khmer court had moved east in a simple search for safety from that threat. With kings and palace ritual removed, there would have been no need to keep up the temples. Moreover, the conversion to Theravada Buddhism, with its rejection of material things, could have undermined devotion to huge monuments and provided religious justification for walking away and starting anew in the east. A phenomenon called 'social exhaustion' was also posited: in the empire's latter years, the job of building and maintaining an ever-increasing number of mammoth temples was said to have overwhelmed the Khmer people's emotional and physical fortitude. Wholescale abandonment was the result.

These and other theories of foundation and demise were tossed about. None could be proven as fact, except in the minds that thought them up. In the years ahead, new evidence and yet more theories would emerge, but none would totally sweep away the uncertainty.

5: Deciding to Reconstruct

The romance of ruins versus an urge to rebuild: French thinking about how to care for Angkor evolves toward putting the monuments back how they were – or must have been.

By the start of the twentieth century, the French presence at Angkor had moved beyond a succession of visiting missions. Now small but generally permanent groups of men were on the ground, overseeing projects of rubble clearing, re-enforcement, photography, and archaeological study. Charles Carpeaux is among the best documented of these people, because he was a devoted journal keeper and writer of letters to his mother back in France, who preserved and later published them.

His father was a famous sculptor of the times, Jean-Baptiste Carpeaux, whose works are found on the facade of the Paris Opera House. Charles had trained in casting techniques and photography, and, after working for a while at the Trocadéro museum in Paris, he went at the turn of the century to Cambodia to join the École française d'Extrême-Orient, newly founded with headquarters in Saigon. He had special reason to leave France, legal fall-out from a duel in which he'd wounded an opponent who was said to have insulted the family honour.

He arrived at Angkor in September 1901 and was assigned by the EFEO to the Bayon. The French didn't control Angkor yet, but were increasingly acting like they did. Working as deputy to another Frenchman, the architect Henri Dufour, Carpeaux would spend a total of nine months at the temple. He kept busy with his camera and portable dark room but much of his work consisted of overseeing heavy labour by Cambodians. 'It's a rough task to move the huge lying stones in ripped-open galleries and toppled pillars,' he explained to his mother. 'Nevertheless, it's necessary to clear things away to understand the temple's plans and to classify the stone sculptures in order to reconstitute the bas-reliefs, which are custodians of sacred history.'

Though the French were largely indifferent to local people's spiritual concerns about interfering with the ruins, Carpeaux

Charles Carpeaux peers from an Angkor window in this photo from the book that his mother published. (Bibliothèque nationale de France)

Opposite page: Banteay Srei temple was completely disassembled, then rebuilt in the 1930s, in the first experiment with the restoration approach known as anastylosis. (École française d'Extrême-Orient)

70

Carpeaux frequently went to this minor palace in Siem Reap to meet with the local Siamese lord. Image from *Les Ruines d'Angkor*.

couldn't help but wonder about the huge sculpted faces, each with an enigmatic smile, for which the Bayon would become world-famous (in part due to his photographs). He felt that their eyes followed him as he moved about the temple, reproaching him. 'One is struck with the hostility that emanates from these superb ruins...The stones defend the secrets of things, and nature comes to their aid in covering them with an almost impenetrable veil.'

Carpeaux had the periodic duty of riding an ox cart to Siem Reap to seek (that is, purchase) permission from the Siamese lord for various projects, among them the building of a permanent house for EFEO people like himself, and the acquisition of supplies at the usual inflated prices. He appears to have become something of a diplomat. In addition to the temples, he wanted to record the local culture through photography, but one senses he also had in part a goal of better relations with the Siamese when he volunteered to take family portraits of the lord, who posed proudly with three children.

Another subject of Carpeaux's camera was local wildlife. One day, a baby monkey fell from a tree and lay injured on the ground. Carpeaux got the idea to set up his camera right by the baby (apparently with some kind of pull string to trip the shutter) and get close-ups when its mother came to the rescue. Crowds of monkeys gathered in the temple's heights, seeming to recognize that some kind of trick was afoot, and let out a great whooping. The mother came close, but never close enough for the photos Carpeaux wanted. After an hour, he gave up and walked away. Before he had gone twenty metres, the mother swooped in and scooped up her child, throwing ferocious looks toward the Frenchman.

As time progressed, illness, probably dysentery and malaria, became a painful fact of life. Stoicism was the usual response. One day in late December, both Carpeaux and Dufour were laid up, and they began sharing their wishes for final arrangements. Dufour wanted to be buried on the east side of Bayon, where he had found some sculpted lions the previous day. 'He asked that a lock of his hair be sent to his family. For me, I want to be cremated, so that my ashes can be sent home, with some hair taken for my mother before cremation. Also, so that something of me lies in our family tomb.'

But by the next day, Carpeaux was up and around again, back at work. On this day, his tool was a chisel, with which he removed some termite residue from a bas-relief. He spent two hours developing photographs. He tripped over a banyan root, injuring his foot. The day after that, he put in eleven hours. He worked again in his darkroom, and saw a 'superb snake' measuring about two metres long.

On New Year's Day 1902, he and Dufour had a little party for themselves in the new EFEO house. They had no bread, so they ate a substitute fashioned from glutinous rice, lightly fried.

During his stay, Carpeaux became well acquainted with the monks of Angkor Wat. Mostly relations were friendly, judging by his writings. When malaria sickened people in the monastery, he provided quinine. He gave lozenges of opium-based laudanum to the abbot for one of his parents, who was suffering severe stomach pains. He attended an elaborate Chinese funeral held inside Angkor Wat and, to entertain the crowd, fired his revolver into the air.

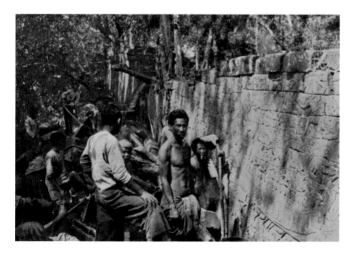

These men at the Bayon bas reliefs, working for Dufour and Carpeaux, were among the first of many thousands of Cambodians who would carry out the actual labor of France's conservation efforts at Angkor. The photo is from his mother's book. (Bibliothèque nationale de France)

But other times, familiar tensions over rights to heritage came to the fore. One day, monks came to take prompt custody of three Buddha images the French team had newly unearthed. Carpeaux considered this "shameless" and insisted on photographing and sketching the images first.

There were periodic visits by other Europeans, early tourists to Angkor. These included, arriving on a gunboat, the bishop of Saigon, a French couple, and the boat's chaplain. Carpeaux arranged lunch for the party at the Bayon under some mango trees, on a table thrown together from buffalo cart pieces and the tops of boxes.

Word that money had arrived in Phnom Penh from the EFEO led him to go back to the capital with these companions, enjoying for a while the French comforts of the gunboat. On his return to the Bayon, he reported progress on the bas-reliefs that today delight so many visitors. 'With the moss barely removed, I have the intense pleasure of seeing all of these moving scenes arise. Grand canoes of war, full of rowers, of which you can see only the heads with short hair... A big canoe, almost a ship, carries sails and a pavilion. The pilot, standing in the back, commands the manoeuvre'.

Early in 1902, Carpeaux left Angkor for what became two years of work in central Vietnam documenting temples of the Cham civilisation. When he headed back to Angkor, illness was again weighing on him. He arrived exhausted on 18 March 1904 after an eight-day cart ride. He got back to work, but found he needed more time for rest. Sometimes, as he sat in his house, he was entertained by natural music. 'What an insect orchestra – thousands of beings that live in sun and light,' he wrote. 'Around the hut, they make a muted music in

Early in the twentieth century, an artist depicted workers building a pavilion for EFEO at Angkor. (John Burgess collection)

Construction, dans la forêt d'Angkor-Thom, d'une *Sala* pour l'École française.

which each one gives his note, from the enormous cicada of sonorous chant down to the tiny firefly with a pointed voice like a needle.'

Slowly, however, his strength was slipping away. 'I drag myself as if I have a great disease,' he wrote on a day on which he nonetheless developed photos of the Bayon's central tower.

By May, he had admitted defeat. He prepared to go home to France. Local people put on some farewell entertainment for him, including a comedic skit in which a woman was rescued from water. He distributed tips to various hirelings and agreed with Dufour that the two of them would meet in the autumn in Paris.

When he arrived in Saigon, he was quickly hospitalized. Doctors tried various treatments and some seemed to work. He was well enough to write to his mother, saying he'd soon depart for France and that for his first meal home he'd like a leg of lamb and pureed potatoes. He acquired a gift for her, a gong with a wooden base.

On 28 June, he wrote in a hurried hand to his brother-in-law. 'Serious dysentery. Hospital. [I] embrace you all. Courage. Charles.' Two hours later, he was dead.

Carpeaux is remembered fondly in the community of Angkor devotees. The French government would later publish a large-format two-volume study of the bas-reliefs containing 250 photographs that he and Dufour took. With this, the world would get its first detailed look at these fascinating depictions of daily life in the Angkor era. Carpeaux was also honoured with a memorial stone erected near the southwest corner of the Bayon.

* * * *

As it turned out, Carpeaux was among the last of a generation of French amateurs at Angkor. Starting with Father Bouillevaux, continuing on to Mouhot and Aymonier, these were people who had no formal training in Asian art, conservation, or archaeology, just passion for the subject and willingness to work hard and learn in the field.

But as the nineteenth century gave way to the twentieth, things were beginning to turn formal. The EFEO was founded, with its journals, annual budgets, internal protocols, and formal appointments to positions. As of 1907, it became Angkor's overseer – giving way to military and political pressure, the Siamese bowed out. The French and the EFEO could now begin to fulfil their plans in earnest.

74

Some Bad 'Best Practices' in Conservation

Monument conservation is a field in which best practices are always evolving, and first conservator Jean Commaille made some decisions that would appall his modern-day successors. Prime among them was his treatment of fallen stones at the Bayon.

When Commaille arrived on the scene in 1907, the Bayon grounds were littered with huge numbers of toppled sandstone blocks. To open up vistas and

Fallen stones remain piled up around the Bayon today.
(John Burgess)

work space, he ordered his men to move them and pile them up beside the main temple. Archaeologists today believe that many of them had formed outer walls and possibly more of the face towers for which the Bayon is famous. Had the blocks been left where they fell, they might have given clues that would allow those structures to be pieced back together. Instead, the stones are randomly jumbled together in what are to this day known as the 'Commaille piles'. Reconstruction is essentially impossible.

Another common practice concerning the stones was even more shocking by today's standards: Commaille's labourers broke up unknown numbers of Bayon stones to produce gravel for spreading on Angkor roads. It seems to have been a matter of convenience and budget-stretching. Bringing in gravel from far away would have been time-consuming and costly.

Henri Marchal, who became conservator in 1919, continued this practice, which drew protests from at least one visitor. In a 1925 report to EFEO headquarters in Hanoi, Marchal wrote: 'I think I should bring to your attention the following fact: I authorize the engineer of public works to use for his paving of the roads around the Bayon the numerous blocks of stone which unpleasantly clutter the external pit'. That was a preamble to explaining that he'd heard that a tourist, someone with high-level connections in Hanoi, had noticed the grinding of the stones and had taken pictures as evidence. Marchal ended: 'I want to warn you so that you will know what to do with this'. The report is silent on what, if anything, happened in Hanoi, but later on that practice came to an end.

A young man called Henri Parmentier embodied the new generation of Angkor specialists. After studying architecture at the École des beaux arts in Paris, he worked in Tunisia on an excavation of the Temple of Saturn, a Roman creation. In 1900 he came to Indochina to be EFEO's resident architect. Hardly had he arrived than he was publishing a learned treatise on the correct way to excavate the ruins of Indochina.

'A hill of a few dozen metres at the foot, which widens at its summit like a volcano, often hides the base of a tower of a *prasat* [temple]. Extended bulges announce the walls.' This he wrote in 1902, in an article that in places amounted to a rebuke of the techniques his predecessors had employed. Trenches must be dug to expose some of the walls and provide a clearer understanding of size and lay-out, he said. It is crucial to document every step of the work; otherwise valuable archaeological evidence will be lost. 'If an excavation brings the discovery of an interesting object, it's wise not to give in to the urge to extract it immediately for study. It's prudent, when it's still stuck in the ground where it was found, to first carefully note its position and then make a sketch or photograph.' As they work, teams must not dump debris in depressions that are common in temple grounds, because these are important architectural elements, having once been moats and pools. Labourers should sift the soil they remove, lest they miss small artefacts. And they must maintain security at the site, so that ancient things don't disappear.

* * * * *

For all their architectural brilliance, the ancient Khmers nonetheless built monuments that were unstable over the long term. The problem, the French were finding, was in what was out of sight. Foundations were often minimal. Though from afar a Khmer temple can give the impression of being sandstone through and through, the stone is often little more than a facing, a covering up of a core made of the clay-like substance laterite, hard-packed sand, or plain old dirt. Under pressure from monsoon rainwater, gravity, and intruding roots, stones wandered from their original places, a migration that, continuing long enough, can trigger catastrophic structural collapse. The eleventh century Baphuon temple, located next to the old palace compound, was a prime example of this dynamic.

Other common construction techniques also assured deterioration. In erecting walls, for instance, the Khmers often

27.- ANGKOR-THOM. - Temple du Baphuon (X°-XI° s.) - Vue générale Est

The eleventh-century Baphuon, shown in a vintage postcard, was among Angkor's most structurally unstable and overgrown temples. (John Burgess collection)

took no care that each block would overlay the vertical seam of the two blocks below it. This allowed dangerous vertical cracks to develop, and not just in walls. Some of the faces on the Bayon towers came to brutally split this way. The Khmers did not know the standard arch, using instead the less stable corbelled arch in which stacked elements progressively stick out further from two sides to bridge a gap. If a doorway was too wide for a stone lintel to span, the builders sometimes reinforced the lintel with wood, hardly a permanent aid in view of the wet climate and hungry termites.

So, early on, the French set about arresting some of the damage that these shortcomings and the onslaught of nature were causing. Around early twentieth-century Angkor could be seen a plethora of propping-up contraptions – timber beams, steel clamps, cement pillars – that sought to stabilize and to prevent further collapse.

A Startling Discovery at the West Mebon

In 1936 there came to light a bronze statue that was much bigger and more exciting than anything found to date.

It was found because a Cambodian farmer at Angkor had been telling people that he'd had a significant dream. He had learned that an image of the Buddha lay buried at the centre of the West Mebon, the island-temple situated at the precise centre of the eight-mile long reservoir called the West Baray. The image wishes to be freed, he said. The farmer had gone to try to dig it up himself, but became frightened by a storm (perhaps it was a divine warning) and left. Word reached the conservator, Maurice Glaize. Excavations soon unearthed three sections of an enormous image of not the Buddha but the Hindu god Vishnu. One would normally call it larger than life, but who can say what is life-size for a god?

The biggest piece, once inlaid with precious stones, was the head, upper torso and arms. It was a depiction of a god whom some believe came to earth as the Buddha, the incarnation the farmer had spoken of. Vishnu was reclining, a hand supporting his head, serenely carrying out one of his main functions in Hindu cosmology, a slumber beneath the Sea of Creation to dream into existence the next cycle of the universe. The image would have rested on a platform at the centre of the West Mebon, and been lapped on all sides by the water of the *baray*. In that way, statue, temple, and *baray* were a mammoth depiction of the primordial sleep in the sea, the largest such tableau that the Khmers ever created.

Many scholars believe that the Chinese visitor Zhou Daguan saw this statue, but mistakenly identified it in his writing as a Buddha located in the East Baray: 'In the middle of the tower is a bronze reclining Buddha with water constantly flowing from its navel.'

The condition of the fragments and their location, in pits right at the temple's centre, suggest that the image was deliberately cut up and buried, apparently during a time of religious upheaval late in the empire's history. The head section is today on display in the National Museum in Phnom Penh. Loaned out to foreign museums, it has enchanted people all over the world.

The bronze statue of reclining Vishnu, unearthed at the West Mebon temple in 1936, is today on display in the National Museum of Cambodia in Phnom Penh. (John Burgess)

The French repaired fallen statuary at Angkor Thom's Victory Gate. Image from *Les Ruines d'Angkor*.

But conservation work was about more than buildings. During the course of their work at Angkor, the French unearthed countless artefacts. Many were stone statues of the Buddha and Hindu deities. Others were ceramics, sometimes complete cups and plates. A few were metal and generally small, such as idols of personal devotion, spear points, and caps for wooden and bamboo poles – *nagas* that graced the ends of the handles of palanquins, for instance.

* * * * *

For years, the French did not try to rebuild ruined temples, due both to cost and philosophy. They put back in place a few stones that had fallen, such as the heads of *nagas* on Angkor Wat's grand avenue and gods and demons at the gates of Angkor Thom. But in general, they believed their job was to lock in place the tumbled-down romance of the ruins. They would not try to make a temple more than what had been found. In early French writings from Angkor, you can find occasional digs at Eugène Viollet-le-Duc, the architect and aesthetic theorist who back home, enjoying big budgets and popular acclaim, was renovating some of France's greatest medieval creations, Notre Dame Cathedral and the walled city of Carcassonne among them. Viollet-le-Duc restored, but he also augmented, adding new architectural elements to achieve the appearance he thought best. At Notre Dame, he designed a spire of his liking, the one that tragically burned and collapsed in the fire of April 2019. He added picturesque roofs to wall towers at Carcassonne. In this, the experts at Angkor saw disrespect for great buildings and for history itself.

But over time they began to reconsider. This was mainly due to conservator Henri Marchal, a goateed man of minor physical stature and major energy, curiosity, and good cheer. As a Beaux Arts-trained architect, he had a refined interest in building design and construction. This was on tap in 1930, when he spent three months in Indonesia, then a Dutch colony. There he tasted of natural beauty, traditional dance, and also stone temples that had been built by other Indian-influenced civilisations that flourished there around the same time as Angkor. He got an introduction to a restoration technique the Dutch had begun using: anastylosis. The term is derived from words in ancient Greek meaning 'to erect again.' Early forms of the technique were used in the nineteenth century on the Acropolis in Athens.

Essentially it means restoring an ancient building to what it is believed to have looked like when new, using elements found at the site and newly created replacements for ones that are damaged or missing. The process starts with a detailed survey of a ruin. Then comes its total disassembly, its pieces being laid aside nearby, each bearing a code that identifies its original position. Reconstruction can now begin. Restorers typically create solid foundations with modern materials such as concrete, taking care that these will be hidden from sight once the project is complete. In service of architectural honesty, new elements are often crafted to be recognizable as such, through such attributes as a different hue or lesser ornamentation. In ancient times, temples were often dressed up with bright colours of gilding and paint. Anastylosis or not, most rebuilt

Not only temples but water structures got attention from the French conservation program. In this image circa 1920, the now pristine Srah Srang reservoir is hardly distinguishable from an ordinary pond. Image from *Les Ruines d'Angkor.*

temples are left as bare stone, as modern visitors expect of antiquities.

Marchal spent extended time at the eighth-and-ninth century Buddhist temple Borobudur, already rebuilt in this way, and at the tenth-century Hindu complex Prambanan, where anastylosis was underway. There his hosts allowed him to provide hands-on help in returning stones to their original spots. He arrived back in Angkor with detailed notes and determination to try this approach. In terms of cost and scale, it would be impractical for large temples such as Angkor Wat and the Bayon. But not at smaller ones.

He chose to try it experimentally at Banteay Srei, a tenth-century edifice located about twenty-five kilometres northeast of the main Angkor group.[1] The temple was not so big, and its stone had a particularly high level of carved detail, which would simplify the job of figuring out how fallen pieces fit together (in the same way that a flowerbed section of a jigsaw puzzle is easier to assemble than plain blue sky). Visitors today sometimes wonder how Banteay Srei could possibly have survived in such pristine condition. The answer is that it did not.

Work began in 1931. At the time, Banteay Srei was in the typical decrepit condition of an old Khmer temple, with large trees growing in its courtyard, sculpture buried under the soil build-ups of centuries, and many structures sagging or tumbled down. Comparatively few elements had been lost to looters, however. The unusually hard quality of its sandstone meant that many fallen elements had not split or eroded and could be returned to their old places. Teams dug away the soil to reach the original base level, sometimes coming upon buried sculpture. Everything was documented *in situ* with photos, plans, and drawings. Then major structures were rebuilt one at a time (see page 68).

First was the south tower. Workers disassembled it using primitive winching equipment to lift the stones, which they laid out nearby. In its now exposed base, Marchal later wrote, were what he'd expected, weak foundations. 'I came upon an inner filling of very rough laterite blocks with the interspaces filled in with soil, which accounts for the sinking in the pavements and the fall of the walls of the temple. When the ground was cleared of all the building material, I had this free area levelled, and topped with a concrete bed of cement mortar, meant to distribute the pressure and avoid subsidence.' With the foundations strengthened, his men then began reconstructing the building itself. Finding the right place for fallen stones was often a tedious trial-by-error process in which extremely heavy

1   Marchal first saw Banteay Srei following a fitful night in the forest. He and two Cambodian assistants had set out for the temple on horseback, but got lost in the sparsely-inhabited area as the sun set. He scarcely slept, battling insects and worrying that wild elephants would spook the horses.

A young Henri Marchal (left), an unidentified Cambodian assistant, and George Groslier posed for a camera at Ta Prohm temple in 1910. Photo courtesy of Groslier Family Archive and DatAsia Press.

blocks were placed together on the ground, re-arranged by winch or labourers' heft once, then twice, then again until the right combination was discovered. The ensemble was reassembled once again up at its proper place in the tower. When elements were missing, masons crafted new ones, but with a lower level of decoration, making them recognizable as new. Slowly the tower's walls rose again. Finally, roof elements were fixed in place. Then attention turned to other structures and the process was repeated. It was not until 1936 that the job came to an end.

The technique remains controversial to this day. Indeed, seeing a beloved ruin undergoing anastylosis can be a disconcerting experience, with the building reduced to rows of component pieces laid out nearby. It's something like seeing a sick friend sedated on the operating table with torso open and organs exposed. When the job is done, a tiny something is subtracted from the viewing experience, the knowledge that, say, a lintel being admired was not hefted into place by sweating Khmer labourers a thousand years past, but was lowered by a crane not so long ago. Beyond the question of undermining romanticism and creating a 'Disneyland effect,' there is the question of historical accuracy. Because restorers aren't working from the original plans, the fear is that no matter how careful they are, they might end up creating a building that's different from the original. Marchal said there is no room for the hypothetical in anastylosis – the architect must be certain that everything done is historically accurate. 'Not everyone has the genius of Viollet-le-Duc,' he wrote, in a sarcastic dig at the man. But there can be no doubt that, no matter how careful they are, anastylosis rebuilders do occasionally err and give us something that never was. The evidence is the collection of odds-and-ends pieces that in many projects is left over at the end, because no one can figure out where they belonged.

Marchal was proud of the rebuilt Banteay Srei, saying it would 'seduce' visitors who'd reluctantly taken the long bumpy ride from Angkor. EFEO agreed. Writing after the project's completion, linguist George Cœdès said good riddance to the old thinking: 'Respect for the "ruin" had become a kind of superstition.' (And he was speaking of Frenchmen, not Cambodians, who of course had superstitious respect from the very start and never gave it up.) Rebuilding Banteay Srei 'had

Banteay Srei today can seem to be in the precise condition it was when it was consecrated in the tenth century. Photo by Kotchasi Charoensuk/Shutterstock.com.

Nature and ancient architecture come together at Preah Khan temple, which the French decided to leave in something resembling the condition in which they found it. (John Burgess)

the advantage not only of restoring for the visitor the original state of the monument while consolidating it. There is also major scientific interest, because it permits the study of the ancient processes of construction and identification of the different modifications that the edifice underwent.'

Indeed, there's no denying that it's impossible to fully understand Khmer construction techniques without taking buildings apart. Marchal noted that the Banteay Srei project had yielded new inscriptions and new insights into ancient building methods, such as the use of iron crampons to lock adjacent blocks together. His Cambodian workers had been surprised at how difficult it was to take the things apart.

Anastylosis would remain in the Angkor conservators' quiver going forward. It was applied to discrete sections of larger temples, and in neighbouring countries such as Thailand. There, with French help, the eleventh century Khmer temple of Phimai was put back together piece by piece. The French also worked to restore water bodies that over the years had silted up.

But at other temples, the French allowed the romance of ruins to live on. They deliberately left things in their overgrown state, albeit in a cleaned-up, safety-engineered version of it. The purpose was both to enchant visitors and give a 'before and after' comparison of the long and costly conservation work the French had undertaken in the mission civilisatrice. Generations of foreign visitors have been glad for it. With its towering trees springing skyward from stone roofs and courtyards, with its fallen blocks that lie in enormous, mysterious piles, the twelfth century temple Preah Khan became – and remains – one of the most visited, photographed, and awed-over temples in the entire Angkor complex.

À LA MÉMOIRE

DE

JEAN

COMMAILLE

Premier Conservateur

d'ANGKOR

Tombé à son poste

LE 30 AVRIL 1916

à l'âge de 48 ans

L'ÉCOLE FRANÇAISE D'EXTRÊME-ORIENT

6: Pushback

The conservators trade barbs with colonial officials and business people – and Cambodians who continue to feel that Angkor belongs to *them*.

From their earliest visits, the French became aware that Cambodians considered Angkor to be a supernatural realm, a place best left to itself. In 1860, Henri Mouhot heard from his guides that it had been built by gods, or had 'built itself.' As French political authority and interest in the temples and their artwork increased, misgivings among Cambodians expanded apace. There were the monks at Angkor Wat, for instance, who grabbed sculpture shards away from Auguste Filoz and images from Carpeaux. But for the most part, Cambodians acquiesced to colonial power, with apologies to the supernatural. The men who led Louis Delaporte around Preah Khan-Khampong Svay in 1873 tossed those rice grains as an offering to local spirits about to be disturbed. Please forgive us, the men were saying. We have no choice but to obey these foreigners' orders. Please forgive us. We must see to our families' well-being by accepting the wages that these men pay.

Most of the Cambodian voices that we hear on this issue come through the filter of French accounts. But one exception is a court poet called Suttantaprija In. He took part in the 1909 reclamation festivities at Angkor and was shocked at some of what he saw. Writing in verse infused with a tone of helplessness, he lamented that Angkor no longer belonged to his people. Changes the French were making in the central tower of Angkor Wat caused him particular pain.

> *Sir Mr. Commaille, the Chief of Works,*
> *Had the statue of Buddha cut out of the southern gateway,*
> *Uprooted from the gateway and taken out*
> *…And broken its neck, the statue was smashed beyond all recognition*
> *It worried me, that they had destroyed the statue.*
> *The time of the religion of the door-deity was over.*
> *…His body was eliminated, he had reached the shore of Nirvana.[1]*

The French were now a major employer at Angkor with their projects of clearing vegetation and repairing structures.

Opposite page: Angkor's first conservator, Jean Commaille, killed in a roadside robbery in 1913, is buried near the Bayon in a tomb built partly from ancient Khmer elements recovered nearby. (John Burgess)

---

1   The poet is quoted in Penny Edwards' book *Cambodge: The Cultivation of a Nation 1860-1945.*

Jean Commaille's tomb stands amidst trees near the Bayon. (John Burgess)

While this may sound like a welcome boost to the local economy, the realities were more complex. Some of the workers were no doubt long-time Angkor residents whom the French had forced out of their traditional – and honourable – vocations of fishing, rice farming, and the raising of pigs and poultry in the shadow of the temples. Toiling in the sun for a foreigner's wage, and on projects that would surely offend the deities, was a poor substitute.

Suttantaprija In had this to say:
I am overcome with pity for the Khmer race, dirt poor,
Working as coolies for somebody else's money.
I watch their bodies, frail and flat-bellied,
Hair thick with dust and grime, stinking like otters.

Moreover, it's unclear if all were taking these jobs voluntarily. When a Frenchman came to a village looking for a team of, say, twenty men, it could be hard to say no. The labour burden reached such a point that colonial administrators feared triggering unrest and disrupting the planting and harvesting cycle. 'The constant requisitions to which local inhabitants are subjected are of the type that might provoke, in the long term, an "*initiation*" and discontent with the potential for far graver serious political consequences,' Indochina Governor General Paul Beau wrote in 1910, in a letter about labour needs at Angkor. He was writing to oppose a proposal from the EFEO to address shortages by bringing in fifty Chinese prisoners or idled workers at a distant rubber plantation.

In later years, however, prison inmates were brought in. For instance, in 1933, the conservator reported to Hanoi that in preparation for a visit by the king, 'the resident of Siem Reap kindly lent me twenty-five prisoners who cleaned the Bayon and its surroundings as well as the royal terraces, [carved] elephants, the Leper King and part of the royal square.' There had been talk of getting an additional forty prisoners from Phnom Penh, he said, but the resident 'cannot ensure their supervision, in view of the reduced size of the militia of this province.'

French relations with local Cambodians received a body blow on 29 April 1916, a Saturday. Jean Commaille was coming by car from Siem Reap with cash wages for his workers at week's end. Along the road, men who had apparently been lying in wait opened fire on the car, wounding him in the stomach. Rather than going on, he told his driver to stop so that he could confront the attackers. He stepped down from the car, and was set upon. He held on until the next day, as friends struggled to secure medical care, then succumbed. Three men were later convicted and executed for the crime.

An obituary that Parmentier wrote for Commaille painted an idyllic picture of his relationship with his workers, but leaves one wondering about the true nature. 'He was much loved by them,' Parmentier said. 'He knew how to direct them without brutality, although with a firmness that they understood and perhaps even desired.' Commaille's remains were later laid to rest a few steps off the road that skirts the southwest corner of the Bayon, where he had carried out extensive work. Colleagues honoured him by building the tomb partly of ancient stone colonnettes and a lintel. The tomb is there today, passed unrecognized by untold numbers of tourists each day.

The fact was that the French at Angkor worked in an isolated part of a not entirely secure country. They were imposing heavy taxes on Cambodians, both in money and labour requisitions. They would inevitably become targets of violence, by criminals or people who objected to their very presence in the country. And if not violence, then resentment – Cambodians who felt that Angkor belonged in Cambodian hands.

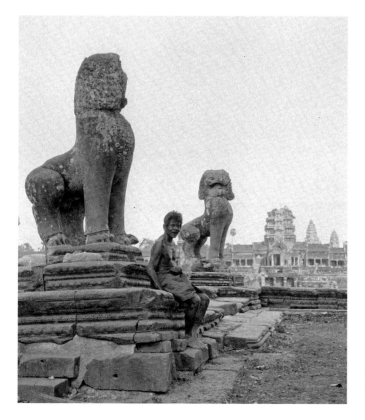

Many Cambodians continued to feel that Angkor belonged to them, not the European power that had colonized the country. Photo from 1920s by J. Dearden Holmes/ Ninskaphotos.

In May 1933, a band of men, whom the French described as 'bandits', was reported to have attacked a village just west of Angkor Wat. The police confronted them, opening fire. Several attackers were taken prisoner. Around the same time, a group of 'evil doers' stopped and robbed a car not far from the spot where Commaille had been killed. Were they simple criminals, or a few of Cambodia's growing numbers of nationalists, taking aim at colonial oppression? Or both? It is hard to say.

In 1949, the French got another telling taste of discontent over their tutelage of Angkor. It was triggered when word spread that workers in the conservation compound were crating up another trove of Khmer sculpture for shipment abroad. In Phnom Penh, the king and various high Cambodian officials received letters signed merely 'inhabitants of Siem Reap.' 'We come to complain to Your Majesty and Your Excellencies of goodness to seek urgent measures to prevent the shipment of these large crates currently in preparation, or if this is not possible, to avoid at least new intrusions into the monuments, which are being more cruelly ruined than by the Siamese in past times.'

The conservation's name, the letter said, ought really to be 'the destruction of Angkor.' All transportable statues of precious materials, the letter claimed, had already been taken away to the Louvre or elsewhere. All that was conserved, really, were things too heavy to move. Rich in metaphor, the letter appears to have been written by an educated person or persons. 'The grey peaks of the monuments, enveloped in the tropical mists of our country, seem to complain to Your Majesty and Your Excellencies that they have painful torments and tortures to bear, as do their people.'

The letter had its share of hyperbole, but underlying it was a very real resentment that had smouldered in many Cambodians ever since the French arrived: the foreigners profaned holy images and treated them as their own disposable property. And indeed, over the years EFEO had overseen the sale abroad of many works of Khmer art. The scholar Pierre Singaravélou, writing in 2000, detailed the policies and practices that underlay this trade.

In the 1920s, he found, the transfer was comparatively minor and low-grade, consisting of small items and fragments that EFEO's people deemed not of scientific or artistic interest. Sold at tourist-oriented spots, these pieces sometimes went for the equivalent of just a few dollars each. But quality of sculpture and amounts paid grew dramatically in the 1930s, which happened to correspond with the colonial administration

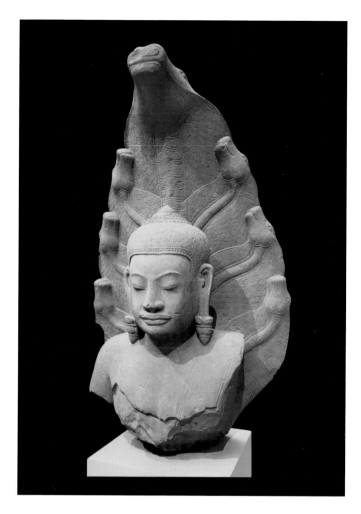

This late twelfth- or early thirteenth-century statue of Buddha protected by a seven-headed *naga* serpent is among a trove of art works that EFEO sold to New York's Metropolitan Museum of Art in 1936. (John Burgess)

cutting funding to the EFEO due to the Great Depression.

In this period, museums in many parts of the world acquired top-tier Khmer artwork. In a 1936 transaction with the Metropolitan Museum of Art in New York, six exquisite sculptures were sold for a total price of $19,500, about $350,000 in today's dollars. The records suggest that the EFEO at times behaved like a for-profit art dealer, testing the limits of the market, Singaravélou found. An item that didn't fetch a hoped-for price might be marked down the following year.

Other ancient artworks had long been adorning colonial offices around Indochina. Writing in 1902, the newly arrived archaeologist Henri Parmentier lamented that he constantly came across priceless artefacts functioning as decorations in gardens and offices, with no one knowing where the things had come from or appreciating what they were. 'Is it not regrettable to see, perched upside down, in the Nha Trang residence [the

88

The Yearning for a Farewell Souvenir

Senior French officials completing tours of duty in Indochina sometimes leaned on the EFEO to sell them additions for their salon back home. At those times, the EFEO might quietly seethe, but also give in.

In a 1930 letter that Pierre Singaravélou quotes, the EFEO's chief of archaeology addresses the soon-to-depart *résident supérieur* of Hue, Vietnam. The chief has just sent the resident's wife two heads that she picked out at an Angkor depot. 'I don't want to create a precedent,' he writes, 'that receiving an Angkor tribute will become a prerogative of successive resident superiors in Cambodia.'

He asks that the resident keep things quiet. Sending the heads to the wife rather than the resident, it seems, was intended to make the sale look like the routine acquisition of a pair of souvenirs, not an official farewell thank you.

seat of the senior French representative in that Vietnamese city], the venerable stone of Vo-can? It is one of the oldest Sanskrit inscriptions in existence, exiled far from the place where the centuries had respected it piously.'

Parmentier noted that there was general indignation (among the French, at least) against Britain's Lord Elgin, who early in the nineteenth century took from the Parthenon in Athens the fabulous pediment marbles that now bear his name at the British Museum. Yet at the same time, everyone claims the right 'to exploit the Khmer or Cham monuments for his own profit. When you consider it closely, the taking of something that is called a travel souvenir is nothing more than theft poorly disguised.'

Khmer art could also function as a political gift. Over the years, the EFEO 'declassified' certain protected pieces of artwork for sale to people whom the institute wished to thank, perhaps. or seek a favour from. In a 1937 letter to conservator Maurice Glaize, the EFEO director George Cœdès endorsed the declassification and sale of four stone heads for a total of four hundred piastres. They were to be 'provisionally reserved' for the Swedish archaeologist Olov Janse, he wrote. Janse was conducting important excavations in Vietnam in the 1930s.

In 1873, the French officer Auguste Filoz faced hostility from monks over the stonework that Louis Delaporte had taken away. Filoz won them over in part through assurances that the statues would go on display in 'splendid palaces' in France. Half a century later, the EFEO officials sometimes cited a similar objective – enlightening the world about Khmer glories – to justify their sales. And indeed, many Cambodians today are proud to see artworks of the Angkor heritage on display abroad.

The EFEO also cited a practical concern for the sales, theft prevention. Many tourists were determined to go home with a stone souvenir, one way or another. Why not bow to the inevitable and sell them insignificant antiquities through a well-regulated channel? Likewise, it could be argued that if foreign museums could buy high-grade pieces legally, professional art thieves would have less incentive to carry things off in the night. Generally the EFEO denied it was trying to make money to bolster the institute.

* * * * *

The 1949 letter to the Cambodian king was a belated reaction to one of the big-ticket transactions of a decade earlier.

In 1938 and 1939, the EFEO had concluded a deal with the Musées Royaux d'Art et d'Histoire in Brussels for the purchase of seven elaborate pieces of Khmer art. But the disruptions of World War II prevented the pieces from leaving Cambodia. They were still there at war's end, and it wasn't until 1949 that the EFEO moved to finally complete the deal by shipping the items to Belgium. Apparently it was the preparations of packing them up that sparked the writing of the letter.

The writers weren't expressing hopeless anguish. They seemed to know of recent political events in Phnom Penh that might work to their advantage. In 1946, the French had offered a measure of autonomy to Cambodia, including the election of a national assembly with limited powers. That body was now considering a law to ban the export of antiquities.

The letter provoked a flurry of nervous communications between French officials, including men embedded in agencies of the semi-autonomous royal government. It was vital, these officials agreed, to hurry things up so that the shipment could leave the colony before any export ban took effect. One French official involved in this 'delicate question' said he had received assurances that if the crates were not officially impounded, the royal government would turn a blind eye to their dispatch abroad.

The sculpture made it out of the country. Despite having given Cambodia a small dose of independence, the French remained the real power in the country. Today works of art from the shipment form part of the permanent collection of the Brussels Art & History Museum. As of this writing, two near life-size sitting Buddhas from Angkor Thom and an elaborately carved lintel are proudly displayed in the images gallery of the museum's website.

* * * * *

In their dealings with Cambodians, the French tried to present a front of unity and common thinking. Among themselves, they were plenty prone to feuding and back-stabbing, and over the years the French community in Siem Reap got its share of this. Surviving records of the disputes make some of them seem petty, even comical, the pursuits of people with an excess of time or self-importance. (Official A: If you had a problem, why didn't you just tell me when we met the other day, rather than filing a formal complaint with my boss? Official B: I'm surprised you're surprised. I'm only treating you in the way you've treated me.)

Yet it was inevitable that conflicts, some of them real and very serious, would arise within the French community, given its members' varied social backgrounds, education, and professional objectives. The conservation team was heavy with academics and aesthetes, people whose prime purpose in life was archaeology and the preservation of ancient beauty. French civil servants in the local government were out to make a name for themselves by running Siem Reap province efficiently and preserving the peace. Tourism operators, meanwhile, wanted to make money. Moreover, the laws, decrees, and regulations underpinning the Angkor park could be a confusing and overlapping mishmash, distorted further by years of customary practice. The park was run by the EFEO, but it lay in the province of Siem Reap, which was run by the resident, the ranking French official in the province. So who was ultimately in charge?

In 1931, the conservators tangled with a resident called Maurice Meillier over his actions concerning an ancient image of the god Vishnu that local people had unearthed on a river bank west of Angkor. It was given the sacred name Sema and soon sparked religious fervour. People began coming from far away to kneel before it and pray for rain or other godly gifts. After hearing of this, Meillier gave orders that the image be brought to Siem Reap. It was placed outside his offices, and the veneration continued. People applied plaster to it so that gold leaf could be affixed, a common gesture of respect for religious images in Cambodia. After a few days, again by Meillier's orders, it was moved to a local Buddhist temple.

In a letter to Meillier's superior in Phnom Penh, the EFEO director Cœdès protested the moving of the image, saying it violated rules governing antiquities. This was only the latest example of a 'spirit of independence' that Meillier had displayed concerning those rules, Cœdès said, asking that the man be reminded of the need to follow them.[2]

Meillier replied that he had moved the image for 'political reasons.' Leaving it in the isolated, unsupervised location where it was discovered risked that the adoring crowds it had drawn 'might fall prey to troublemakers.' As for the plaster, it could be easily removed. He scolded the conservators for treating the image solely as an object of archaeological study, saying this trod on the rights of local Cambodians to practice their religion.

Meillier also made a legal argument. He had no obligation to consult with the EFEO on moving the image: 'It was about indigenous politics, not archaeology.' Furthermore, he said,

2 Correspondence concerning this and other cases of disputes among the French at Angkor is preserved in the EFEO archive in Paris.

Classical dance at Angkor Wat was for tourists, but also for Cambodians, such as those who watched this performance circa 1920. Image from *Les Ruines d'Angkor.*

'the authority of the representative of the protectorate exists on the park of Angkor as on other parts of the province. The decision that appointed me head of this province made no mention that my powers were reduced there.'

Henri Marchal was flabbergasted. In a private letter to Cœdès, he complained in detail. 'The Cambodians are not such a dangerous race. I do not think the country would have been in great danger if the stone had remained a few more days *in situ*' to allow him or his assistant to examine it.

Meillier 'never loses an opportunity to publicly demonstrate the contempt he feels for all the regulation of the EFEO, which, according to him, falls under his direct control.' What next? Marchal asked bitterly. Mr. Meillier will want 'to demolish the Bayon because he will judge that its too-dark galleries could shelter plots threatening the security of the country.'

Conflicts like this would continue. A few months later, the EFEO formally complained that Meillier had exceeded his authority by sending police officers to close off Angkor Wat for two hours and admit only people who had bought a ticket to a classical dance performance inside. The resident responded that he did in fact have such authority, and that in any case, his men had admitted tourists who didn't have dance tickets but just wanted to see the temple. He mockingly suggested that the next time there was a cremation ceremony for an abbot, which would attract large crowds, he would be happy to send no police and leave security up to the conservation staff. They would 'be solely responsible for public order.'

Later on, a new resident, a Mr. Rouan, took office, but there was no let-up in the bureaucratic tensions. In 1934, the EFEO took issue with Rouan having personally given a visiting Swiss colonel a tour of the monuments. This violated protocol, it said, by which VIP tours are the prerogative of the conservator.

Marchal departed his post, and in 1935 was replaced by his deputy, a boyish but archaeologically accomplished man called Georges Trouvé. More sniping ensued. The temple guards were not doing their job to prevent stealing, Rouan told Trouvé. 'Remind them of their duties. A piece of carved stone was taken and returned, but I've decided that no charges will be brought'. To this Trouvé objected, suggesting that he had sole authority to make such a decision. On that particular claim, his superiors in Hanoi declined to support him.

Trouvé wrote an anguished letter to Cœdès, now the head of the EFEO in Hanoi, describing the fights and closing with a surprise request: 'As I cannot work in such conditions, I ask you…to kindly relieve me of my duties as conservator of Angkor.'

A stunned and cajoling Cœdès wrote back. 'You have the best job in the school, where the work is exciting. You are starting to make a name for yourself. And you want to leave it over a miserable quarrel of self-esteem? You can't be serious!' He advised Trouvé not to respond to troublesome letters immediately, but to get a good night's sleep, and then answer as briefly as possible. 'A spat will be quickly forgotten,' he assured him. In any case, he said, Marchal was going to be visiting Siem Reap shortly, and he would see about restoring friendly relations.

Five months later, Trouvé was dead in Siem Reap at age thirty-three, a suicide.

The obituary that appeared in the EFEO's journal later that year cited his many professional achievements and called his death tragic and premature, while offering no explanation for it. But years later Marchal suggested in an unpublished memoir that it was not entirely a surprise. Marchal had made the promised visit to Siem Reap. There he had witnessed 'every stage of the drama that was being prepared.' Trouvé's marriage was a wreck. By Marchal's account, the dispirited man spoke of his spouse as a *poule de luxe*, literally 'luxury hen,' a term that can variously mean trophy wife, high-maintenance girlfriend, or courtesan. Bored in Siem Reap, she had moved out to go live the high life in Phnom Penh and Saigon. The abandoned husband was turning aside advice that he divorce her, continuing to hope she would come back to him. 'On the morning when Madame Trouvé made clear to her husband that it was she who demanded a divorce,' Marchal wrote, 'the blow was so unexpected and hard for him that he killed himself.'

So it was more than the stress of bureaucratic in-fighting that unravelled his life, but that could not have helped. Perhaps in trying to resign, Trouvé imagined moving with his wife to one of those larger towns, where she would be more content and open to reconciliation.

Near the tomb of Jean Commaille off the Bayon's southwest corner, Trouvé was laid to rest as a new martyr to the cause of Angkor. In the years that followed, the French community in Siem Reap gathered annually at the graves for prayer and the sombre placement of flowers.

Angkor's many Cambodians took notice too, of course, and remembered. They had their own explanations. Six decades later, Japanese anthropologist Keiko Miura was told during interviews with local people that Ta Pech, a powerful and sometimes malevolent spirit resident in Angkor Wat's south gate, had borne responsibility for the death.

7: HOLIDAY DESTINATION

As Angkor gains fame in the world, it is deemed too exciting to be left to the archaeologists. By steamboat, seaplane, and Model T Ford, adventurous tourists come calling.

If you had opened a British newspaper in the 1860s, you might have found an article about a woman called Therese Yelverton, orphaned daughter of a prominent manufacturer. You'd have learned that she had taken private vows of matrimony with an Irish nobleman, William Charles Yelverton, but that he soon moved to discard her, arguing that the bond between them was never legal. He seems to have expected her to go quietly. Instead she fought back with a series of very public lawsuits. Newspapers went to town with this tale of a woman of high rank and education rendered poor but hardly voiceless. She was variously cast as gold-digging or grievously wronged. As the suits progressed, her celebrity grew – at one point, a crowd of fifty thousand was said to have gathered outside the courtroom.

After six years, her fight finally concluded with a failed appeal to the House of Lords. That might have been the end of her in the public eye, but she went on to do something very bold and unusual: she became a solo travel writer, touring the world on her own, without a protective man (though she kept the name of the man whom she insisted she had validly married). She became known for long and thoughtful accounts of far-away places. In 1872 she decided to add Angkor to her list.

It's hard to say when Angkor drew its first foreign tourist. In one sense, Henri Mouhot was a tourist, traversing oceans to behold a fantastic sight (and paying a fee to get in). But ultimately he was there for 'science,' as Father Bouillevaux was there for religion. In the following years came westerners who were there for the sheer joy of seeing the place, and perhaps to make some money afterwards by penning a book or article. Therese Yelverton was among the very first such people.

Therese Yelverton posed in 1870, two years before she visited Angkor. Photo by James J. Reilly, courtesy of the Yosemite National Park Archives, Museum, and Library.

Opposite page: Charlie Chaplin and Paulette Goddard tour Angkor in 1936, caught in a photo that found its way into one of Goddard's albums. © Roy Export Company Ltd.

The 18 June 1864 edition of the *Manchester Times* carried a lengthy report on day five of Yelverton's appeal to the House of Lords. The article began with a quote from a letter she wrote to the man trying to cast her off, whom she addressed as 'Carlo'. Newspaper image © The British Library Board. All rights reserved. With thanks to The British Newspaper Archive (www.britishnewspaperarchive.co.uk)

Her interest was sparked in Macau, then a Portuguese colony on the coast of China, when one day a Frenchman asked if she had seen the wonder in the Cambodian hinterland. She resolved to go, but getting there was no easy task. Only six years had passed since the Mekong commission visit, and facilities for western travellers remained non-existent. Writing later in the American publication *The Overland Monthly*, she recounted making her way first to Phnom Penh. There a French colonial administrator arranged an audience with King Norodom, in the hope that he might help her reach her destination. This was one of many dicey situations for this woman traveling on her own. The king, after all, maintained a large harem, and she had received what seem to be serious warnings to watch her step. But she got through the audience without problem, she later wrote, joking that she had left without being 'shut up in a seraglio.'

On the contrary, the king provided her with a ten-metre boat with rowers, guards, interpreter, pages, and a junior courtier. In seven days of travel across water, she slept and ate in a bamboo-shuttered chamber in the boat's centre. She gazed on forests passing on shore, she rejoiced in the calls of birds. 'There is a sweet satisfaction in self-reliance,' she wrote, 'when a purpose, for which we have to fight to gain every inch of ground, is nearly accomplished. There came over me an indescribable feeling of awe and curiosity as we penetrated into that unknown wilderness, which the face of a white woman had never looked upon.'

The boat reached the northwestern Tonle Sap, then turned up the Siem Reap River. Soon Yelverton got aboard an oxcart for a jarring half-day ride to Siem Reap town. There she met with the Siamese lord, as European men before her had done. She travelled the final distance on the back of a pony that he provided. Then, in a flash, there it was. 'Raising my eyes, I was almost paralyzed at beholding the full glory of the temple of Angkor Wat....For awhile, I could not speak; my faculties seemed absorbed and overcome.' Once again, the great temple had exceeded expectations.

Yelverton stayed for twelve days. She explored the corridors of Angkor Wat, taking photos, using smelling salts against the smell of bat dung. With no guide book and only basic communication with her hosts, she did her best to make sense of the bas reliefs, drawing on her western cultural literacy. She saw Darwinesque significance, for instance, in scenes of battles between humans (gods, in fact) and monkeys (also gods) in the *Ramayana* epic. She climbed to the very top of the temple and gazed in awe on gilded images of the Buddha.

She went on to visit Angkor Thom, believing it was probably the mythical *Sinarum Metropolis* mentioned in the writings of the Roman mathematician Ptolemy. She was closer to the mark about dimensions, saying its walls measured eight to ten miles around (about eight is the actual figure). She passed large Buddha images in the forest. Sometimes she watched and listened as monks chanted prayers before them.

There was no hotel or guesthouse, of course. She passed her nights in a grass-roofed hut that the lord had ordered built for her inside Angkor Wat's walls among the monks' dwellings. Her bed was a mattress the king had provided, sheltered by a mosquito net. She rose early. She had no choice, in fact, because roosters strutted around her hut from dawn, crowing all the time. But she did have morning coffee, no doubt specially brought along.

European men in Cambodia drew gawkers; Yelverton got even more attention. 'All the time I remained, there was an ever-changing crowd of people from the villages, far and near, coming to see me, as the first White woman they had ever beheld.' Among these daily visitors was a somewhat wild-eyed older woman. Her garment was ragged. Her hair formed a strange cone that stood half a meter high. She was said to be the sister of Angkor Wat's abbot – and possessed by a demon. Yelverton was warned to keep her distance, but she felt sympathy and gave the women rice each time she came. Perhaps she saw some kind of parallel to her own cast-out situation back home. 'Poor body! she was another victim to circumstance, for I was told she had been possessed from her youth, and no one would marry her.'

Yelverton left Angkor feeling it was proof of spiritual universality, that all religious faith flows from some common attribute in the human species.

Through these ruins I wandered,…living in a world of by-gone grandeur, of beautiful conceptions and delicate fancies; in communion with high minds and great thoughts that never die, but speak for centuries and tens of centuries in those massive stones, as they will speak to souls yet unborn – telling us plainly that not Solomon alone built temples to the Lord, but that all creatures between earth and heaven have worshipped Him with their highest aspirations, with their utmost labor – bearing testimony to all future generations that the great Supreme has ever been praised with the deepest devotion.

Author Pierre Loti was serving as a French naval officer when in 1901 his ship called in Vietnam and he was able to realize a childhood dream of visiting Angkor. Wikimedia Commons.

* * * * *

Many years passed with Angkor gaining no formal facilities for tourists. But a few foreign sightseers came anyway. In November 1882, when Étienne Aymonier arrived by steamboat on his inscription-collecting mission, a handful of other Europeans stepped off with him, headed for get-aways at the monuments.

In 1901, the big foreign guest was a literary celebrity, Pierre Loti. He had first gone abroad as a French naval officer. Over the course of his life, he penned a collection of travelogues and exotically set novels that built him a world reputation. Turkey, Egypt, China, Japan, India – and now Angkor. All were inspected and dissected by Loti.

He arrived at Angkor Wat at midday. His first act on arriving was…to take a nap, as the French in Indochina habitually did after lunch. During his stay, he explored Angkor Wat and Angkor Thom, returning for siestas inside a mosquito net at a pilgrim hut. It was all far removed from life in Europe, except for something that happened during one of his midday rests. His reputation had preceded him. He was brought three calling cards, bearing the names of three Frenchmen who were requesting the honour of paying him a visit. One of the men was Charles Carpeaux, then at work at the Bayon. In a letter to his mother, Carpeaux would describe having Loti to his house later for a meal. Things did not go smoothly, however. A fire that had been lit to drive off mosquitos suddenly filled the house with smoke, causing the company to hurry outside gasping for air.

Loti stayed just three days, but he made the most of them, authoring some years later *Un Pèlerin d'Angkor.* It was a slim volume made large by soaring prose. By his account, he had dreamed of visiting Angkor as a boy, ever since he'd read an article in a colonial journal. But on seeing the place in person, he was, very much unlike Yelverton, troubled by feelings of suspicion, even revulsion.

Was this another case of the cultural anxiety that often hit the French when they came face to face with the magnificent place? It's impossible to say. But to Loti, the forest and creepers of Angkor seemed ever-threatening. He felt menace in the gaze of the stone faces at the Bayon. In his book he recounts waiting out a sudden downpour in an Angkor Wat chamber that was filled with dust-covered wooden images, mouldering in the humid air, with masses of bats hanging overhead.

This, then, is the sanctuary which formerly haunted my childish imagination, which I have only at last reached after many journeyings about the world, in what is already the evening of my wandering life. It gives me a mournful welcome. I had not foreseen these torrents of rain, this confinement amongst the spiders' webs, nor my present solitude in the midst of so many phantom gods. There is above all one personage over there, reddish like a flayed corpse, with worm-eaten and crumbling feet, who, in order that he may not fall altogether, leans crosswise against the wall, half-upturning his face with its pitted lips. It is for him, it seems, that all the silence and all the unutterable sadness of the place proceed.[1]

* * * * *

There was no such moroseness of heart for French aristocrat/adventurer/motorist Ferdinand d'Orléans, the Duke of Montpensier, who arrived in 1908. For him, Angkor was also a dreamed-of destination, maybe not from childhood but from some time earlier when he and friends hatched the idea of being the first to go by motor car from Saigon to the old Khmer capital. Their ride was a Lorraine-Dietrich, an early French roadster shipped to Saigon for the purpose. In a subsequent book, he recounted a bouncy journey by roads and tracks traversing southern Vietnam and Cambodia. When necessary, he and his traveling companions mobilized local people to build bridges to cross culverts and rafts to cross rivers.

The group reached Angkor in twenty-nine days, on 14 April 1908, after the hasty construction of one more bridge, in Siem Reap town, to pass from the east side of the river to the west. Arriving at the entrance causeway of Angkor Wat, the duke was not satisfied – he insisted on taking the car inside the temple. With roaring engine, it climbed the two steps from road to causeway. The duke knew he was violating local sensibilities. 'A crowd of Cambodians are watching us... many of them may be waiting for the thunderbolt, suddenly breaking out in the clear sky, to chastise the impious ones who dare disturb the peace and the set of sacred buildings. But the Buddhas who guard the threshold of palaces and temples do not seem to care about our approach.'

The car made its way across the causeway and through the entrance complex's stepless Elephant Gate. Then came another challenge: five more steps to reach the level of the processional avenue. We can only hope there was no damage to the stones.

---

1 This is from the 1996 translation by W.P. Baines and Michael Smithies.

The duke's Lorraine-Dietrich was pictured in his book parked below the insurmountable steps at Angkor Wat. (Library of Congress collection)

[The car] ascends in a masterful style and without losing any of its dignity, any more than its bolts. A legitimate pride mingles with the exhilaration we feel, my dear traveling companions and myself: we drove the first car to Angkor and no one else could ever go further into the temples. This moment of happy triumph repays us for all the bad hours and all the fatigue we have had to endure.

The Lorraine-Dietrich rolled down the avenue to the very entrance of the temple, the base of the steps that lead up to the cruciform platform. Thankfully these were too many and too steep even for this car and its superpowers. So it was parked there, and, after the taking of photos to mark (and prove) the great automotive feat, the duke went off on a tour of the temple with Jean Commaille, the newly arrived first conservator.

* * * *

In the first years after the French took formal control in 1907, Angkor remained without western-style facilities for visitors. A handful of people, such as the Duke of Montpensier, came nonetheless. He stayed at Commaille's house; others had to fend for themselves. 'Each traveller had to bring his bedding and grooming things, food, and a food service accompanied by a cook,' wrote EFEO's chief archaeologist Henri Parmentier, after a visit in 1908. 'It was a tiring and costly expedition for those – and most are this way – who do not normally live the life of the bush.'

Parmentier looked forward to better transport, a western-style hotel, and a campaign of international promotion. 'When leaving London or New York,' he noted, 'we know in advance when and how to visit the Pyramids or the island of Philae in Egypt. But we do not know Angkor or when or how to get there.'

The colonial authorities wasted no time. By 1909, it was possible to buy an all-inclusive package tour to Angkor from Saigon for 245 francs. Visitors boarded steamboats operated by the monopoly shipping company Messageries fluviales de Cochin-Chine and chugged up the Mekong to Phnom Penh. After a day's layover there, the water journey continued on into the Tonle Sap. At the lake's northwest reaches, visitors switched to sampans, in which local men paddled them up the Siem Reap River toward Siem Reap town. From there they continued north, by oxcart, to the place where they would finally unpack their bags: The Bungalow.

This first western-style hotel at Angkor opened in 1909 as a simple wooden guesthouse with ten rooms, fourteen beds, a salon and a large dining room. It would be known in ensuing years by other names – Hôtel des Ruines and Auberge d'Angkor – and acquire a storied history of its own. Depending on what they were accustomed to, guests saw it as unimaginable luxury in a remote place or just one step up

The Bungalow in 1912, with foreigners riding small ox carts known as *norgelettes*. Photo courtesy of DatAsia Press Archive.

from camping out. But there was one thing whose value could not be denied, something that many guests, arriving tired in the gloom of night, didn't appreciate was so close until they rose the next morning and looked out the window – Angkor Wat, right there in all its glory, the sun rising behind its towers. The hotel had the ultimate premium location: at the temple's western moat, a few steps from the entrance causeway.

Owned by the colonial administration, the Bungalow was managed by the same shipping company that brought tourists in. Under a contract signed in 1910, Messageries fluviales committed to have a European manager on the premises at tourist high season. It would offer a continental breakfast for half a piastre and a full for one piastre. Dinner, to include a soup, entrée, vegetable dish, salad, cognac, and wine, would cost three piastres. Someone came up with the idea of providing a true European vacation treat – ice cream. Packed cold for the long journey by boat, it would appear on the menu in the two-day window after a steamboat had arrived.

By October 1911, the Bungalow was doing a modest business of roughly one guest per day. Records show it took in a total of thirty-seven people that month. Guests included a Mr. John L. Laid and a Mr. and Mrs. Blanchard and their daughter.

For guests taking a serious interest in the temples' architecture and history, the hotel's salon had reference books to consult. For getting around, horses were available for one

Tourists who came at the right time of year could catch such sights as these boat festivities, circa 1920, in Angkor Wat's west moat. Image from *Les Ruines d'Angkor*.

and a half piastres a day with a saddle, or one piastre without. There were also conveyances known as *norgelettes*, mini-oxcarts with spring suspensions. (Traditional Cambodian ox carts, tourists were warned, were quite uncomfortable.) And there might be an elephant available as well.

The hotel's social centre, where guests gathered at day's end over aperitifs to compare the amazing things they'd seen, was a large veranda furnished with rattan chairs and potted plants, looking out on Angkor Wat.

By bringing in foreign visitors, the French hoped to show the world that they were a rightful, responsible steward of this historical gem. But mercantile considerations were in play as well. Even early in the twentieth century, colonial administrators had settled on tourism as an engine of economic growth for Indochina as a whole. From his office in Hanoi, the governor general took a close interest. Around Indochina, hotels were built, roads constructed. Costly promotional campaigns in Europe and the United States sought to catch the eye of wealthy travellers (and wealthy was basically the only kind, mass-market international tourism remaining uninvented). Indochina even tried to promote itself, the Angkor area included, as a destination for big game hunting. Wild boar, buffalo, deer, tigers, Asian rhinos, even elephants were all waiting to become stuffed trophies on the walls of homes back in Europe and the United States.

But from the beginning, the government's tourism arrangements at Angkor drew criticism as poorly planned, uncomfortable, or even so bad as to scare tourists off.

In a 1911 letter to France's Angkor Society, Charles Gravelle, head of its Cambodia subcommittee, depicted the water journey to Angkor as a steerage-class ordeal. 'We cannot reasonably expect that people, some of them old, who travel for leisure and without concern over cost, will accept with good humour and resignation thirty-six hours of complete misfortune, dispiriting food, and the sleep of Italian emigrants.' The word was getting around, he warned. 'Last summer's American visitors, while expressing enthusiasm, said they would wait for improvement of the river trip before encouraging their many friends who would be likely to come to Cambodia.' This was not to mention the wobbly sampans into which tourists stepped from the arriving steamers.

To the critics, there was little to admire about the Bungalow either. Policies of favouring guests who were colonial officials (visiting either on business or holiday) with set-aside rooms and discount prices tended to crimp the flow of bigger-spending

'Indochina is the tourist paradise,' declared this 1929 advertisement in the publication *L'Éveil économique de l'Indochine*. Image from collection of Bibliothèque nationale de France.

international tourists – and wasn't bringing new money into the colony the whole point of tourism? Even the prices on the hotel's menu drew questions. Surely, critics said, it wasn't fair to charge the same for a dinner that had ice cream and one that didn't.

Improvement was promised, but a decade later, many of the same complaints were still being aired. In a 14 February 1920 letter to the Touring Club of France, the ranking French official in Cambodia, the *résident supérieur*, acknowledged that the steamboat trip was unpleasant and the hotel primitive, not in line with the high fees that tourists were paying. We're working on it, he essentially said. Further issues had arisen concerning how the Bungalow was run. The steamboat company was trying to renegotiate its management contract, saying the current government subsidy of fifteen hundred piastres a year was too low. Furthermore, complaints had been voiced against the hotel's French manager. Despite a shortage of rooms, he was said to be putting up family members who had nothing to do with the hotel's operation. The company firmly instructed him to occupy just one room.

Slowly, slowly, facilities expanded and improved. By 1924, the Bungalow had twenty-one rooms, electric lights, and a telephone line connecting to the French colonial office in Siem Reap. Beds were made up in white linen; mosquito nets hung overhead. Photographs, postcards, and guidebooks were on sale. Model T Fords were available for touring the temples, though people who preferred a more 'authentic' experience could still go around by elephant, horse, or oxcart. Depending on how many sites they wished to visit in Angkor, visitors followed a *petit circuit* or *grand circuit* that the EFEO had helpfully mapped out. There was as yet no post box at the hotel for sending cards and letters home, something that a visiting colonial official noted with disapproval. The hotel got one soon afterwards.

Foreigners eating a picnic lunch at the gate of Preah Khan temple in Angkor, as Cambodians looked on in this postcard from the early twentieth century.
(John Burgess collection)

Cambodians, such as these women depicted on a vintage postcard, continued to come to Angkor during the early tourist age.
(John Burgess collection)

2   Candee makes no mention
    in the book, but this form of
    disembarkation surely recalled
    to her the terror of ten years
    earlier, when she was among
    passengers of the Titanic who
    boarded lifeboats at night and
    survived.

But no matter how comfortable (or less uncomfortable) the steamboat trip might become, nature had put limits on that mode of access: the dry-season shrinkage of the Tonle Sap made it navigable for the boats for only about half the year. The Bungalow, in fact, was open for business only in that period, roughly September 15 to February 15. Angkor would need practical access by road. That came around 1925, with completion of Highway 6 linking Siem Reap and Phnom Penh. In places, French civil engineers routed it right across surviving Angkor-era bridges. Rainy season wash-outs remained a problem, but arrivals by motor car and public bus increased steadily. Another road connection to Siem Reap was also opened from the Thai border town of Aranyaprathet.

* * * * *

The American writer Helen Churchill Candee, who arrived in 1922, was typical of the well-heeled, adventurous foreigners who were putting Angkor in their travel plans.

In her book *Angkor the Magnificent*, she recounts the disconcerting experience of stepping down at night from her steamboat into a sampan for the paddle to shore.[2] But once there, things looked up. Ford motor cars were waiting. She and other visitors were driven with their baggage through the night to the Bungalow, where the manager welcomed them. Morning brought the view of Angkor Wat.

In the 1920s, some tourists arrived in Angkor aboard public buses like this one, operated by the colonial postal service. It was photographed crossing what appears to be the Tonle Sap River at Phnom Penh. Photo by J. Dearden Holmes/Ninskaphotos.

One of Douglass's etchings depicted the Bayon at sunset. (Metropolitan Museum of Art)

An American Devotee's Final Resting Place

The American artist Lucille Sinclair Douglass was another westerner who became enraptured with the old capital, to the point of deciding to stay eternally.

'Angkor is one of the really great experiences of my life – a more intellectual than emotional experience,' she wrote after her first visit, in 1926, in the company of the writer Helen Churchill Candee. 'Not that it left me cold, quite the contrary – but it was more of an uplift – an inspiration...I have never had a place affect me so peculiarly.'

Born into a genteel family in Tuskegee, Alabama, Douglass became well travelled and accomplished early in life. She studied art in France and worked as an art instructor and journalist in China. On a second visit to Angkor in 1927, she put down roots, staying for five months. She wandered the monuments day after day

Lucille Sinclair Douglass, in an undated portrait. Photo courtesy of Birmingham, Alabama, Public Library Archives.

with an artist's kit and eye. The Bayon, Angkor Wat's moat, the stairway to the third tier were among the places she depicted in sharply drawn etchings.

She became friendly with Henri Marchal and other members of the French archaeological community in Siem Reap. Later on, she lectured on Khmer antiquity in the United States and Britain, becoming known as a sort of unofficial Friend of Angkor. Her etchings of the old capital entered the collection of New York's Metropolitan Museum of Art.

In mid-1935, Douglass began making arrangements for another visit. She inquired from the United States about the cost of a flight from Saigon to Angkor for her and a friend. But no such trip occurred – she died in Massachusetts on 26 September 1935, aged 56.

She may have known she was terminally ill when she contemplated this trip, and one is left wondering if she intended to die in Angkor. According to Marchal, writing in an unpublished memoir, she had declared in one of her last letters that 'no matter what happens to me, my spirit will always be in Angkor.'

At her request, her ashes travelled back to it, in a sealed cylinder. Marchal attended a 'simple but quite moving' ceremony at the lawn off the south gallery of Angkor Wat on 5 February 1936. Those attending formed a circle around a mango tree there and spread her ashes on the grass. 'In line with her wishes,' Marchal wrote, 'the spirit of Miss Lucille Douglass did not leave these monuments which she loved. Her remains were returned to the beautiful Cambodian nature, whose memory had illuminated her last moments.'

This pencil and watercolour of monks and guardian images at Angkor Wat was the work of Dutch artist Marius Bauer in 1931. Image courtesy of the Rijksmuseum, Amsterdam, Gift of J. Bauer-Stumpff.

In ensuing days, Candee experienced the architectural wonders up close, but also classical dance and an elephant ride up Phnom Bakheng. A Ford took her to the further-off Neak Pean temple. She bought a souvenir bracelet. She watched a fellow tourist, a young woman from Boston, set up an easel and paint. She heard another, apparently familiar with some of India's ancient sculpture, remark that he hadn't found anything off-color in the Bayon bas-reliefs.

There seems to have been no reliable system of advance booking at the Bungalow – when you arrived, it either had a room for you, or it didn't. Sometimes an ad hoc arrangement was made. Candee, who took pleasure in observing fellow western travellers, recounts that during her stay the manager announced that twenty more people would arrive that evening, though every room was occupied. In ensuing hours, he cajoled various of his already checked-in guests to double up in rooms to make space. On arriving, the newcomers were appalled to find that *they* had to double up as well. 'Impossible!' 'I cannot sleep two in a room!' 'Unbearable!' Those were the protests heard, but the manager had the last word. His hotel, after all, was the only place in town.

Scenes like that are really only asides in Candee's book. What really interested her was Cambodia. Unlike Loti, she had great admiration and empathy for the heritage on display. She explored temples thoroughly, expressing wonder over them, and admitting that she might remain unable to grasp their full complexities. She had this to say about the *devatas* of Angkor Wat: 'I am made shy in their presence, while they remain unperturbed. They are so many to know all at once, and their character to me is unfathomable. Coming into the court where they abound is like being shown into a room full of living strangers...They have the ease of those to whom self-consciousness is unknown, the air of the rich aristocrat.'

* * * * *

Acquaintance, sometimes real friendship, with French archaeologists at Angkor was something a foreign visitor might take away.

After a society wedding in New York in April 1920, an American couple called Augustine and Jeanette Reid Healy left for a two-year round-the-world honeymoon. By January of the following year, they had made it as far as Angkor. On their first day, a prominent archaeologist joined up with them. 'Mr. Goloubew, a charming Russian, lunched with us [at the Bungalow], an explorer, traveller, and savant,' Jeannette wrote admiringly in her diary. After siesta, he took them to temples, explaining along the way his 'methods of deduction and classification.' He was back at their service the next day. 'We started with Mr. Goloubew after breakfast to Angkor Thom, the old city built by the Khmers between 900 and 1400 AD. He piloted us about, showing one ruin of past grandeur after another… We wandered around all morning listening to his vivid reconstruction of the life and colour of the Khmers.' The morning ended with a drink of milk from a coconut that a local man plucked fresh from high in a tree.

The hoped-for effect of EFEO men tending to prominent visitors was a spreading of the word back home of the temples' grandeur and the French work on them. Goloubew might seem to have been going beyond the call of duty, however. Perhaps he wanted some western company, or was engaging in a little fund-raising, cultivating two people capable of writing a large check for deposit in Angkor's accounts. Jeanette Healy didn't address these questions in her diary, but noted that on their way to the steamer for the trip back to Phnom Penh, she and her husband stopped at his house to bid him adieu.

* * * * *

Many tourists who came to Angkor were determined to go home with a stone memento of the place, by whatever means required. Some bought illicitly from locals. Others engaged in do-it-yourself purloining direct from temples. But occasionally someone had a change of heart. The American writer Arthur Davison Ficke, onetime lover of the poet Edna St. Vincent Millay, was one such person, according to an account he published in 1921 in *The North American Review*, a literary journal of the University of Northern Iowa.

Walking alone one day in the Ta Keo temple, he came face-to-face with a statue of the goddess Parvati. 'From a delicately but powerfully moulded woman's body rose the head that was the statue's chief glory; a head severe and magnificent, noble and sensual, disdainful and exquisite. Among all the sculpture I had ever looked at, nothing had ever moved me as did this.'

Then he was shocked to notice that that enchanting head had been 'broken free' long ago and was merely resting on the shoulders. Before he knew it, he had put it in his bag.

That night in his hotel room he couldn't sleep. He kept looking at the 'beautiful cold proud face.' But he began to feel uneasy. He told his readers that this was not due to moral misgivings. Rather, 'I was profoundly disturbed by the thought that the head and the body of this remarkable statue were now to be separated forever.' He could not go back for the rest of the statue – it would be too heavy. But he found himself reflecting on the tragedy of the Winged Victory, the Greek sculpture treasure in the Louvre in Paris, its head eternally unknown. Early the next morning, he returned Parvati's to her place, though afterwards he felt somewhat of a fool for having given her up.

Not many thieves put things back, of course. Pilfering would remain a chronic problem. That is why a visiting American donated one hundred piasters to place in front of the Bungalow a sign bearing this message in English and French: 'Help us preserve these ruins. Unlawful to destroy or remove any objects.' The EFEO, meanwhile, began taking the precaution of moving major sculpture to depots for safe-keeping. And, seeking to remove the incentive for theft, it put on sale in the Bungalow some genuine items that it deemed to be of no archaeological interest.

* * * * *

To cater to the tourists, professional photographers produced an oeuvre of postcards, samples of which survive today in private collections and on-line auction sites. Many bear no stamps or messages, because buying a packet of the cards to take home was often a substitute for taking your own snapshots. But here and there can be found words in the elegant handwriting of the time. In February 1931, an H. Sourisse sent an Angkor face-tower card to a Mademoiselle P. Grec in Paris with the message 'Best memory of unforgettable days passed at Angkor.' A note to an object of admiration who was far away?

Not everyone was impressed, however. A Frenchman whose name is illegible – he seems to have been a new resident in Indochina – used an Angkor card to express homesickness to a couple back in Vincennes, France. 'I'm getting used pretty well to my new life, but even so, I confess that I'm a little disappointed. The country is not very remarkable and the city even less so, but in the end it is only a moment that will pass.'

The Great Heist of 1923

In 1923, the young writer André Malraux was in a bind. He was already semi-famous in France as a brash new presence in literature and philosophy, but he had run short of cash, due to bad investments in a Mexican mining company. He had read an article that Parmentier wrote about the sculptural riches of Banteay Srei, then still in its unguarded, pre-anastylosis state of isolation and ruin. To the headstrong young man in Paris, the temple seemed just the thing for a solution to his financial problems, and some adventure to boot.

So Malraux and his wife Clara set off on the long sea voyage from France to Saigon, where they met up with a childhood friend of Malraux's. The three made their way to Angkor and checked into the Bungalow. Their cover story was that they had come to make an artistic study of the temples. They toured the main ones, then, with a caravan of buffalo-drawn carts and hired Cambodians, set off toward the north. At Banteay Srei, the team hacked and sawed off about 650 kilograms of sculpture and loaded it into the carts. After a week away, the group returned to the Bungalow. Its manager, a Mr. Debyser, became suspicious that the carts seemed so heavily laden.

The plan was to sell the loot in New York, but thieves and treasure made it only as far as Phnom Penh. Debyser had alerted authorities; George Groslier had the group taken into custody at the city's waterfront.

Clara was allowed to return to France, but the two men went on trial in Phnom Penh. Convicted and sentenced to three years in prison, they never served the time, in part because Clara managed to make her husband a *cause célèbre* in literary circles back in France. His defenders made legalistic arguments that removing the sculpture wasn't really a crime because Banteay Srei hadn't been formally listed as a protected site. They also suggested that, whatever the rights and wrongs of Malraux's acts, it would be a travesty to imprison someone of his talent and intellect.

André Malraux in 1962, during a visit to the United States as minister of state for cultural affairs. Robert Knudsen. White House Photographs. John F. Kennedy Presidential Library and Museum, Boston.

Malraux returned to France, deprived of the sculpture but not of material for his typewriter. He fictionalized the Cambodia escapade into a dark and tendentious novel called *La Voie Royale* (The Royal Way), the tale of two Frenchmen who amidst jungles and hostile indigenous people seek their destiny in a quest for a trove of exotic sculpture. The world would hear much more of Malraux in later years. He would become an iconic figure of modern French culture and history, writing more (and better) books, fighting the Nazis as part of the resistance in World War II, and serving in the 1950s and '60s as France's minister of culture.

Six years after his contact with Malraux, Bungalow manager Debyser had his own run-in with the law. An audit of the hotel's books had turned up numerous discrepancies, including a gap of more than ten thousand piasters in the wine accounts. He was put on trial, accused of using his position to skim five percent on wine orders. His defence argued that breakage and spoilage were to blame, but the court did not believe it. Debyser was sentenced to six months in jail.

Another Angkor tourist, visiting in 1931, jotted complaints on a card mailed to a woman in France. 'The ruins of the Angkor region are ruins, nothing more. In my opinion, they're not worth the tiring and long road trip in the blazing sun.'

A few returning travellers wrote Angkor articles for magazines and newspapers. Headline writers often summoned their best swashbuckling tones. In 1924, the American newspaper *Hartford Courant* gave its readers a very long account by Gertrude Emerson, who later in life became known as a distinguished writer and geographer.

IN THE DEAD CITY OF THE JUNGLE
American Girl Wanders Alone in Ghostly Ruins of the
Ancient Cambodian Capital
Leering Bats Only Live Creatures Met By
Traveler in Place Once Larger Than
Rome in the Days of Nero –
Array of Smiling Gods.

In 1926 the *Minneapolis Sunday Tribune*, another American newspaper, had one by a man called Richard Halliburton.

FROM THE FANGS OF DEATH TO A MAGIC CITY
Caught in the Coils of a Cobra in the Depths of a Siamese Jungle
Daring World Traveler
Braves Flooded Tropic
Wilderness in Struggle
to Reach Ancient Ruins

Halliburton cast almost his every act of the trip as an exploit, even acceptance of the Bungalow staff's ride to the hotel. From his boat he 'splashed ashore' and saw 'an archaic Ford – unescapable even in these jungle wilds.' "How far is the bungalow?" I asked the native French-speaking chauffeur, expecting to be told only a few stops. "Twenty-five kilometers" – 15 miles. And the tourist bureau in Saigon advertised that their river steamers deposited one at "the very gates of Angkor!" '

An Angkor experience might also became grist for the lecture circuit in the United States and Europe, where people paid for the privilege of listening for an hour. In December 1925, the American photographer and film-maker Burton Holmes, said to be the coiner of the term 'travelogue,' held forth on Angkor in Washington, DC's National Theater, whilst showing clips of silent film shot at the temples.

* * * * *

As tourism expanded, private entrepreneurs were opening a few small, low-cost hotels in Siem Reap. Still, officials in Indochina worried that a dearth of good accommodations would undermine their plans for tourism on a grade scale. Momentum began building for a large, modern, *dignified* hotel offering the era's equivalent of five-star luxury. But where to site it? In the view of one group of officials, it only made sense to put it among the temples, where the tourists would

The Grand Hotel, shown here around its opening in 1932, brought tourist luxury to new heights in Siem Reap. © Lynda Trouvé / Christophe Fumeux.

want to be, though, like the Bungalow, it would have to be low-rise and obscured by forest leaves to fit in with the ancient monuments.

That point of view eventually lost out. The Grand Hotel d'Angkor opened in 1932 in Siem Reap town, a full five kilometres from Angkor Wat. With a design in colonial art deco style, it was one in a series of tourist palaces going up in French Indochina under a plan drafted by the architect and town planner Ernest Hébrard. It had four floors and more than sixty rooms, each with a private bathroom. Guests rode a bird-cage elevator to upper floors and walked corridors tiled in patterns of black and white.

Hébrard himself was among those who favored keeping the temple zone free of tourist development. 'It's not just a matter of preserving the masterpiece ruins,' he wrote in 1935 in *Urbanisme: Revue mensuelle de l'urbanisme français*. 'It's necessary as well to protect against modern buildings becoming inappropriate neighbors, able to damage the charm through the brutality of a strange element appearing in their setting.'[3]

Though the new hotel was far from the temples, it was not entirely removed from them. From its top the central tower of Angkor Wat could be seen. And it sat right on the north-south axis of Angkor Thom, seven kilometres south of the city's South Gate. This siting appears to have been a deliberate decision, though whose is not clear. It's been suggested that George Groslier was consulted. However it happened, the hotel kept with the ancient architects' beliefs that all must take its proper place in the cosmic design.

An early guest, British author H.W. Ponder, called it an

3   Hébrard wrote in his article that the governor general had decided to demolish the Bungalow. But that did not happen.

On New Year's Eve 1934, a Grand Hotel guest called Nicholas, staying in Room 101, signed for a Badoit mineral water and glass of Bordeaux. (John Burgess collection)

'immense and dazzling white concrete palace that would look more at home on the Côte d'Azur that in its present setting in the middle of the Cambodian plains.' At the time of her visit, the Bungalow had been temporarily closed, apparently so as to channel business to the new creation. But an exception was made for Ponder. She slept nights at the old place, with its view onto Angkor Wat, but took meals in the fancy dining room of the new.

French colonial offices kept up the promotion. A booklet entitled *Les Hotels en Indochine* noted that in Siem Reap 'good French cuisine is served everywhere, while excellent wines and liquors from France can be had if desired.' An American travel film of the time, however, stuck with the enigmatic and exotic. 'Angkor Wat reminds me of the tale of the mystery ship,' intoned narrator Deane H. Dickson, 'found deserted on a calm sea, with all sails set, a fire burning in the galley, and a table laid for lunch. Not a soul was aboard. Nor was there a hint of what had happened. That is Angkor Wat. It is no ruin. In its beauty and state of preservation it is unrivaled.'

* * * * *

With hotel swimming pools a thing of the future, Angkor tourists sometimes cooled off in water bodies built by the ancient Khmers. Here the camera caught foreigners and local Cambodians in a carefully posed tableau, circa 1930. © Lynda Trouvé / Christophe Fumeux.

Connection to the world's growing network of air travel was getting underway.

France had been a pioneer in the development of what people there called *hydravions*, hydro-airplanes, 'flying boats' that could take off and land on water. Early biplane versions flown by goggled aviators in open cockpits had been arriving off and on for years (archaeologists' early aerial surveys were often conducted using these types of planes). But it wasn't until 10 April 1929 that Angkor got, with some promotional pomp, what was billed as the start of a regular commercial service by Compagnie Aérienne Française. That day, a Schreck FBA 17 flying boat took off from Saigon, set down on the river at Phnom Penh, then took off again for Angkor. At the controls was a well-known pilot of the time, Fernand Robbe. His passengers were a very game shipping executive and a colonial government representative, selected apparently as symbols of public-private cooperation in tourism. At 5 pm, the aircraft set down on the south moat of Angkor Wat, where conservation workers had carried out a special clear-up of floating vegetation.[4] Watching was a crowd that included local French notables and Cambodian monks. The monks must have been particularly amazed, both at the sight and noise, and at how the local spirits might react to this intrusion into their abode. The aircraft taxied on its floats into the west moat and beached on the bank right in front of the Bungalow. Robbe and his passengers stepped ashore to be greeted by the resident of Siem Reap.

The colonial government did its best to promote 'aerial tourism,' in Angkor and elsewhere in Indochina. The flight from Phnom Penh to Angkor took only an hour and forty-five minutes. But speed of travel was not the only advantage, the government pointed out – there was no substitute for the thrill of seeing the monuments from above. One of its writers described it like this:

> '*To arrive over Angkor in full flight, at a thousand meters of height, to see beneath in a striking miniature and like a precise synthesis, the stately ruins enveloped in the folds of the millenary forest, to see springing from the ground and growing the large copolas which surmount the stairs, the temples, the passages, the monasteries, to distinguish better second by second the details of the architecture,*

MESSAGERIES MARITIMES

"ANGKOR"

The ocean liner *Angkor*, shown here in a vintage postcard, took on passengers at Marseille for the trip to Asia. (John Burgess collection)

4   Not for free, however. The EFEO gave Mr. Robbe a bill for fifty-two piastres.

This four-seat flying boat, a Schreck FBA 17 operated by *Compagnie aérienne française,* landed on the Angkor Wat moat around 1930. Three people who appear to be proud passengers posed with the seated pilot. *(Collection Ville de Biscarrosse (France)—Musée de l'Hydraviation, Origine Tixier)*

the elegance of the buildings, the set-off of the sculptures, the patine of the stones, the entwining of the boughs and branches and, in a dizzy descent, to repose on the still water which splashes around you in carbuncles of an incomparable design, it is to accumulate in a few rapid instants, which one regrets not being longer, an infinity of sensations of which nothing else can give an idea.'

In addition to the Angkor Wat moat, the West Baray was functioning as a hydroplane runway. In 1931, minister of the colonies Paul Reynaud, later to become prime minister, arrived at Angkor by land as part of an inspection trip and departed by air, from the *baray*. He was paddled out to a floating airplane, which lifted off, then turned in the direction of Phnom Penh.

By now construction of a proper airport was underway on land northwest of town. Opened in 1932 with a short runway, the airport soon began receiving the smaller passenger planes of the time. The French carrier Air-Orient added flights to what for years would be known as Angkor Wat Airport. An aerial view of the temple graced some of its travel posters.

* * * * *

Much of the development of tourism in the 1930s could be traced to an indefatigable, some would say combative, man called Alfred Messner. A military officer turned brewer, hotelier, restauranteur, and all-around disrupter of established ways, he was named manager of both the Grand and the Bungalow in 1932.

In his view, the old place had degenerated into a rank embarrassment – overpriced, undermaintained, and lacking in modern comforts. It had become known, he said shortly after his arrival, for 'the merciless exploitation of the tourist.' Messner worked to improve it. Around this time, likely by the new manager's doing, it acquired the more alluring name of Hôtel des Ruines.

But his real focus would be the Grand. Under his tutelage, the area in front became a European-style park, while a golf course was built to the back. He operated hunting excursions beyond town – prey seems to have included birds and wild boar. He offered guests 'nautical attractions' at the West Baray, including water polo, boating, and at least one diving board. Visitors wanted souvenirs, so Messner promoted the

Buses lined up at the Bungalow, now rechristened Hôtel des Ruines, in December 1936. Photo by Robert Larimore Pendleton, from the American Geographical Society Library, University of Wisconsin-Milwaukee Libraries.

Hôtel des Ruines' salon, or reading room, shown here in the 1930s, provided background material on Angkor for visitors. ©Archimages@AngkorDatabase

production and sale of jewellery, paintings, and replica stone sculpture. Visitors would not want to wait to return home to see their photographs, so he had a darkroom installed in the Grand. He was an amateur photographer himself, and no doubt had his own film developed there.

Maximizing tourist numbers was of course a prime goal. Messner felt these were being held down by the cost of the road trip to Angkor from Saigon and the Thai border town Aranyaprathet. 'Tourists were unanimous in complaining about high prices; I looked for a remedy,' he wrote. He bought five cars and created his own service, offering the same rides for (by his account) thirty to fifty percent less. This was done in part to force down the prices of a firm operated by a Mr. Henri Vergoz, who was a formidable presence in the Indochina tourism business, being the local agent for the Thomas Cook and American Express travel firms. It was the start of an energetic, sometimes pugnacious, competition between the two men at Angkor.

Another of Messner's focuses was dressing up some of the monuments for tourists. Angkor Wat was illuminated at night in an early form of *son et lumière*. Classical dancers performed for tourists on the cruciform platform at its western side, the temple towers bathed in magical glowing hues above them. In an odd union of disparate religious traditions, the Hindu and Buddhist edifice became known among the French of

Indochina as a place to go for special Christmas-season dance performances.

As his six-year contract progressed, it seemed there was nothing *touristique* that Messner didn't want to improve. He proposed working with the Siamese rail system to operate overnight sleeper cars on the rail line linking Bangkok and the Cambodian border. And why not put European welcome staff at the border? The 20,000 promotional pamphlets that were being distributed abroad were drawing people, but were not enough, he warned – print at least 50,000! How to replace wooden bridges that give out after a year? Make them of old train rails instead. How to regulate tipping? Add 5 percent to bills and share the proceeds among staff at the end of the month.

One of his more unusual (and largely unrealized) proposals was to turn Angkor into a destination for Buddhist and Hindu pilgrims from beyond Cambodia, much like, he said, Mecca was for Muslims. He consulted on the idea with the Buddhist Institute in Phnom Penh. There would be a need to involve shipping and railroad companies if the pilgrim numbers were to become truly large. Ancient religious festivals could be revived as an extra draw. In general the cost would not be high, he said: Monks coming to Angkor would need only rice and shelters that could be built at low cost. And there might be a bonus effect that the buzz of religious activity would draw more western tourists to come for a look.

'Mr. Messner is a man who knows that he's talking about, says what he thinks…and isn't afraid to have ideas,' wrote a commentator in the publication *L'Eveil de l'Indochine*. 'He's a worker and a man of initiative.'

EFEO and the conservation staff continued their own lower-key, old school-style promotion of tourism. They paid special attention to Banteay Srei, into whose rebuilding they had put so much time and capital, partly in hopes of drawing tourists. But the head count remained paltry. In a December 1937 letter, Angkor's new conservator, Maurice Glaize, lamented that rains made the road to the temple impassable three months a year and that local government authorities weren't helping much with repairs. 'Many tourists have had to give up excursions they were planning, while others who are more tenacious have had to spend an entire day, and after many incidents on the road, make part of the trip by foot or oxcart.' Other countries, he said, wouldn't tolerate such conditions concerning a great monument; foreigners were getting 'a pitiful impression of our touristic organisation.'

Nonetheless, the numbers were slowly rising, even though the Great Depression was biting into international travel. A report that Messner sent out on his fancy stationery showed 999 tourists visiting in the first six months of 1931, 1,015 for that period in 1932, 1,150 for 1933, 1,582 for 1934, and 1,695 for 1935. The annual totals were something less than double these figures, because muddy roads and aversion to rainfall on holiday lowered tourist numbers in the years' second halves.

Some of the Indochina French turned their noses up at the foreign visitors, viewing them as charmless rubes who crowded the good hotels and restaurants. One columnist likened them to herds of cattle but noted that, like it or not, they could have a positive effect: they 'leave a manure which enriches the ground,' he wrote, 'and which in Angkor would allow the arrangement and consolidation of the ruins as well as scientific or artistic work.' Still, the overall numbers could seem pitiful in light of the government's long and costly campaigns of promotion and investment. And so many of the visitors continued to be Indochina French, who brought no new foreign exchange into the colony, merely redistributed what was already there.

Various ideas were tossed about for pushing the tourist numbers up. A rail line was being built from Phnom Penh to the Thai border, but it ran south of the Tonle Sap. Why not build another line on the north shore with a stop at Siem Reap, so that tourists could arrive in the comfort of night trains with sleeper cars? Why did the EFEO have to be so restrictive with the sale of antiquities to tourists, limiting it to cast-offs? Surely many more people would come if they could legally buy quality pieces of Khmer sculpture.

Some contended government policies made it hard for tourists to do what many wanted to do, visit just Angkor. The tourism bureau tried instead to channel them into costly, weeks-long visits to Indochina with Angkor as just one stop. In a 1931 commentary, Henri Cucherousset, editor in chief of *L'Eveil économique de l'Indochine*, cited a hypothetical English family that wants to cross from Thailand for a low-cost three or four days at Angkor. French travel officials would be aghast. No, no, don't! they would say. 'You're going to first take a long detour to Singapore and then take a French boat to Saigon. There you start by touring the city. Then you can rent a car at great cost to go visit Angkor, and above all, don't take the bus.'

'The main stupidity is to bully the tourist by considering him a bit too much like a cow to be milked,' Cucherousset wrote, in another use of the bovine metaphor. 'Result: he does not come.'

Visitors listening to a guide at the Bayon in December 1936. Photo by Robert Larimore Pendleton, from the American Geographical Society Library, University of Wisconsin-Milwaukee Libraries.

But others did come. A booking aboard the twin-stacked ocean liner *Angkor*, operated by the company *Messageries Maritimes*, was one way to come out to the region from Europe. There was also a growing selection of package tours, organized from far away by groups such as the Touring Club of France.

But after French residents of Indochina itself, the biggest foreign group visiting Angkor was not Europeans but Americans. Some were military, coming from the not-so-far away Philippines, then an American colony. In 1938, Hyman Rickover, a young officer stationed there who would go on to become the father of the American nuclear navy, arrived with his wife Ruth. That same year, three American destroyers docked at Saigon, and twenty-four of the men aboard went in a group to the old capital.

Angkor had long begun drawing the occasional VIP visitor. In 1922, it was the writer Somerset Maugham. In 1930, it was King Prajadhipok of Siam. In 1936 Charlie Chaplin and his co-star and possibly (they wouldn't say) newly wedded wife Paulette Goddard arrived as part of a five-month tour of Asia that drew media attention every step of the way. Dressed in the loose cotton whites of western tropical vacationers, Chaplin and Goddard climbed and poked around the major monuments. Once again, the charming Victor Goloubew turned out as

5   Three decades later, Chaplin published his voluminous *My Autobiography*. He offered memories of time in Japan, Hong Kong, and Bali, but had not a word to say about Angkor, or Indochina at all. His accounts of the other places focused not on sights but on personalities, culture, and political intrigue. Perhaps Angkor did not engage him in those ways.

guide for important visitors. As if *he* was the Hollywood star, he presented Goddard with an autographed photo of himself. It's not known whether she returned the favour.[5]

One VIP made great effort to visit Angkor, but didn't get there – Antoine de Saint-Exupéry, author of the children's classic *Le Petit Prince*. This multi-talented man was also an aviator and sometime ambassador for the newly established Air France. In July 1934, on a visit to Indochina for the airline, its Saigon station lent him a flying boat – a single-engined Lioré et Olivier 190 – for a trip to Angkor with four colleagues. The plane took off from Saigon. But twenty minutes into the flight, it developed engine problems and Saint-Exupéry guided it in for an emergency landing on river water. After on-the-spot adjustments, the flight resumed – and more problems quickly ensued. He brought the plane down for a second time. The group passed the night aboard it on an isolated riverbank, awaiting pick-up the next morning by boat. Saint-Exupéry's plans to see the temples came to an end. A fuel shortage was eventually blamed for the engine's malfunction.

Yet another VIP *probably* visited Angkor. The surrealist painter Max Ernst arrived (with the other two members of his *marriage à trois*) in Saigon by steamship on 11 August 1924. He departed on 13 September. There is no record, but he seems to have made his way to Angkor in that one-month period. He later told a biographer of having visited Khmer ruins. Some scholars, in fact, feel that the view of Angkor Wat from the Bungalow's terrace is reflected in his 1934 painting 'The Entire City' (*La Ville Entière*), now in the Tate collection in London. But there is no ticket stub, no diary entry, no recorded sighting of the great artist at Angkor.

* * * * *

Given his propensity for shaking things up, it was no surprise that Alfred Messner got tangled in disputes, with the EFEO and other members of the tour business. In 1936, he had one going with the same Mr. Vergoz whom he had faulted as overcharging for rides from the Thai border. By now, Vergoz had a hotel that was in direct competition with Messner's, the New Siem Reap Hotel, located on a corner in the old part of town. ('If you visit Angkor, stay at Vergoz's place,' read one of his ads. 'Great cuisine, rooms with every modern comfort. The least expensive hotel in Angkor.') He also still had his motor car business. The substance of the dispute is unclear, but whatever it was, it was important enough to rise all the way to the desk of the governor general in Hanoi, who ruled that Messner should retain his contract as hotel manager but be monitored to assure that he met its full conditions.

In 1937 there came more trouble for him, a very public complaint about the Bungalow, now the Hôtel des Ruines. The Siam Society, a prestigious Bangkok organisation with royal patronage, had organized a Christmas holiday trip to Angkor with a party of twenty-four people. The firm overseeing the trip, the Borneo Company, was not happy about the accommodations and wrote a letter saying so. 'The number of boys was quite inadequate for so many persons staying in the hotel; the boys seemed inefficient; and the food was poor. In particular several of the luncheon baskets supplied to our clients on leaving Angkor were found when opened to contain, among other things, bad eggs.' Correct these problems, the firm said, or we won't recommend this hotel.

The *Bangkok Times* added to the embarrassment with an article by a tour participant, who said the visit had been wonderful save for the 'legalized banditry' practiced by the hotel. This was all brought to high-level government attention. Cœdès weighed in with a private letter to the governor general, warning of harm to Indochina's tourism reputation and noting that the EFEO's people in Siem Reap had had 'too many opportunities for friction' with Mr. Messner.

That friction came to a head in May 1938. On a Tuesday afternoon that month, conservator Glaize got a tip that something untoward was going on at a small temple, Prasat Patri, located just off the road linking Siem Reap and the airport. Glaize went immediately to the scene and found a Grand Hotel van and several employees breaking up fallen stones by sledgehammer and loading the pieces. He ordered them to stop. One of the broken stones was a carved lintel. Glaize then went to the hotel and confronted Messner's deputy, a Mr. Legrand, who acknowledged that these were his men, instructed to gather sandstone blocks – but only ones with no carving – that would be sent to Saigon for carving into replica sculptures for tourists.[6]

The EFEO filed a formal complaint with the French resident. There followed a series of letters back and forth. Messner began one to Glaize in a sarcastic tone: 'I have just learned from Legrand that I have become a big thief of the stone of Angkor in my old age. I've really finished up badly...' But he went on to defend himself and his team in detailed and sober terms, depicting the stones as 'abandoned,' coming from a place outside the Angkor zone, and having no value. It

6   Documentation of this dispute is preserved in the EFEO archive in Paris.

was permissible to take them. 'The removal was done in broad daylight in good faith and not clandestinely,' he noted.

He also could not resist pointing out the EFEO's long practice of improving roads with gravel made by grinding up loose stone quarried by the ancients.

In sum, Messner wrote, 'we are currently making a lot of noise for nothing.' The EFEO's decision to file a formal complaint 'lacks elegance,' he complained, suggesting that if officials at the institute had a problem, they should have just brought it to him for an explanation. 'I have always believed myself until now to be an auxiliary of the EFEO and not a gentleman à la Malraux who plunders ruins.' But he gave no ground on selling the sculpture: 'No one can forbid me to copy subjects from Angkor, because the ruins and their stones are in the public domain. The only thing I cannot do is sell a copy as an original piece.'

In a private letter to his boss in Hanoi, Glaize lamented the whole affair, noting how awkward it was to get into a feud with people whom you see regularly. (Members of Siem Reap's small French community were intimately acquainted, and one gets the impression that Messner could be intimidating in person.) Glaize had initially wondered if the whole thing could be settled privately, with Messner agreeing to pay compensation and stop making statues. But he noted that another tourist operator, that same Mr. Vergoz, had found out about the incident and gone to the resident. If Messner was not brought to book, Vergoz was saying, he would send a truck of his own to Banteay Srei to haul away stones. Moreover, Vergoz had a brother in high places who would mount a press campaign. Vergoz hoped that

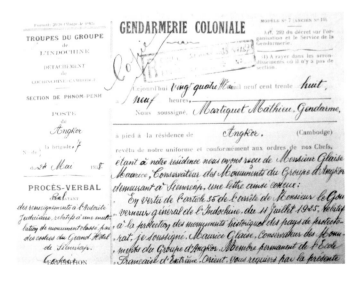

With exquisite penmanship, a colonial gendarme wrote up his findings after investigating the broken stones at Prasat Patri. Document from EFEO archive.

a court finding against Messner would bring his dismissal from the hotel, 'which cannot keep a thief in its service.'

The colonial police formally interviewed Glaize, Legrand, and the Indochinese men who had been at the temple (history records their names as Nguyen Van Tri, Truong Van Ut, Thach Doeuk, Nop Buth, and Nuon Tim). Messner was not formally questioned. The police also went to the scene, where they confirmed that there was indeed a broken lintel with carving. A court case ensued, with charges against the five Indochinese men and Legrand. In August, the court acquitted one of the Indochinese, Nguyen Van Tri, fined the four others five piastres each, with the fines suspended. It fined Legrand fifty piastres, with no suspension.

Messner did not face prosecution, but soon he was to leave the scene. It's unclear whether the trouble with the stones helped bring on what came next, or whether it was simply the matter of a six-year contract expiring and a logical successor being named. However it happened, travel decals that were stuck on the suitcases of guests at Siem Reap's premier place to stay soon bore the words '*Grand Hotel d'Angkor, Concessionnaire H. Vergoz.*'

* * * * *

This and other dust-ups notwithstanding, as the 1930s drew to a close French plans for Angkor were by and large on track. The ancient capital was revealing more and more of its history and archaeological secrets. It was drawing a growing, if still small, number of free-spending admirers from foreign countries – even a man who'd been the world's most famous movie star. More tourists seemed sure to come: Siem Reap airport was upgraded in 1938 to give it a paved, seven-hundred-metre runway, long enough for the biggest passenger planes of the era.[7]

In French minds, Angkor was offering daily proof that colonial rule was justified and bringing vast benefits, both to Cambodia's people and the world at large.

In the new decade, the Second World War would close in. A broken lintel? Mud on the road to Banteay Srei? How trivial such concerns would come to seem.

7   Whether the reason was real estate availability or the direction of prevailing winds, the runway had a spiritually jarring alignment of northeast-southwest, at odds with Angkor's strict respect for the four cardinal directions.

8: In the Path of
an Invading Army

Thailand attacks a weakened French Indochina, aiming to recover territories it surrendered in 1907 – Angkor included.

What began the undoing of French plans for Angkor – and Cambodia as a whole – were events not in Asia, but Europe. In May 1940, Nazi Germany invaded and quickly conquered France. It divided the country into an occupied zone and Vichy France, the notorious collaborationist republic. Vichy had control of the country's south, but also its overseas empire, Indochina included. Nazi Germany was a friend of Imperial Japan, and therefore so were Vichy and French Indochina.

At the time, the Japanese were fighting a long and inconclusive war in China. Following the changes in Europe, they requested – in effect demanded – that the French move to cut off supplies that were flowing through Indochina to Japanese foes in southern China. The French agreed. The Japanese followed up with a request-demand to station troops in northern Vietnam. The French were appalled with that idea; it was one thing to have cordial relations with Japan and another to host its soldiers. They recognized that whatever the legalities of such an arrangement, it would in effect mean surrendering sovereignty, and to an Asian power at that.

The newly appointed governor general of Indochina, Admiral Jean Decoux, had sworn allegiance to Vichy, but could see no help coming from its direction. So in September 1940, he opened the door, agreeing to accept 6,000 Japanese troops in northern Vietnam. Perhaps to show who was truly in charge, one imperial army commander subjected the French *after* signature of the agreement to several days of attacks at the border town of Lang Son, causing extensive casualties.

Peace was restored. The Indochina French continued their privileged lives as colonial overseers. But everyone knew that it was now through the charity of the Japanese.

The very visible humiliation soon brought the French more problems. The military men who now ruled Thailand saw a chance to take back parts of Cambodia and Laos that

Opposite page: Preah Enkosei in Siem Reap town was the only Angkor-era temple to be damaged – and only a little – by bombing in the 1941 war with Thailand. (Photo Don Guiney)

Tirailleurs Indo-Chinois

This postcard depicted protection of Angkor as a prime function of Indochinese men who served in the colonial armed forces. Courtesy of Joel Montague.

their country had ceded under military pressure to France in 1907. Returning the land was only fair, the Thai legation in London said. 'There has been no thought in the mind of the Thai government of taking advantage of the present plight of France and Indochina,' though that was precisely what it seemed to be doing. Thailand demanded negotiations – perhaps the French would cave as they had to the Japanese. They did not. By late 1940, skirmishing was breaking out on the border, and full-scale attack from Thailand was looking increasingly likely.

In response, the French began reinforcing western Cambodia and Laos with French and colonial troops. Some of these men came to Siem Reap. In October, Glaize and the conservation staff were unsettled to find that colonial commanders viewed Angkor Wat as an available military barracks. Newly arrived Cambodian soldiers entered the temple and laid out their bedding in the shelter of its famed bas-relief corridors. Glaize's team protested, saying no one had consulted them and pointing out that the billeting might bring bombardment of the temple if war did begin. Glaize found a friend in the French sector commander, who went to see the scene himself and quickly gave orders for the men move. No damage was done during their stay of several days.[1]

Beyond the temple, there was more unwelcome pressure – military teams began cutting down large numbers of trees for construction material. Again, the conservation contacted the commanders, this time asking that trees along roads not be cut and that things worthy of conservation be respected.

Another threat to antiquity came at Siem Reap airport, where a long-delayed expansion was finally moving forward amidst the military build-up. A French civil works official wrote to the conservator asking his permission to demolish the brick towers of an officially listed Angkor-era temple located next to the airport, Trapeang Ropou. They are hazards to aviation, the official said, and 'should disappear.' Glaize responded that he could give no permission to demolish listed edifices. The engineers tried again: then couldn't you get them delisted? The airport work has 'extreme urgency.' Again Glaize refused, joined by the EFEO headquarters in Hanoi. Governor General Decoux's response was to order a new study that would satisfy both conservation and the needs of aviation. The civil works people soon backed down. The conservation submitted to the public works authorities a detailed diagram of the area that they would have to respect, measuring forty by thirty-one metres. Trapeang Ropou was safe, for now.

1 This chapter draws on EFEO documents, notably monthly status reports that Glaize sent to the institute's headquarters in Hanoi. They mostly concern progress on various conservation projects, but *divers* (miscellaneous) sections at the end often describe war-related and political events at Angkor and Siem Reap.

Tensions continued to rise. In November 1940, Decoux officially cancelled all Angkor tourism due to the military situation.

Full war began in early January. Thai troops began advancing into western Cambodia and Laos, with Thai warplanes flying raids against multiple towns and cities there.

At about 4 pm on 8 January, seven Thai planes appeared in the skies over Siem Reap. There was no time for a general alert; people were caught in the open as bombs exploded on both sides of the Siem Reap River. Glaize would report to the EFEO that about ten people died, including monks, women, and children, and about fifteen were wounded. Town inhabitants streamed into the countryside seeking safety; subsequent bombing targeted only the airport.

Field Marshal Plaek Phibulsongkhram oversaw the war against the French in Indochina. Courtesy Franklin D. Roosevelt Presidential Library and Museum.

In what seems a one-in-a-million chance, a single bomb found its way to the only significant Angkor-era structure in Siem Reap town, the tenth century Preah Enkosei. Its two brick towers stood (as they do now) in the grounds of the later-era Wat Enkosei. Detonating a few metres away, the bomb made a hole in the edge of the laterite platform on which the towers stand and dislodged some bricks. It did more serious material damage elsewhere in the grounds of Wat Enkosei, smashing roof tiles, felling trees, and leaving rooms filled with debris. And two of the estimated ten fatalities were at the temple.

After securing the Cambodian border town of Poipet, Thai troops pushed toward Sisophon, with great public support at home. Thais were elated by news that their fighting men were at long last taking on a resented imperialist power. Angkor lay not so far beyond Sisophon. 'These ruins that encompass Khmer art and civilisation – are they going to again know a Siamese invasion?' Writing in the magazine *l'Illustration*, a journalist posed this question to the French public.

French legionnaires and colonial infantry resisted the advancing troops near Sisophon but were unable to stop them. So far, the war was going badly for the French. But a naval battle on 17 January in the Gulf of Siam helped even up things. French warships sank a good portion of Thailand's navy.

The next day, the French conservation staff and other French civilians in Siem Reap got orders to evacuate. Conservation work was suspended; records and photographs were boxed up and sent to the safety of Saigon. Glaize himself withdrew to Dalat in Vietnam. Cambodian staff remained behind, with the precaution of air raid trenches and look-out posts for Thai aircraft.

On 24 January, Thai planes struck Siem Reap airport

again. Damage there from that raid and the previous one was considerable, including three French bombers destroyed on the ground. The French managed to shoot down at least one Thai plane, which ended up as a pile of scrap on the airport road.

The 24 January raid turned out to be the last for Siem Reap. Shortly after, Japan again showed itself to be the real power in the region. Its commander in Indochina instructed the two sides to stop fighting and offered his country's 'good offices' to mediate the conflict. A ceasefire took hold.

Glaize and other French team members were back in Siem Reap by early February. They found little damage to the conservation buildings, though some had been requisitioned by the French military. Ten rails for a small-gauge Decauville train in use at Preah Khan had been stolen.

Governor General Decoux came to town with his wife, and on 6 February the couple spent the morning at Angkor. Decoux put his support behind getting conservation work restarted, so as to build confidence among local people that normal times had resumed.

Tokyo had been selected as the venue for talks toward a peace treaty. On the same day that Decoux and his wife walked through the temples, Thai and French delegations arrived by air in the Japanese capital within an hour of each other.

From the beginning, the French knew that the offer by Japan to mediate did not mean it was going to be neutral. The Japanese were preaching a doctrine of Asia for the Asians. They were courting Siam, the only country in the region to have escaped colonization. The Tokyo conference was shaping up as a place where the French would be giving up considerable territory. But one card they still could play was their unique expertise on Angkor. They would argue that whatever happened, the temples deserved to remain in their hands. French media sounded the message. 'The Angkor ruins from the 18th Century to Today: Forgotten under the Siamese masters – Resurrection through French science.' That was the headline of a front-page article in Saigon's *L'Echo Annamite* newspaper on the day after the delegations arrived in Tokyo. It was the old claim of the *mission civilisatrice*, refashioned for the new realities: French experts were preserving the Angkor marvel for the world and were the only ones up to the task.

At home in France, the newspaper *L'Ouest-Éclaire* made a similar argument as the talks continued. Would, it asked rhetorically, the temples of Angkor have been 'drawn today from the thick shadow which concealed them without the patience and tenacity of the French scholars who have leaned over these stones, have deciphered their inscriptions, investigated their frescoes, and restored to them their ancient grandeur?' Angkor in fact has no frescoes, but readers didn't know that and in any case a point was being made. 'It is French work,' the newspaper declared, 'that is far from completed and will have to continue for many years to come, because not everything has been said about the marvels of Angkor.'

In March, Japanese Foreign Minister Yosuke Matsuoka, who was basically steering the talks, put forth a 'compromise' proposal by which France would give up the three western provinces of Cambodia as well as substantial Laotian land. French ambassador Charles Arsène-Henry accepted the plan in principle. It was a bitter pill – sixty-five thousand square kilometres of Cambodia and Laos would pass to Siamese control – but in the proposal was an important consolation prize: 'ANGKOR reste française,' proclaimed *Paris Soir* newspaper on 13 March. Angkor remains French. Though just barely – the new frontier line would pass immediately north and west of the main temple group. In Thailand, of course, the settlement was cause for celebration, a ratification of victory against France.

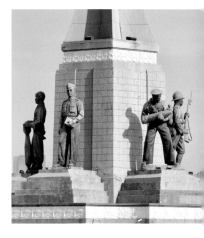

The Victory Monument in Bangkok, erected to commemorate Thailand's 1941 war with France, includes larger-than-life statues of Thai military men. Photo by Imwaltersy/Shutterstock.com.

On 9 May, representatives of France and Siam gathered at the official residence of the Japanese prime minister, Prince Fumimaro Konoe, and signed a treaty formalizing the transfer of territory. Even with keeping Angkor, the treaty caused considerable anguish among Cambodians. The 1907 regaining of the three western provinces had given the Khmer people immense pride, commemorated with a monument at Wat Phnom in the capital, in which bas-reliefs of three women representing the three provinces were shown returning to the king's fold. Now the provinces would again enter the national consciousness as 'lost territories.' The Thais, meanwhile, would build a large Victory Monument in their own capital, with larger-than-life heroic-realist statues of Thai servicemen and a civil servant, to commemorate the defeat of a European imperialist power.[2]

The ceding of Cambodian territory formally soon took place. The French lowered their flag in the three provinces and handed them over to Thai administrators. Some local people opted to move east to territory that remained French-Cambodian; most stayed put under Thai control.

2   Today the monument, located inside a giant traffic circle next to a Skytrain transit station, is known by most everyone who lives in Bangkok, though few know what it commemorates.

With the hostilities over, Siem Reap was inching uneasily back toward normal. Routine research resumed at Angkor. A team investigated a widely held belief that the ancient Khmers had gone to the enormous trouble of paving the floor of the Srah Srang reservoir, which measures roughly four hundred by eight hundred metres. It was true there was silt on the bottom now, but beneath it surely were paving stones. Experts' guidebooks said so. So researchers sank iron rods deep into the bottom of the pool at multiple points and nowhere did they strike paving stones. One more facet of the Angkor myth had been cleared up.

Hanging on to Angkor-Era 'Enclaves'

From the time the French accepted at the Tokyo talks that they would have to give up large swathes of Cambodia, they began campaigning to hang on to major Angkor heritage sites located in areas that would now be Thai. This effort to create French 'enclaves' focused on Banteay Srei and the Kulen hills.

Governor General Decoux sent almost daily telegrams to his team in Tokyo giving guidance on this and other issues. In a 29 March 1941 telegram, he backed a deal by which Thailand would get administration of an island in the Gulf of Siam and land in Stung Treng province in exchange for Banteay Srei and, if possible, the southern Kulens. 'I ask you to

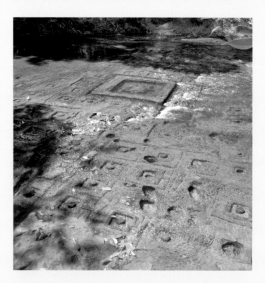

In 1941 territorial negotiations with Japan and Thailand, the French struggled to hang on to the Kulen hills, which contain artefacts of Khmer antiquity such as these stream bed *lingas*. They sanctify water as it passes by, headed for the plain below where the main Angkor temples are located. (John Burgess)

insist on this point,' Decoux cabled, noting that these places were part and parcel of Angkor history and were only of archaeological interest.

The May 9 treaty left the main Angkor group with the French and Cambodians but was silent on Banteay Srei and the Kulens. The effort to keep them continued at the joint Thai-French-Japanese commission that was formed to delimit the border and had discretion to make minor changes in precisely where it ran.

As delimitation proceeded, the French courted the commission's president, Japanese ambassador to Indochina Makoto Yano. They gave him a special tour of the Angkor monuments. They 'declassified' a stone head in EFEO's protected collection, making it available for sale to Yano at a cost of 225 piastres. Conservator Maurice Glaize telegrammed Hanoi suggesting that it assemble a private photo album for him showing scenes from Vietnam, Cambodia, and Laos.

Border details announced in September gave the French much of what they wanted. An EFEO telegram to Hanoi proudly announced the news: 'We retain Banteay Srei and half of the Kulens.'

EFEO director George Cœdès later wrote that this win came courtesy of 'the energy and tenacity of the Japanese delegation of the border delimitation commission, particularly its president, His Excellency Makoto Yano, which has supported the point of view of the French delegation. It was thanks also to the spirit of understanding and conciliation of the Thai delegation.' What he was saying was that Yano had decided in France's favour, and the Thais had fallen into line.

The French stationed a few militiamen at Banteay Srei, but the place was sufficiently deserted most days that wild elephants were said to knock over stone posts on its processional avenue. In subsequent years of World War II, high-ranking French and Cambodian visitors to Angkor would make a point of going to Banteay Srei, under armed guard, if necessary, to exercise the hard-won right to be there.

French archaeologists investigated
the Srah Srang reservoir to test a
widely held belief that the ancient
Khmers had paved its bed.
(John Burgess)

But despite the lowered tensions, Siem Reap remained a
military town. Along the Angkor grand circuit roads, soldiers
of the colonial army had set up camp for extended stays.
Some of these men visited the temples, alone or in groups,
creating the spectre of off-duty misbehaviour. It was to soldiers
that suspicion turned when a frieze of seven ascetics at the
tenth-century Pre Rup temple suffered a terrible mutilation –
one carved figure was carried off, while another lost its head.
The conservation consulted with commanders to try to find a
solution.

Numbers of tourists remained low, and those who did
come were increasingly Japanese: sixty-eight of the ninety-
five people who paid to enter Angkor Wat in June 1941. The
conservator's report attributed this to Japanese being exempt
from wartime restrictions on the use of cars. Some of the
Japanese visitors that month were VIPs, such as university
professors and a cabinet minister's secretary.

In early August 1941, the first of another kind of Japanese
arrived: soldiers of the Imperial Army, in uniform, with
weapons and field equipment. They moved into the largely
empty Hôtel des Ruines/Bungalow and established camps in
two Buddhist temples in Siem Reap, Wat Enkosei (where that
Thai bomb had exploded) and Wat Bo. Japanese warplanes
landed at Siem Reap airport, which was now undergoing
conversion into a base for the imperial forces' air power.

A general build-up was underway. The peace seemed
unlikely to hold for long.

佛印南西部を進む北山部隊

八月三日木村派遣員撮影＝台北より無線電送

9: THE JAPANESE OVERLORDS

**Angkor remains safe from the bombs and bullets
of World War II but it becomes a battleground in
the 'peace' that follows.**

In 1941, the world was watching Japan, wondering what its
huge armed forces were going to do next in East and Southeast
Asia. The United States had imposed economic sanctions and
was demanding, among other things, that Japan withdraw its
troops from Indochina. Japan was refusing and was, on the
contrary, sending more soldiers there. The signing of the
Franco-Thai treaty in Tokyo, in fact, coincided with the landing
of Japanese troops at Cam Ranh Bay in Vietnam to set up a new
base there.

In Siem Reap, people experienced the suspense close-
up. Japanese soldiers continued to arrive. A detachment of
them climbed to the top tier of Angkor Wat in uniform, a
comrade with a flag in the lead. These men were clearly not
tourists. The Japanese newspaper *Asahi* noted the event with
a photograph, turned into an illustration in the journalistic
style of the day. The temples of Angkor were now under
the protection of the Imperial Army, a related article
announced.

By late in the year, the Japanese force in Siem Reap had
grown to about 1,400 men, Glaize told his superiors in Hanoi.[1]
He reported no 'grave incidents,' but there were plenty of
minor ones that come with hosting large numbers of military
men. The Japanese were driving trucks through the gates of
Angkor Thom at full speed, the vibration risking knocking
loose stones from their places. They were cutting trees
indiscriminately. They had taken bamboo that was part of a
memorial to Charles Carpeaux, the man who had surveyed
the Bayon four decades earlier. Some of the soldiers were
visiting the temples unsupervised, raising fears of theft or other
misbehaviour. Glaize worked with Japanese commanders
to address these and other problems, but his influence was
limited. The Japanese might or might not listen. Commanders
did pledge that their soldiers would go to temples only in the
company of superiors. But in a report to EFEO headquarters,
Glaize revealed a certain feeling of helplessness on this point:

Opposite page: Japanese Imperial
Army soldiers climbed Angkor Wat in
August 1941, as pictured at the time
in the Japanese newspaper *Asahi*.

---

1 As in the previous chapter,
Glaize's monthly reports and
other documents in the EFEO's
Paris archive were crucial
sources for this chapter.

'We believe that the religious character of the monuments will be their best safeguard.'

One day there came a 'request' from the Japanese for something that surely dismayed him: the creation of a live-ammunition firing range by a small hill inside the Angkor zone, about a kilometre from Preah Khan temple. Glaize signed off, noting that the requested area had only scrub and no ancient structures.

At the airport, meanwhile, the Japanese were now doing their own construction work – and paying better wages than the conservation. Many of its workers defected to jobs there. And soon the Japanese were pressing for the same thing the French civil engineers had wanted: removal of the ancient towers near the runway.

It was in this period that a new king ascended the Cambodian throne, Norodom Sihanouk. He was a nineteen-year-old feeling his way. The French were convinced they could easily manipulate him, but in the years ahead he would become a seminal, wilful figure in the country's modern history, as well as Angkor's.

Shortly after his coronation, the young king paid respects at the old capital, Maurice Glaize at his side. He visited the various anastylosis sites, showing detailed interest in the reconstruction work underway there (he was given a photo album including before-and-after shots). But perhaps his most important purpose was attending a large-scale religious ceremony at Angkor Wat. It was really more of a mass display of patriotic sentiments unleashed by the recent loss of the three provinces. In the presence of five hundred monks, the young king was solemnly presented with a silver box containing soil collected from the provinces. It would stay at Angkor Wat until Cambodia regained sovereignty over those lands. A flame that Sihanouk lit burned for a night in the central tower, then began an Olympic-style relay that French officials had organized as a demonstration of colonial unity. It would wind around Indochina and end up in Hanoi.

International tensions with Japan continued to mount. As a precaution, conservation workers created a protective dug-out near their buildings.

On December 7, the wait came to a close. In coordination with the attack on the U.S. fleet at Pearl Harbor 11,000 kilometres away, Japanese troops staged a general offensive in Southeast Asia. They struck the Americans in the Philippines and the British in Malaya. And the Thais in Thailand. Siem Reap, now a border town due to the shifting of frontiers earlier in the year, was a natural jumping-off point for this assault. Thailand had failed to promptly grant permission for Japanese forces to pass through its territory as part of the offensive, so troops simply stormed across the border at Siem Reap under cover of darkness, treating Thailand as a hostile power. Japanese planes took off from Siem Reap airport to attack the Thai town of Aranyaprathet. War with Thailand proved very brief – its government capitulated in less than a day,

The French colonial government issued this passport to archaeologist Victor Goloubew shortly before his departure for Japan in 1941. Document courtesy of EFEO archives.

letting the foreign army enter unopposed. Western colonial powers in neighbouring countries kept up resistance, though they would succumb too. By some accounts, Japanese planes flew support missions from Siem Reap during the two-month campaign against the British that ended with their surrender in Singapore.

As it turned out, the ignition of total war across the region was good news for Angkor. It meant that almost all of the Japanese troops there moved into Thailand and did not return. Soon the Japanese warplanes at the airport flew away as well. All that remained at the end of December, Glaize noted in a report to Hanoi, was a Japanese guard post at the Bungalow. 'The most complete calm' had settled in, Glaize wrote.

At the airport, the towers near the runway remained undemolished. Glaize had again resisted that pressure.

* * * * *

Despite the constant tensions of the relationship with Japan, the French authorities in Indochina did their best to pretend that all was normal and friendly. One aspect of this was 'cultural cooperation.' In November 1940, the Japanese military proposed to Governor General Decoux an exchange of scholars. It was decided that a senior Japanese academic called Masao Ota would come to Indochina, while the archaeologist Victor Goloubew would go to Japan. Compared to many of the French in Indochina, Goloubew seems to have had genuine enthusiasm for working with Japan.[2] He had helped set up a French-Japanese friendship association and had long wanted to visit Japan to see its art and culture first hand.

So, on 25 May 1941, he arrived in Japan, shortly after the signature of the Franco-Thai treaty there. He came with photographs, maps, and a collection of stone-age artefacts.

2 Goloubew seems to have had conflicting ideas about Nazi Germany, however. In 1941, as the German army advanced into the Soviet Union, intending to overthrow communist rule, he voiced hope that he might finally be able to return to his country of birth. However, when the Red Army forced the Germans into retreat, he expressed patriotic joy over the bravery of his Russian compatriots.

In the following six weeks, he delivered two major lectures on Angkor and the French work there, illustrating his words with projected slides, and two lectures on art and archaeology in Vietnam. He also opened a photo exhibit and met with senior Japanese academics. He was the consummate diplomat, flattering his hosts with praise for their temples, museums, flowers – and discipline. 'In his modest black uniform, the Japanese student is both a soldier and intellectual worker,' he told Japanese radio near the end of his visit. 'Gathered in a conference room, the young men to whom I spoke about Indochina and the temples of Angkor constituted a model, attentive, and collected audience. I felt a real pleasure in addressing them.' Goloubew also took the opportunity to sample Japanese culture. Among other sites, he visited the ancient wooden temple of Horyuji in Nara while in Kamakura he took part in a tea ceremony.

Goloubew returned to Hanoi by air, his plane climbing high to dodge a typhoon. He was greeted as something of a hero – they'd loved him in Japan. He'd produced some rare good news in what was a troublesome relationship. Governor General Decoux asked that he come see him. Arsène-Henry, the French ambassador in Tokyo, wrote a laudatory letter suggesting that Goloubew had confirmed to the Japanese the wisdom of the decision to leave Angkor in French hands.

Besides the charm of his society, our countryman had the merit of filling a void created by circumstances. It had been a long time since Japanese intellectuals had had the opportunity to hear a qualified lecturer from our country…[His visit allowed] a timely reminder of the achievements of French science, by the objective presentation of precise results obtained by our researchers in the entire field of archaeological art. The personal remarks of Mr. Goloubew brought to life…the stages of the resurrection of Angkor; the screenings that he presented delighted his audiences.

In the meantime, French authorities in Indochina had hosted Goloubew's Japanese counterpart, Masao Ota, at a similar round of lectures and conferences, one of them attended by Decoux. Ota was a medical doctor, and so his events focused on such subjects as surgery and infectious disease. But before going home after a two-month stay, he toured the temples of Angkor.

Official statements proclaimed both visits a rousing success, but there remained the sentiment among some Japanese that, given the new era in Asia, it was Japan that should be doing the job at Angkor. It was fired by the photograph of soldiers climbing Angkor Wat in the *Asahi* in August 1941, with a related article that depicted the monuments as essentially lying untended in the forest, awaiting Japanese attention. In a similar vein, the Japanese translator of one of Groslier's books took the opportunity at publication to call for Japan to carry out its own archaeological work. 'Angkor is close to us,' the translator wrote. 'Angkor belongs to the East. It is a place that Japan must know and study in depth. We cannot be content to rely on the studies of European experts.'[3]

In 1942, the Higashi Honganji temple in Kyoto put that idea into practice. In December that year, a team from the temple, led by a painter of Buddhist art called Tetsuro Sugimoto, arrived in Angkor for a month and a half of study. Photographs from the time show three team members posing at various Angkor monuments, dressed in white tropical attire. The group assembled more than a thousand rubbings and photographs, plus some Buddhist paintings.

At about the same time, Professor Shoji Mehara of Kyoto Imperial University toured and lectured in Indochina as part of Japanese-French exchanges. According to a Japanese radio broadcast of 2 March 1943, he noted that northern and central Vietnam had 'many old ruins of Chinese culture which have not yet been explored' and said he planned to return with a team of explorers for a two- to three-year 'grand-scale' tour. The prominent Japanese archaeologist Sueji Umehara also visited Indochina as part of the scholarly exchanges.

A few of the other Japanese whom the war brought to Indochina took a covetous approach with which the EFEO was long familiar. In mid-1943, two men from the Saigon office of the semi-governmental Nanyo Kyokai (South Seas Society) were said to have stolen a small head from a bas-relief at Preah Khan. Questioned by the French police, they denied taking it. No legal action resulted. 'We did not think it appropriate to put their word in doubt and create an incident, because of the small value of the stolen item,' the EFEO's Hanoi headquarters was told. Earlier in the year, four Japanese visitors were accused of taking four fragments of sculpture from the Bayon after giving a guard a five-piastre bribe. He reported the theft anyway, and was allowed to keep the money as a reward. Again, there seems to have been no legal follow-up. Was this lenience influenced by reluctance to tangle with people who were the de facto masters of Indochina? Perhaps, but it's also true that over the years the French had generally not responded harshly when European and American tourists were caught doing similar things.

3   The translator's remark is quoted in an article by Professor Sadao Fujihara of Ibaraki University, *'Les échanges entre le Japon et l'Indochine française durant la seconde guerre mondiale,'* published in the journal *Ebisu, Études japonaises.*

*****

Angkor figured in another aspect of cultural cooperation with Japan, the exchange of museum pieces. In the past, the French had conducted multiple high-priced sales of Khmer antiquities to foreign institutions. But in 1940 an idea arose for a cash-less arrangement in which the two sides would provide each other with museum-quality objects of interest. Certainly the exchange fit with the EFEO's long-standing objective of educating the world about the ancient Khmer heritage and the French work to preserve it. For Japan it fit with the wartime ideology of glorifying Asian heritage under Japanese guidance.

Shipment was delayed as officials hashed out exactly what each side would give and receive. By 1943, the deal was set: the EFEO would make what seems to have been its biggest-ever single export: sixty-nine objects, including ancient Khmer images of Vishnu, Buddha, a female deity, and the god Ganesh and a collection of ceramics. Japan proposed a like number of items, including paintings, swords, a wooden Buddha image from the Kamakura period (twelfth to fourteenth century), a writing desk decorated with gold powder; armor, masks used in No drama, an elaborate kimono, and dishes. These would go not to Cambodia, however, but to French-run museum halls in Vietnam.

The Khmer items, packed in twenty-three crates weighing eight tons, left Siem Reap in April 1943 aboard French military trucks. In September, they were the focus of a send-off ceremony in Saigon, with Japanese ambassador Kenkichi Yoshizawa, EFEO director George Cœdès, and other dignitaries in attendance. Japanese transport faced severe danger from Allied attacks by this point in the war, but in January 1944 the shipment reached Japan safely. The items were intended for display at the Imperial Museum in northern Tokyo, but due to the danger of American air raids, they soon went instead into safekeeping storage. The Japanese items, meanwhile, had arrived in Indochina, reduced in number to about half of what the French had provided.

The French went along with programs like this, but privately fretted over what Japan's true long-term objective concerning culture and archaeology might be. In 1942, a series of memos and letters flew back and forth within the EFEO and colonial offices about how to rebut a Japanese magazine article that had denied that the French had 'discovered' Angkor. Discovery in fact was by Japanese pilgrims who had visited centuries earlier, the article said. Decoux asked the EFEO to organize a series of what he called 'propaganda conferences' to refute this claim. Writing in response in a letter marked 'secret,' EFEO director Cœdès pledged to do so. But he noted that 'these conferences would have, like all our conferences, a strictly scientific character and not manifest any trace of counter-propaganda. But intelligent listeners won't fail to reach the conclusions that you intend.'[4]

In the end, the Japanese did not displace the French at Angkor. Perhaps that picture of soldiers climbing Angkor Wat was intended mainly for consumption on the home front. The Kyoto temple's delegation staged some exhibits of Khmer culture back in Japan, but otherwise seems to have made only modest follow-up. Nonetheless, during this period many ordinary Japanese came to know the name Angkor for the first time.

* * * *

In 1942, Angkor settled back again into its routines. Reconstruction work resumed, as did research. Tourists began again coming, though just a trickle.

The Japanese soldiers were gone, but not the economic effects of war. Shortages developed. Lack of fuel and motor oil began making it difficult to supply and supervise conservation projects (there was talk of reverting to ox carts). Other specific items necessary for the work were running out as well: photographic supplies, key to creating the meticulous visual documentation that normally accompanied restoration work, paper for drafting designs, and the steel rods used in reinforced concrete.

But that would change after mid-1942, when Decoux came for another visit. The admiral had been twice before, but with limited time available. This time, he announced in advance, he wanted to get thorough briefings on conservation work and see it up-close in the field. Moving about with an entourage dressed in the white suits and pith helmets that marked colonial administrators, he visited the four major anastylosis projects that were underway at the time, at the Bayon, Bakong, Banteay Samre, and Preah Khan temples. During the visit, Decoux offered praise and encouragement, and elicited some good will with a promise of more funds. The money would go mainly to the work on Preah Khan, which officials said was the project with which he most hoped his name would be associated.

At the time, the work force at Preah Khan included some 500 Cambodian young people, who were moving fallen stones

4   The author did not find out whether these conferences actually took place.

weighing a hundred kilograms and more to their former places along the west entrance avenue. The French saw this as a kind of vacation work camp that would promote what they intended as a benign, controllable kind of national pride in young people. 'They appreciate the joy of selfless labour for their country, work that ennobles and strengthens their patriotic feelings,' wrote an approving colonial journalist. The workers were variously boy scouts, local youth, and refugees from areas newly taken over by Thailand. Some of them slept in the wooden hotel by Angkor Wat.

Last stop on Decoux's tour was the 'enclave' of Banteay Srei, where the governor general exercised the right of visit won by the border commission.

As the Pacific conflict progressed, Japan further stepped up its demands on the resources of Indochina, in particular rubber and rice. In 1944 and 1945, famine and widespread death occurred in Vietnam. Conditions were less severe in Cambodia but still tough. Nonetheless, Decoux somehow came through with his promise of more money for Angkor – 50,000 piastres in 1943, 100,000 in 1944. Glaize was able to expand conservation operations to about ten sites, with a total of 425 workers. Among the new projects was the West Mebon, the island temple where the bronze Vishnu statue had been unearthed. Between 1942 and 1944, the EFEO teams rebuilt the eastern wall of the largely collapsed temple.

While American, British, and Dutch civilians who had fallen into Japanese hands in neighbouring colonies grew thin on meagre rations behind barbed wire, the French of Siem Reap and the rest of Indochina enjoyed ample meals and slept in their own beds at home. 'The country lived in security and peace,' recalled Joseph Schilling, who as a young military officer spent two years in wartime Siem Reap. 'Cut off from the outside world, it lived with the simplicity and rhythm of buffalo carts.' His account, written in 1999, recalled an almost idyllic time. He was billeted at the Grand Hotel, his room affording a view of the tallest tower of Angkor Wat. Most Sunday afternoons he took a walk out to the temple. Along the way he stopped and chatted with local people; sometimes a peacock's cry broke the silence. When he reached the temple, it was usually deserted. He only saw tourists there once, 'a group of very discreet Japanese officers.'

Intellectual inquiry, debate, and publication about Angkor continued. In 1943, Cœdès and the scholar Pierre Dupont came out with a new translation of the Sdok Kok Thom inscription. In 1944, Glaize published a new Angkor guidebook, and reported the discovery of near-flawless statues of the gods Vishnu and Shiva at the Bakong temple. Their faces, Glaize wrote, bore 'imperceptible smiles' that suggested the gods' 'consciousness of their greatness and unquestionable power.'

And at a house in Phnom Penh, a retired but still very engaged Henri Parmentier kept busy. Surrounded by stacks of documents from his many years in the field, he worked on private writing projects. One of them was an ambitious revision and expansion of a cornerstone reference work on Khmer antiquity, *Inventaire descriptif des monuments du Cambodge.*

In February 1945, a flight of American B-29 warplanes like this one bombed Phnom Penh. U.S. Air Force photo.

* * * * *

Beyond Cambodia, Japan and Germany were losing the war. In 1944 the allies overran France. Vichy died on the home soil, but a phantom version of it lived on in Indochina. Though it made covert contact with the new French government of General Charles de Gaulle, Decoux's administration continued to collect taxes, lock up nationalists, and run ports and hospitals, all under the watchful eyes of the Japanese. Some members of the French community got involved secretly with allied intelligence and De Gaulle's Free French movement, which by August 1944 had agents operating in the colony.

Still, at Angkor, as 1945 opened all seemed as before. The *résident supérieur* of Cambodia visited Banteay Samre and awarded a medal to a Cambodian called Eam Suon for his long work on the temple's reconstruction. Colonial soldiers who'd come for a short stay at Angkor made off with some heads from Chau Say Tevoda temple. The Baphuon temple suffered another of its periodic landslide-like collapses, leaving the insides of part of its north face exposed. King Sihanouk arrived for another visit. He made a point of going to Banteay Srei.

But on 7 February 1945, four years of insulation from hostilities for Cambodia came to an abrupt end. A flight of nineteen American B-29 bombers struck Phnom Penh, with great destruction and loss of life.[5] A few refugees from the attack later straggled into Siem Reap.

Having suffered defeat after defeat in the Pacific war, the Japanese were now worrying that the Allies might invade

5   Phnom Penh was not the intended target, however. The bombers diverted there from Saigon due to heavy cloud cover. U.S. military records report an attack on 'targets of opportunity,' resulting in damage to jetties and buildings. Dityvon Le Rumeur, a child in a French family in Phnom Penh at the time, recalled in an interview with the *Cambodia Daily* in 2007 that some of the bombs fell on a Chinese neighborhood near the central market and that her mother went looking for the body of a Cambodian friend. By the adult Dityvon's recollection, more than 200 people died and at least 200 were injured.

This two-way radio in the Phnom Penh home of George Groslier drew the interest of the Japanese military police, ending in Groslier's arrest and death by apparent torture in 1945. Photo courtesy of Groslier Family Archive and DatAsia Press.

Indochina. They were also becoming increasingly sceptical of the loyalties of the colony's French. So on 9 March, they ended the long charade. They staged a coup against the French administration and abolished it. Japanese soldiers seized colonial offices and military bases. Some French military fled Hanoi for China. Those who stayed behind and resisted were dealt with harshly, in some cases executed after capture. In Phnom Penh, in cooperation with the Japanese, Sihanouk declared a new, theoretically independent Kingdom of Kampuchea. At the Buddhist New Year celebration the following month, the historian David Chandler has written, he told his people that the way was open for the country to soon regain the greatness of Angkor.

French civilians living in the provinces were transported to Phnom Penh for internment in a camp that was really just a hastily fenced-off section of the city north of the rail station. In Siem Reap, however, the Japanese attempted to make an exception of Maurice Glaize, asking him to remain on the job. 'He refused this offer with dignity, in order to share the fate of his compatriots,' a colleague later wrote. The Japanese seem to have chosen not to try to force him. He left for internment in Phnom Penh, having placed Cambodian subordinates in charge of conservation sites. He would later say that he remained in secret communication with them from internment, issuing instructions.

It was a difficult time for French civilians – thieves looted the homes of Glaize and Parmentier – but most survived. Among antiquity scholars, there were two major exceptions. George Groslier was one. His health had long been failing; he had been in a Phnom Penh hospital for months. The Japanese military police came there to question him about a two-way radio that he had operated in his house for years. They appeared to believe he was using it for espionage. Later they returned and arrested him, over the objections of hospital staff. He was held in a cell and interrogated. On 22 June his daughter Nicole and son-in-law were summoned to the office of a Japanese commander and given a death certificate, cremation ashes, and a few personal effects. The exact circumstances of his death have never emerged, but all evidence points to him succumbing during torture. Some people believe he had been helping the allies and Free French in some way, but the facts remain unknown.

Angkor and the Vichy Legacy

Vichy France's legacy was forever stained by the association with Nazi Germany; French Indochina faced a similar reckoning for its work with Imperial Japan.

After the war, Decoux was brought back to France and held in jail pending investigation of various allegations of criminal collaboration with the Japanese. Maurice Glaize was among the Indochina French who filed affidavits of support, essentially depicting him as an honourable man caught in impossible circumstances. These can be found today on microfilm at the *Archives Nationales* in Paris.

Glaize portrayed the French position in Indochina in 1941 as hopeless (he mentioned 40,000 French versus 120 million Japanese). He praised Decoux for securing increased funding for Angkor during the war and keeping it out of Thai hands. 'During the negotiations that followed the hostilities with Siam, Admiral Decoux's insistence with the border delimitation commission and his instructions to members of the French delegation contributed in a major way to retaining Angkor in our zone of influence, and in particular the small temple of Banteay Srei, one of the jewels of Khmer art.' It's unclear what if any influence this statement had on the legal proceedings, but charges against Decoux were dismissed in 1949.

In a similar way, Victor Goloubew's postumous reputation was sullied by his enthusiastic cooperation with the Japanese. He and his work received relatively little attention in the post-war years. But, in a lengthy article in the EFEO Bulletin in 1965 on the twentieth anniversary of his death, EFEO director Louis Malleret signaled a desire to give him his due, recounting in detail his long career and many accomplishments in the field of archaeology.

Malleret described a recent memorial gathering at the Guimet museum in Paris. 'The ghost of Victor Goloubew was present at this rendezvous of memories,' he wrote, 'in one of the places where the seductions of his words had so often manifested themselves. [The ghost] was present, like those old soldiers of the Tommies' song on the front of the First World War, which he had undoubtedly heard. *Old soldiers never die. They only fade away.*'

Malleret wrote that the timing of Goloubew's 1941 trip to Japan was perhaps 'badly chosen.' But he noted that neither France, Britain, nor the United States was at war with Japan at the time, and that Japanese Emperor Hirohito had labeled as an act of insubordination the Japanese attack on colonial forces at Lang Son in 1940, which was remembered with bitterness in the Indochina French community for its many casualties.

George Groslier's legacy suffered no suspicion. In 1947, the French government honoured him with the official designation of a man who died for his country, *Mort pour la France.*

The other fatality was Victor Goloubew, though with him the causes were natural. Like Groslier, he had long been ill, a condition said to have been aggravated when the unpressurized plane that was bringing him back from Japan in 1941 flew at high altitudes for two hours to avoid a typhoon. He died at the Saint-Paul clinic in Hanoi on 19 April. The Japanese allowed three colleagues, including George Cœdès, to accompany his body on its journey to the cemetery. Other friends gathered there to give farewells.

In their places of internment, the French dreamed of rescue and release. They cheered the news that arrived in mid-August: Japan had announced its surrender. But there was no quick restoration of the status quo. French military forces did not return and re-impose colonial authority until October. Even after that, many French citizens remained in their internment quarters out of fear for their safety outside.

* * * * *

Glaize did not make it back to Angkor until December. There he relieved of duty a Cambodian aristocrat, Prince Kethana, whom the short-lived Kingdom of Kampuchea had appointed as conservator. This was apparently done on friendly terms – the prince remained on the scene to work with Glaize and conduct his own research. In the chaos of the previous months, various EFEO possessions such as cars and cameras had gone missing, but overall there was little serious damage. Once again, Cambodian work teams re-assembled to go back to work on conservation projects.

Some physical changes had occurred in Glaize's absence: French-language signs around Angkor had been replaced with ones in Khmer script. This was in line with a key cultural initiative of the defunct government, pride in use of the Khmer language. The government had quickly stopped an unpopular colonial program to retire the Khmer writing system in favour of an easier-to-learn one based on the roman alphabet. With Glaize's return, the Cambodian signs were scrapped and French ones put up. Also junked was a Japanese and French language sign at Angkor Wat pointing the way to a Japanese-language inscription, believed to have been created by a Japanese pilgrim in the seventeenth century.

Conservator Maurice Glaize (left), newly returned to Angkor with his family, posed in late 1945 with a visiting American, Kenneth P. Landon, a former Presbyterian missionary in Thailand. Landon was representing the United States in post-war negotiations in the region. Photo courtesy of Special Collections (SC-38), Buswell Library, Wheaton College, Illinois.

Monks at the ninth century Lolei temple had used the French absence to resume doing things their own way at a place of worship that they viewed as belonging to them. They had demolished a wooden pavilion and put up a new one that masked part of the ancient structure. Glaize found this unacceptable. He alerted the provincial governor and moved to have the new structure taken down.

By March 1946, things were sufficiently back together to allow a visit by important VIPs: Lord Admiral and Lady Mountbatten of Britain (he was at the time serving as viceroy of India). Cambodian classical dancers entertained the couple in the evening at Angkor Wat.[6]

The war was over, but Siem Reap was now hosting more than its share of military men. The Grand Hotel had become a convalescent centre for French soldiers; other members of the armed forces were visiting on leave, as tourists. With many off-duty military men around, the usual unwelcome things happened: in April, a man staying at the hotel shattered two of the heads of a *naga* serpent at Banteay Srei. In July, some

6 Among the couple's French hosts was the military officer Joseph Schilling, newly returned from internment in a Japanese camp.

airmen about to depart for France came under suspicion when four *devatas* at Angkor Wat were mutilated.

* * * * *

In Japan, meanwhile, the Khmer sculpture that the EFEO had provided during the war was drawing the attention of U.S. occupation authorities. In post-war Europe, a corps of 'monuments men,' academic specialists in art, was helping track down artwork that the Nazis had looted. Documents unearthed in the U.S. Archives by Ricardo J. Elia, a Boston University associate professor of archaeology, show that a 'monuments woman' called Ardelia Hall set in motion an investigation of how the Khmer artefacts came to be in Tokyo. Before the war, Hall had begun her career at the Museum of Fine Arts in Boston. During the hostilities, she took a job with the OSS, the precursor to the CIA, and later joined a State Department team on wartime theft of artwork. On 5 February 1946, she wrote a memo drawing attention to the twenty-three cases of Indochinese archaeological material that had come to Japan. Her interest had apparently been sparked by reading transcripts of wartime Japanese radio broadcasts about the exchange. '[T]ransactions of this sort,' wrote an occupation official, 'negotiated in countries which were the victims of Japanese aggression and at a time when the country was occupied by the Japanese army, are considered to have been conducted under duress.'

Japan's Imperial Museum, which had received the sculpture, provided correspondence and other records of the exchange, including cordially worded letters from EFEO head George Cœdès. Occupation officials wondered, however, about the valuation that had been placed on the Khmer objects – it seemed much too low to them, suggesting that the paperwork had been doctored to mask that what France was sending was much more valuable than what it was getting in exchange. But U.S. authorities eventually concluded there was no cause for action. A major reason for that finding was that the French were not seeking the sculpture's return.

According to Professor Sadao Fujihara of Ibaraki University, the Japanese public did not see the Khmer artwork until a short-lived exhibit in 1949, after which it went back into storage, until some came out for a display in 1968. The full

Walter Vella, shown here at Banteay Srei in late 1945, was a young officer in the U.S. Office of Strategic Services, forerunner of the Central Intelligence Agency, who was accompanying Landon. Vella went on to become an academic specializing in Southeast Asia. Photo courtesy of Special Collections (SC-38), Buswell Library, Wheaton College, Illinois.

collection finally saw the light of day in 2013, in what is now Tokyo National Museum. Khmer items are now part of its permanent display collection. The Japanese museum pieces, meanwhile, had reached Indochina in 1943, and, like their Khmer counterparts in Japan, they largely disappeared from view. However, in 2013 twenty-one of them were rediscovered at the Vietnam National Museum of History in Hanoi.

Like the French, the successive governments of independent Cambodia have never requested the return of the sculpture. Not many Cambodians know it's in the Tokyo museum, and those who do may well view it as a proud statement of their country's heritage.

* * * * *

Save for that single bomb that fell by Preah Enkosei in Siem Reap town, ancient Khmer monuments had eluded weapons damage all the way through the great conflict. That was going to change in the war's immediate aftermath.

The reason was that restoration of French rule had angered Cambodia's growing numbers of nationalists. A *Khmer Issarak* (Khmer Independence) movement had begun to operate clandestinely. It was getting help from Thailand, which for its part was unhappy with the return of French colonial rulers and their demands for the return of the three provinces that had gone to Thai control in 1941. For the time being, however, these provinces remained Thai, with the border right on the doorstep of Siem Reap.[7]

On 7 August 1946, an estimated 500 Khmer Issarak guerrillas, led by a charismatic commander called Dap Chhuon, staged coordinated attacks in the town. They overran a small French military base and attacked a prison, freeing its inmates. According to Glaize, they killed a French customs official in front of his wife. Perhaps their most concentrated assault occurred at the Grand Hotel, a target apparently chosen for its symbolism of French authority and the presence inside of about 100 French military men. The guerrillas opened fire at about 4 a.m., riddling the facade with bullets. Two French captains organized a defence; attackers who got inside the lobby were shot dead in the lobby in front of the bird-cage elevator. By the time the attack ended, as many as thirty-five guerrillas had been killed, according to French media reports, the bodies strewn in the park in front of the hotel. Three French soldiers lost their lives.

The conservation compound drew the guerrillas' attention

7   In an agreement signed in Washington with France on 17 November 1946, however, Thailand agreed to give up the provinces. The actual handover took place the following month. This was France's price for ending a veto of Thai entry into the newly formed United Nations.

as well. A group sent to seize it arrived too late to find Glaize: he had been warned and went to hide in a nearby forest. He later made his way to safety in the Grand Hotel, which was secured by late morning.

It was a great shock for the French, who less than a year after their return to power in Indochina were on edge over nationalist uprisings. In Vietnam, hostilities with the Viet Minh were already underway, and this seemed to presage an expansion. In Siem Reap, officials made much of the fact that the attackers had crossed from Thailand and were getting help from its government – khaki uniforms, weapons, and advisers. These were not the 'bandits' of old.

It took a while, but French reinforcements began arriving – commandos, foreign legionnaires, and tanks. Dakota transport planes, flying from Saigon, dropped close to a hundred paratroopers at the airport. Others floated down into the park in front of the Grand.

The attackers withdrew to Angkor. Perhaps that was intended as an assertion of Cambodian pride, or an appeal to resident spirits for protection. Perhaps it was in belief that the French wouldn't dare fire on them there, out of fear of damaging the monuments. Whatever the motivation, Angkor proved to be no haven. French soldiers were told to protect the monuments, but turning back an uprising seems to have had a higher priority. They moved to Angkor in force and began confronting the guerrillas. Captain André Briend, leader of a commando group, was killed in action on 9 August at the south gate of Angkor Thom.

On 10 August, the guerrillas staged another attack in Siem Reap but were again beaten back, this time at a cost of four French dead. Taking advantage of continuing chaos, the guerrillas returned to the conservation compound and looted and burned some of its buildings. Glaize had been able to remove various cameras, logs and some of the photos and drawing, but archives, photographic supplies, other photos and drawings, and automobiles were lost. So were many of his personal belongings.

With gunfire, the French soon dispersed guerrillas who'd taken over the Bayon and Terrace of the Leper King. On 13 August, the troops moved on Angkor Wat, firing machine guns at doorways of the western entrance (they did not use artillery that they had on hand). The guerrillas put up little resistance, but did manage to kill the driver of a French armored car. Within an hour, the guerrillas had left, and French flags were flying over the temple. A journalist looking inside Angkor Wat

In 1969, Angkor Wat's western entryway was still showing bullet scars left by fighting in the late 1940s. (David and Alice Burgess collection)

found a few souvenirs of the guerrillas' stay, cartridge casings, blood stains, and, for whatever reason, a sewing machine.

Glaize went to have a look too. The worst damage, he wrote in a rather dispassionate report to the EFEO, was at the western entrance of Angkor Wat, where he counted close to two hundred bullet scars. Some *devatas* had been hit; some window colonnettes were pulverized, but in sum he called the damage 'not very serious.' He found two bullet holes at Phnom Bakheng. At the south gate of Angkor Thom, where large stone gods and demons pull on the body of the *naga* serpent, the guerrillas had toppled a few stones to create cover from bullets, but Glaize deemed this easily repaired.

Peace had returned, but it was unclear for how long. The conservation staff moved valuable sculpture to the lower floor of the Grand Hotel for safe-keeping. A French officer who was particularly helpful in these efforts, lending a car, received in appreciation the head of a small female deity found at Preah Khan.

King Sihanouk, back in the good graces of the French despite his support of the Japanese coup the previous year, condemned the 'vandals of the monuments of Angkor, sacred to all Cambodians.'

In Angkor, French soldiers stood guard against the guerrillas. Things were secure enough that French military convalescents were coming out to visit some of the temples. Theft again became a problem. 'At the present time,' Glaize complained in November, 'the task of the curator is to advise the military and civil authorities when a theft occurs, to protest continually, and to check that the guards and maintenance workers are doing their jobs.'

Glaize set his men to work cleaning up the wreckage of the torched conservation buildings. He scrounged supplies and equipment. Perhaps, he proposed, some EFEO member going back to France on holiday could return with such basic supplies as paper and pencils for drawings.

On 23 December, the Khmer Issarak attacked again at Angkor Wat. They were driven back, but the violence signalled the start of a period of broader insecurity in neighbouring areas. Guerrillas became particularly active around the Western Baray, Srah Srang, Pre Rup temple, and in the Kulen hills. They attacked cars on the road to Kompong Thom. They paid menacing visits to the homes of Cambodians who worked for the conservation team. Some Angkor residents appear to have gone over to their side, whether out of fear or patriotic sentiments.

The only saving grace of this period, Glaize told Hanoi, was that the guerrillas were not causing any further deterioration to the temples.

Angkor Wat was one of the few temples that French conservators could visit without armed escort. And as of June 1947, there was plenty more work to do there. Early on a Saturday morning, the temple's southern bas-relief gallery suffered a major spontaneous collapse. It destroyed or damaged forty-five metres of gallery extending west from the temple's southeast corner. Vaulting, roof, columns, and bas-relief panels depicting Heaven and Hell had come tumbling down, creating 'indescribable disorder.' Thanks to the early hour of the collapse, no one was hurt.

In 1947, Glaize bowed out to Henri Marchal, who returned to the conservator job at age seventy-one. This man of seeming eternal youth did his best amidst the continuing major insecurity and minor budgets. Long known and held in affection in the Siem Reap area, by French and Cambodian alike (his wife was Cambodian), he seems to have been accepted at some level even by the Khmer Issarak. The historian and museum curator René Grousset recounted that during a 1949 visit he and Marchal were driving in a car when they came upon a band of guerrillas setting up a roadblock. Rather than retreating, Marchal got down from the vehicle and walked toward the men, who lowered their rifles and greeted him warmly.

Around Siem Reap, the insurrection largely had died out by the end of 1949. King Sihanouk had granted amnesty to Khmer Issarak who showed repentance, and many of them pledged loyalty him. Going forward, the war to drive the French from Indochina would take place mainly in Vietnam.

In 1953, Cambodia became a fully independent country. It was no surprise that at the centre of the new nation's flag was an image of Angkor Wat.

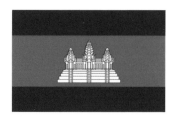

This flag, with a three-towered Angkor Wat at its center, was first adopted when Cambodia achieved partial independence in 1948. It continued as the national banner after full independence in 1953. (Wikimedia Commons)

10: FRAGILE TRANQUILLITY

Though war devastates much of Indochina, Angkor remains at peace. Sihanouk, Cambodia's politician-prince, takes a special interest in the old capital, coming to it often as a film-maker.

When the gunfire of the Khmer Issaraks finally died out, there began at Angkor a two-decade period that many would remember as a golden age of tranquility.

King Sihanouk abdicated in 1955 to rule as Prince Sihanouk, politician and autocrat. Intrigue, arrests, and violent demonstrations became common in Phnom Penh. But the turmoil rarely reached Siem Reap and Angkor. In the 1960s, the war in South Vietnam began spilling across the border into eastern Cambodia. Communist Vietnamese forces built sanctuary bases there; American B-52s dropped loads of bombs in hopes of destroying them. However, Angkor remained safely insulated from this threat too – the battle zone was hundreds of kilometres away.

Like the colonial authorities before him, Sihanouk sought both to show off Angkor to the world and make it an economic driver through tourism. The Bungalow was open again, doing business now as the Angkor Auberge. The Grand remained Siem Reap's upscale tourist address, though staying there did not guarantee basic amenities such as functional plumbing (nor dining flexibility – the hotel was known to demand that anyone renting a room pay for dinner in its restaurant as well). But by fits and starts the foreigners' numbers headed upward after the disruptions of the 1940s.

A new generation of Cambodians earned livelihoods as guides, cooks, drivers, elephant keepers, conservation workers, and vendors of soft drinks and small stone sculptures that might or might not be real. A new generation of monks sought enlightenment at the Angkor Wat monastery. Prosperity slowly expanded; on holidays, the people of Siem Reap often rode out to Angkor to picnic at the temples and moats. Countless family photos from the period show smiles and pride before the towers of Angkor Wat.

Running Siem Reap province now was Dap Chhuon, the same man who had overseen the Khmer Issarak attack on the town in 1946. Like many Cambodian leaders, he sensed a

In the 1960s, tourists could have an almost so* communing with Angkor Wat. (David and Alice Burgess collection)

Opposite page: Former American First Lady Jacqueline Kennedy and admirer Lord Harlech taking a break during a 1967 visit to Angkor. Photo courtesy of the National Archives of Cambodia.

strong supernatural power in Angkor. On his orders, two large standing images of the Buddha that had been unearthed there in 1950 were brought to his headquarters in town. Bearing the names Preah Ang Chek and Preah Ang Chorm, they were enshrined for prayers and protection.

The temples continued to claim the hearts of Cambodians everywhere in the country. When the architect and urban planner Vann Molyvann began devising a style of building that became known as New Khmer Architecture, he sometimes tapped into Angkor motifs. His design for the lotus-shaped tower of the Independence Monument in Phnom Penh leaves no doubt as to the source of its inspiration. He would leave his mark on Siem Reap airport as well, a large and curving glass-and-metal arrival hall.

With Sihanouk's consent, the EFEO remained in charge of Angkor in independent Cambodia, though the prince did not see that as a long-term solution. He wanted to 'decolonize' conservation. The Royal University of Fine Arts in Phnom Penh inaugurated an archaeology department with a goal of turning out a cadre of qualified Cambodians. One of the early graduates was a young man called Pich Keo, who would have deep importance in the Angkor story, though not right away.

* * * *

In 1964, there arrived at Angkor an unusual group of foreign visitors, a Hollywood production team. Led by American director Richard Brooks, it had secured permission to film scenes for a cinematic version of *Lord Jim*, the revered Joseph Conrad novel. This caused some surprise, given the mood of anti-Americanism prevailing in Sihanouk's government at the time. But it turned out that Brooks had paid a large and unusual price, negotiated with the prince's staff in Phnom Penh. About $600,000 of the film's budget had already been spent to enlarge and modernize the Auberge, which gained forty-seven air-conditioned rooms. Actors and crew would occupy them during the shoot, then leave them for future guests. Sihanouk

Following war-related disruptions, conservation work resumed full-scale at Angkor. Here two men work on a wall reconstruction project circa 1953. Photo by Harrison Forman, from the American Geographical Society Library, University of Wisconsin-Milwaukee Libraries.

had secured what was essentially foreign aid from Hollywood: a free upgrade of what remained one of the country's premier assets of the tourist trade.

For two months, the cameras rolled at various spots around Angkor. In the title role was Peter O'Toole, his career riding high after the success of 1962's *Lawrence of Arabia*. Other big names in the cast included James Mason, Curd Jürgens, and Eli Wallach. The female lead, Jim's love interest, was played by a little-known Israeli actor called Daliah Lavi. Cambodian army soldiers served as extras; in a number of scenes, local Buddhist monks played themselves, coming and going in procession. At day's end, the foreign cast members retreated to the Auberge. 'Everybody was sitting together in the dining room,' Lavi recalled in a 2011 interview with the Phnom Penh Post. 'Only James Mason was a lonely wolf and not very communicative, but Peter O'Toole was good to me and protective like a brother.'

Like all Cambodian leaders, Prince Sihanouk used Angkor as a symbol of his country. Here he presents an Angkor statuette to American President John F. Kennedy in New York in September 1961. Photo courtesy of John F. Kennedy Presidential Library and Museum.

Most of the story takes place in an imaginary realm called Patusan. In the film, its people have some strange kind of hybrid Asian culture – by turns Malay, Khmer, Vietnamese, and Balinese – and happen to live in the midst of some very photogenic stone temples.

Jim is a former maritime officer who torments himself for having abandoned a shipload of Asian Muslim pilgrims in a storm. Now he is making amends by helping Patusan's people cast off enslavement by 'the general' (Wallach), a ruthless European who has turned the twelfth century Preah Khan temple into his headquarters and fortress. As the film progresses, the temple receives some serious special-effects abuse from Jim and his cohort – spears strike its gate, cannon balls land in its courtyard, attackers pole vault over its walls, and in the middle of a melee Jim bravely pushes a keg of gunpowder into an inner chamber. The general, too slow to snuff out the fuse, is blown up. So too, it seems, is Preah Khan.

Filming accelerated after a Frenchman, who was said to be politically well connected, advised that, for safety's sake, the crew should wrap up quickly and leave Cambodia. There was concern that the soldier extras might turn out to be a threat. Shortly after an ahead-of-schedule departure from the country, mobs attacked the U.S. and British embassies in Phnom Penh (though nothing seems to have happened at Angkor). The violence was part of orchestrated demonstrations by which

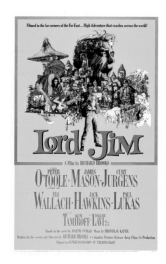

A poster for the 'Lord Jim' movie had a mish-mash of Asian references. LMPC / Contributor via Getty Images.

Air Vietnam played on the romance of a trip to Angkor in this marketing poster. Poster courtesy of Musée Air France.

Sihanouk periodically showed his displeasure with western powers and the escalation of the war in South Vietnam.

The film was released in 1965 to often skeptical reviews and disappointing box office receipts. Sihanouk himself dismissed it as mediocre. But what seems to have most caught his attention were the insults to his country that O'Toole delivered in an interview with *Life*, a photo magazine read by millions of people in the United States. During filming, the actor had shared his complaints with fellow cast members; now he did with the world at large, in an edition timed to the film's release. The Auberge, O'Toole declared, was 'more expensive than Claridge's [a swanky London hotel]. Ten flaming quid a night and a poxy room at that. Nicest thing you could say about the food was that it was grotesque.' There were snakes and insects on set and illness. Cambodian officials treated the film crew as if it had come to the country solely to hand out bribes. 'If I live to be a thousand,' O'Toole told the magazine, 'I want nothing like Cambodia again. It was a bloody nightmare. I really hated it there.'

The actor also recalled that one day Sihanouk arrived on location and in the course of conversations voiced some anti-British rhetoric. 'I walked up to him and said, "I couldn't agree with you more. I'm Irish meself." ' If that was meant to endear him to the prince, it had no such effect.

Sihanouk denounced the *Life* interview as engineered by western governments to undermine his rule. His anger would have a long-term effect. The prince had dabbled in film-making as a young man and now he decided that no one was more qualified than he to make films that would properly present his country to the world. He made at least six between 1966 and 1969, variously functioning as director, star, screen writer, and producer. The films drew patronizing praise abroad, and pride and incredulity at home, where many people wondered how he found time for affairs of state. But out the films came, one after the other, some of them featuring Angkor as a location. Conservation workers grew accustomed to the sight of the prince strutting around temples that had been converted into movie sets cluttered with cameras, lights, and sound equipment.

Le Petit Prince du Peuple (The Little Prince of the People) has as its title character a young royal from centuries past, who is wise and empathetic beyond his approximately twelve years of age. He was played by Sihanouk's son, the future King Sihamoni. In the opening scene, filmed on an Angkor terrace, royals are dispensing justice in a traditional court. They take up the case of a wife who is being detained by a powerful man over her humble husband's unpaid debt. Filled with compassion, the prince intervenes to re-unite the couple, paying off the debt from his own pocket. On the story goes, with songs, comedy, and palace intrigue. Viewers variously get glimpses of the Srah Srang reservoir, sculpted deities performing the Churning of the Sea of Milk, a temple interior set with furniture to create a palace, and a shaman's lair deep in a monument. At the close, the little prince sits in a stone doorway and accepts adulation from a holy man. All in all, the film was a parable of the benefits of rule by an enlightened royal.

There were also political messages in *Shadow over Angkor*, a very loose dramatization of one of the few cases of violence in Siem Reap in this period, the 1959 killing of province governor Dap Chhuon. Accused of turning against the prince and conspiring with the CIA, Thailand, and South Vietnam, he fled his residence on the approach of Sihanouk's security forces. By some accounts, he sought to take his two guardian images with him to Thailand, but they were too heavy. He settled for breaking off some fingers. He was later found and killed, under circumstances that remain unclear. The two images, deeply revered by Siem Reap's people, were removed from his headquarters and taken to a major Buddhist temple in town, Wat Damnak.

Made in 1969, the film is part James Bond knock-off, part polemic, part tourist travelogue. In one scene, a Sihanouk-like character, played by Sihanouk, takes the wheel of a sports car and drives an attractive foreign ambassador, played by his wife Princess Monineath, to Banteay Srei. Pointing to a famous piece of sculpture showing the god Krishna killing a tyrant ruler, he tells her: 'We devout Buddhists believe firmly that a traitor trying to sell out his country to the great powers cannot escape death.' Few Cambodians would have missed the meaning there.

Sihanouk took a close interest in what was shaping up as Angkor's biggest-ever reconstruction project. Like so many Khmer monuments, the pyramid known as the Baphuon had been built on what was little more than a giant pile of sand and laterite. Water that seeped into that core year after year had built up and exerted outward pressure on the stones. Archaeological examination had suggested that the Baphuon, which at the time of its consecration was Angkor's largest temple, had overtaxed the structural capabilities of the pyramid-on-sand form and was unstable from the start, suffering partial collapses through its long history. Yet another collapse had further disfigured the temple in 1949.

Preah Vihear temple stands atop a five hundred-metre cliff. (John Burgess)

Keeping a Temple in the Cambodian Fold

The ancient glories were frequent themes in Prince Sihanouk's speeches and writings. He likened his 'Khmer socialism' to the policies of King Jayavarman VII. At the Terrace of the Elephants in Angkor he staged an ancient Hindu plowing rite intended to assure a good harvest. He of course ruled under a flag graced by Angkor Wat. And he actually saved one of the ancient temples from loss to Thailand.

The temple was Preah Vihear, located about 140 kilometres northeast of Angkor. Standing atop a 500-metre cliff, it had the most spectacular setting of all the monuments the empire's people built. But as history moved borders around, Preah Vihear had the misfortune to come to be right at the frontier with Thailand. It became a conflict flashpoint.

In the late 1940s, Thai paramilitary police occupied it. Requests from Phnom Penh to withdraw came to nothing. So in 1959, Sihanouk's government sued for possession at the UN International Court of Justice in the Hague, commonly called the World Court. Three years of litigation ended with Cambodian victory.

The judges' nine-to-three decision was based largely on Thailand's decades-long failure to protest a 1907 map, produced by a joint French-Siamese border commission as part of Siam's return of Cambodia's western provinces. The map clearly showed the temple as being on the Cambodian side of the border. Saying nothing for so long amounted to acquiescence, the court ruled. The court instructed the Thais to withdraw. After initially refusing, they did.

Wild festivities broke out in Phnom Penh. Sihanouk was celebrated as a hero; protecting Khmer antiquity was a cause that united all strains of the Cambodian political world. In January 1964, the prince and his wife climbed the cliff to preside over a joyous reclamation ceremony attended by thousands of Cambodians and the Phnom Penh diplomatic corps.

This state of general ruin lingered into the 1960s. Then the new conservator, a barrel-chested man known to friends as 'Bear,' stepped in. Son of the late George Groslier, Bernard-Philippe Groslier was a veteran of the French resistance, a trained archaeologist, and an all-around Renaissance man. He decided on full anastylosis for the Baphuon. Cranes began removing stone and laterite blocks one by one. By the time this stage of the job was done, the temple had essentially disappeared, turned into some 300,000 blocks laid out nearby, each bearing a painted code to indicate the precise position it would take in a future rebuilt and reinforced Baphuon. Reconstruction began. Concrete was poured as an invisible reinforcement of foundations, and the temple's bottom tier took form again.

* * * * *

In the 1950s and '60s, Angkor was again attracting international VIPs, often with Sihanouk acting as proud personal guide. U.S. Vice President Richard Nixon came in 1953. Nixon was a man whose passions were politics and global relations, not ancient culture, and even Angkor failed to make a dent in that. In a weighty memoir that he later wrote, he had just half a sentence for it, calling it 'haunting and majestic.' In 1959, the big visitor was UN Secretary General Dag Hammarskjöld, in

U.S. Vice President Richard Nixon, centre right, and his wife Patricia were among the foreign VIPs who visited Angkor in the 1950s. Photo courtesy of The Richard Nixon Foundation.

1960 Chinese Prime Minister Zhou Enlai, in 1966 Charles de Gaulle, now president of France. Among other things, De Gaulle announced French financial support for the work at the Baphuon.

But none of these visits created even a fraction of the international attention that exploded in 1967 when Jacqueline Kennedy, widow of the assassinated American president John F. Kennedy, came calling.

The United States had no diplomatic relations with Cambodia at the time. Sihanouk had broken them off in 1965 as the war in South Vietnam rose in intensity, often intruding into Cambodian territory. But 'Jackie' came nonetheless. She was at pains to say there was nothing political about her visit, that she was merely realizing a 'lifelong dream' of seeing Angkor Wat. But whatever her personal motivations, her trip was also an overture from the United States, which was seeking to repair relations with Sihanouk and see him move against Vietnamese sanctuary bases in eastern Cambodia. From the start, the supposed private vacation felt like a state visit. The U.S. Department of State assisted closely in preparations; Mrs. Kennedy arrived in a U.S. Air Force plane at Phnom Penh's Pochentong Airport, where Sihanouk and a crowd of courtiers waited to greet her.

She was feted in the capital and then flown to Siem Reap, where preparations had long been in progress. Groslier turned out to give her party a personal tour. He led the way through the Bayon, pausing at the famous bas-reliefs that depict daily life. She took lunch at the temple, where white-jacketed waiters served up seven courses on a table set in the open air beneath soaring hardwood trees. Musicians provided traditional music with flutes and cymbals. That night she visited an Angkor Wat lit by candles, torches and floodlights, strolling barefoot across the stones and running her fingers in wonder over carved images (no doubt no one scolded her for that). It was all suitably magical and stage-managed. Her reaction to Angkor: 'It's magnificent, just magnificent.'

Sihanouk depicted it as a sombre pilgrimage. 'She told me that she wants to go to Angkor to meditate,' he said, 'because she is a widow who keeps alive memories of her husband. The press should not disturb this great lady.' But the prince was not about to black out news that he and his country were hosting a guest who was arguably the most famous woman on earth. At the Bayon, a sizeable scrum of reporters and photographers tagged along with Groslier, Kennedy, and her traveling companion, Lord Harlech, the former David Ormsby-Gore, who had served as British ambassador to the United States during the Kennedy administration.[1]

Life magazine had published Peter O'Toole's wounding words about Cambodia. Now it gave the country some salving praise. It put Kennedy on its cover ('Jackie in Cambodia'), showing her walking through the Bayon, communing with its stones. Foreign newspapers and television gave prominent coverage as well. Never had Angkor received such global exposure. The visit is today viewed as the first step in a process by which the United States did achieve a form of reconciliation with Sihanouk. In 1969, he staged another of the turn-arounds for which he was famous and restored diplomatic relations with Washington.

* * * * *

The old hotel outside Angkor Wat continued to operate after the *Lord Jim* crew departed, now with a modern air-conditioned wing. But for some guests, it still lived up to its old reputation for guest exploitation. In March 1966, an American pharmaceutical executive called Ted Behr drove in with family members from their home in Bangkok. On their first night, they were served a fine French wine with dinner at the hotel. Behr asked if he could buy a case of it to take back to Bangkok, where good wine was hard to find. As his brother Pete, who was along on the trip, recounts it, a hotel employee loaded a closed case into the car's trunk on the morning of their departure. After getting on the road, Ted found himself feeling suspicious. He checked the case and found he'd been given twelve bottles of the cheapest kind of Algerian plonk. Ted returned to the hotel to protest. Sorry, the manager said, all sales are final. 'I'll write a letter of complaint to the minister of tourism!' Ted declared. 'Why don't you call him? asked the manager, reaching for the telephone. 'He's my brother-in-law.' Ted conceded defeat.

Perhaps monopolistic arrogance was at the root of this kind of behavior. But late in the '60s, the Auberge stood to get its first competition in the coveted temple-side location. A few steps away, on the north side of the airport road, construction teams were finishing up a hotel designed by French architect Claude Bach, with input from Vann Molyvann. To bear the name Hôtel Angkor, it was a joint venture of Air France, a major player in the Cambodia tourist trade, and local investors.

Like the Auberge, it was low-rise, so as to hide discreetly in the foliage and not distract from the temple. But everything else

Jacqueline Kennedy listening to an explanation by conservator Bernard-Philippe Groslier, left. Looking on was Lord Harlech. Photo courtesy of the National Archives of Cambodia.

1   Lord Harlech was widely known at the time to be a suitor. Letters that went up for auction in 2017 show that he formally proposed marriage several months after the Cambodia visit. He lost out to the Greek shipping magnate Aristotle Onassis, who married Kennedy in 1968.

about it seemed calculated to outshine the old wooden facility. Hôtel Angkor's walls included tastefully arrayed brick and laterite, prime materials of the temples' architects. The hotel had one hundred ninety-five rooms, each with private bath and phone. There were six suites, a restaurant seating three hundred twenty, a discotheque, a bar, and a swimming pool. Its three-hectare grounds would be elaborately landscaped. Guests would be able to hire cars with or without drivers. Boating excursions on the *barays* or the Great Lake would be on offer. For those wanting to tour by traditional transport, elephants would be on call in a special pen out front.

From the start, Sihanouk took a close interest in the project. Bach presented a model of the hotel to him, with a joking suggestion that each room should contain a butterfly. Always a micromanager, Sihanouk is said to have loved the idea. Opening day was set for 15 July 1970.

By now, although the Vietnam War was at its height in the next country over, about 50,000 foreigners a year were coming to Angkor. With aid from China, Siem Reap airport had been expanded yet again. Many people were now flying in directly from Hong Kong, avoiding lay-overs in Phnom Penh. The Grand Hotel, quoting prices in 1970 in U.S. dollars, was offering 'superior category' rooms for $5.35 to $8.90 a night, an 'English breakfast' for $1.20 and lunch and dinner for $3.15.

Watching the growing tourist parade was a retired Henri Marchal. Having finally given up all official duties, he lived now in a house by the Siem Reap River. He continued to write and weigh in on Angkor concerns as he approached, then exceeded, the age of ninety. Though over the years he had done his share to encourage foreign visitors, he now came to feel that their presence altered something fundamental. 'The incessant stream of tourists,' he wrote in an unpublished memoir, 'that the airplane, the ocean liner, or the automobile bring to Angkor accentuates more and more a utilitarian modernism which deforms and trivializes the character of these old temples.' He recalled the Angkor of mystery of his younger years. 'In that distant time, after passing through the south gate of Angkor Thom by cart, horseback, or elephant, one was immersed in an inextricable jumble of vegetation until arriving in front of the Bayon, which was itself buried under the trees and lianas.' Those days were gone, he said, but 'evocation of these visions…will remain the consolation of my old age.'

50,000 tourists a year. How quaint, how redolent of quieter times such a number now sounds. It works out at roughly 1,000 a week, 150 a day.

* * * * *

Beyond Angkor, time was running out for Prince Sihanouk. In parts of the country he was facing a low-grade communist insurgency directed by men he had forced underground (for them he popularized the term *Khmers Rouges*, 'Red Khmers'). He had proven unable to end spillover of the Vietnam war into the eastern provinces. In Phnom Penh, his power and impetuous ways had alienated many members of the political and military elite. (Having to feign enthusiasm for his films was just one of many complaints against him.) The pressures came to a head on 18 March 1970, while the prince was visiting Moscow. His army commander Lon Nol and acting prime minister Sirik Matak staged a coup d'etat and deposed him.

Coup co-leader Lon Nol later became prime minister of Cambodia. © Everett Collection / Historical Highlights Images/ agefotostock.

Sihanouk remained abroad. In the days after the coup he seemed almost wiped from history. The new leaders began dismantling palace authority to transform Cambodia into a royalty-free Khmer Republic. Like all their compatriots, they viewed Angkor as the soul of the nation, and would keep it on Cambodian banknotes. Yet they now had to perform some ideological acrobatics to justify the new form of government. Shortly after the coup, Cambodia's official press agency published an attack on the ancient kings for having created a system that enslaved the Khmer people. King Jayavarman II, widely seen as the Khmer Empire's founder, 'was the promoter of our country's dictatorial regime and considered himself a god-king in order to win the veneration of the Cambodian people...Other kings of the Varman dynasty joyfully exploited the worship of the population and forced our citizens to build monuments to glorify their power.' The clear implication was that Prince Sihanouk, as their royal successor, had continued these oppressive ways and deserved to be overthrown. This did not, however, detract from the accomplishments of the Khmer people of ancient times. Their monuments would continue to receive reverence.

The new leaders pledged to drive the Vietnamese from Cambodian territory and restore peace and sovereignty. In fact, their coup turned out to be step one in a process that would engulf the country in war. No place in Cambodia, Angkor included, would escape the momentous suffering to come.

11: WAR

North Vietnamese forces occupy Angkor for their Khmer Rouge allies. With diplomacy and armed attack, the American-supported Lon Nol government tries but fails to take it back.

War arrived at the ancient Khmer capital on the night of 5-6 June 1970. North Vietnamese forces attacked and overran the newly expanded Siem Reap airport. The din of weapons fire carried to the temples, but there was no real fight there. Lon Nol's troops did not mount a defence, which would have risked damage to the nation's heritage. In any case, they were hardly up to keeping out a foe as strong and determined as the North Vietnamese. In the early morning hours, the foreign soldiers in olive uniforms and pith helmets simply moved in and laid claim.

Fear and confusion mounted as Angkor's many residents ventured from their homes and encountered the new masters. EFEO anthropologist François Bizot, living in a community by the Srah Srang reservoir, set out by van for Siem Reap early that morning and came upon a Cambodian military truck that had been hit by a rocket grenade. Dead and wounded lay scattered about. Bizot's efforts to drive three of the injured to town for medical aid ended with Vietnamese stopping him near Angkor Wat's east moat. Helpless to protest, he watched as rows of the foreign soldiers marched along the roads, fully in control.

In these first day, the lines of control fluctuated; soldiers moved here and there; no one was sure who controlled what. Lon Nol's soldiers shelled areas they thought enemy forces had occupied, often hitting villages. Vietnamese rockets and mortar shells fell on Siem Reap, fired with similar disregard for civilian life. Buddhist temples in town took in many of the people who lost their homes, for what would become extended stays.

Angkor's first hotel, once known as the Bungalow, now as the Auberge, met its end after six decades of operation. Hit by some kind of weapon of war, it partially burned. What remained became an abandoned hulk, littered with ashes and debris.

By this time much of the country was in similar havoc. The pledge by the coup leaders in Phnom Penh to drive the

Opposite page: With war having descended on Angkor, soldiers of the Lon Nol army received a blessing in July 1970 from a Buddhist monk on Angkor Wat's entrance causeway. © Chas Gerretsen, Nederlands Fotomuseum.

Vietnamese from the country had produced the precise opposite effect. From their bases inside Cambodia, the Vietnamese struck out against the inexperienced and corruption-addled Cambodian forces, scattering them. In short order the Vietnamese overran much of the country. Official media in China and North Vietnam attributed the attacks to 'patriotic Cambodians,' but in fact the country's homegrown insurgents, the Khmer Rouge, as they would come to be known, had only scant armed forces in the field. Their North Vietnamese allies did almost all of the fighting at this point in the war.

Far from fading away after the coup, Prince Sihanouk threw his weight behind the Khmer Rouge and a newly formed government-in-exile. Speaking on Radio Peking, he called on all Cambodians to join him in confronting the new government in Phnom Penh, headed by Lon Nol. That government, meanwhile, had its own foreign patron, the United States. Following the coup, the Americans quickly began providing aid, including food, weapons, and diplomatic support. The U.S. Air Force began bombing missions that would broaden to cover virtually the entire country. U.S. observation planes became a common sight in the skies over Angkor, trying to figure out what was going on below.

In the days following the 5-6 June attack, Lon Nol's forces managed to regain control of the airport. Airplanes began landing to deliver food and other supplies and fly out the wounded. For a brief period in July, there came reports that Vietnamese forces had withdrawn from Angkor. But that proved false. The Vietnamese remained. This was a grave blow to the Lon Nol government. It had proven powerless to prevent a foreign army from occupying the spiritual heart of the nation.

It soon became clear that Siem Reap was becoming part of a pattern that set in across Cambodia – government forces bottled up in cities and towns, the other side ruling the countryside. Still, Siem Reap was a special case. Here the countryside included the temples, which, in principle, at least, the international rules of war protected from attack.

* * * * *

In the first days of this chaos, French authorities scrambled to assure that French citizens in the area were safe. At least two were clearly not. From the unopened Air France hotel by Angkor Wat, a plea for help had come from the French manager who had been living there with his pregnant wife during final preparations for opening. The couple felt imprisoned, afraid to leave as guns boomed and Vietnamese soldiers marched past. EFEO ethnologist Jean Boulbet volunteered to try to bring them out. Hervé Manac'h, a young Frenchman doing his military service as a technical consultant to the EFEO, offered to go with him, but that was vetoed on grounds that Manac'h's father was the French ambassador to China and there would be repercussions if the son were taken prisoner. An EFEO archaeologist, Bruno Dagens, offered to go instead.

The two men drove from Siem Reap on the now deserted road. They were in a borrowed French military ambulance, Dagens at the wheel, Boulbet waving a French flag from his rolled-down window. At the Angkor Wat moat, Vietnamese soldiers blocked their way; the two foreigners were ordered out of the vehicle.

Jean Boulbet and Bruno Dagens reached the Air France hotel in this ambulance, shown here on its subsequent drive to Battambang. Photo by Hervé Manac'h.

Boulbet then began what would be a constant role in the months ahead – pleader, cajoler, persuader of soldiers who generally didn't want to help but sometimes would, or sometimes could be defied without deadly consequences. That day he prevailed upon the soldiers' leader to seek permission from up the chain of command for the ambulance to go through to the hotel. But there was a problem – the leader couldn't contact his commander. So, he borrowed the ambulance to go seek permission. Boulbet and Dagens, in the meantime, waited at the hotel, where the French couple greeted them as rescuers. But now there were four 'prisoners.' No one was yet free to go. The woman brought out an expensive bottle of champagne, intended for guests who had never checked in, and they all raised a glass anxiously. After some time, the ambulance returned. The four French people got in; Dagens drove off even though there was no clear permission to leave. Soldiers shouted, but did not stop them. On the way back, the ambulance came upon a column of the other new group, the Khmer Rouge, sinister armed men in black peasant clothing. Again, cajoling and just driving on got the party back to Siem Reap. There they discovered two bullet holes in the ambulance, whether stray shots or intentional they could not tell.[1] Manac'h escorted the couple on to Battambang.

* * * * *

It had been no surprise when the war reached Angkor. In preceding weeks, Siem Reap's people had watched fearfully as Vietnamese attacks drew ever closer to their town. One by one, villages surrounding Angkor passed into the control of

---

1   This account is largely from a memoir that Boulbet later wrote, *De Palms et d'Epines: Vers le Paradis d'Indra*.

mysterious new authorities. Conservator Bernard-Philippe Groslier took the precaution of draping the temples with huge blue-and-white banners signalling that they were protected by UNESCO and the Hague Convention, an international agreement that aimed to keep hostilities away from cultural treasures. Other preparations included sending key documents and portable artefacts to Phnom Penh for safekeeping, and ringing the storage places of things that remained with sandbags and sandstone slabs.

Now, with war having actually arrived, Groslier faced the task not only of protecting the monuments but his conservation staff, who with family members numbered close to six thousand. Many of them lived in settlements now occupied by the Vietnamese. 'The stones will survive,' he told a friend at the time. 'I worry about the people.' However this was accomplished, it was going to mean cooperation from the Vietnamese.

Several days into the occupation, he and Boulbet boldly went into the park to seek out the new authorities. They quickly encountered Vietnamese soldiers who in effect took them into custody and marched them toward a headquarters. En route, at the Srah Srang reservoir, local people turned out with coconut milk and other refreshments. The sight of the two familiar Frenchmen must have been a welcome sign that perhaps things were getting back to normal, never mind that they were essentially prisoners.

They eventually sat down with a Vietnamese commander for an extended, meandering negotiation. Pinning the man down on what could and couldn't be done was frustrating. Groslier and Boulbet stressed a need to respect the protected status of the monuments. The Vietnamese wanted to know, what would his side gain by doing that? The two foreigners were

Crisis consultation in the Angkor conservation compound, June 1970. Left to right, Jacques Dumarçay of the EFEO; the French consul; Bruno Dagens (partially hidden); conservator Bernard-Philippe Groslier; Jean Boulbet; and a French military doctor. Photo by Hervé Manac'h.

sure the man knew the answer already: if he didn't militarize the monuments, his men wouldn't be subject to attack. Angkor would become a sanctuary of sorts. The Frenchmen proposed that they be allowed to move in and out of the zone to continue conservation work. The commander wanted to know what route they would follow on the Lon Nol side's territory. He was told, we can't tell you (it would qualify as military intelligence), but neither will we tell the Lon Nol soldiers what route we follow in your territory. The commander now seemed to see some utility. A deal came together[2] by which twelve conservation people would be allowed to enter and leave the zone, but only on bicycles. They would wear UNESCO armbands to identify themselves.

That was the start of a remarkable, though always shaky cooperation. Groslier and other French conservation staff members gained a new distinction as the only westerners able to pass in and out of the Cambodian 'liberated zone.' Groslier believed initially that the deal would be sufficient only to close up various conservation sites and secure them for a peaceful future in which work could continue. But it came to be more than that. Over the coming weeks and months, many of the Cambodians workers returned to their jobs. Groslier, pedalling a bike, dropped in periodically to supervise work on the bas-relief galleries at Angkor Wat and on the Baphuon. Boulbet handled further-out sites. Groslier would later joke that the bicycle brigades amounted to a 'Ho Chi Minh Trail,' a reference to the covert supply lines between North and South Vietnam.

Groslier now became a man sought out by foreign journalists coming to Siem Reap. Jeff Williams, an Associated Press correspondent, arrived with AP photographer Max Nash shortly after the temples' occupation. Williams recalls chatting with Groslier briefly in the conservation compound. He was not entirely friendly, giving the visitors a brief lecture on the folly of the American intervention in Indochina, a common view among resident French. The journalists left, planning to join a Lon Nol patrol that was going to walk towards Angkor. Groslier's parting words, in French: 'I hope you like dog meat.' It was a gallows humour allusion to what they might be eating if they fell into the hands of the Vietnamese, who sometimes treated canines as food.

From near Siem Reap airport, the patrol walked east along the road that runs to Angkor Wat's entrance causeway, passing deserted rice fields. Ahead, over some palm fronds, the iconic stone towers came into view. Things were quiet. Williams

2   A parallel diplomatic outreach by the French government in foreign capitals seems also to have helped reach this deal.

began thinking that they might get lucky and walk right inside, which he much wanted to do. He'd never been. The patrol came upon two Buddhist monks walking away from the temple. Its leader questioned them about numbers of Vietnamese or Khmer Rouge inside, but the monks denied knowing anything. The patrol walked further toward to the towers, then stopped to radio its position. A mortar shell fell into one of the rice fields, raising a shower of red earth. A second round exploded on the other side of the road. The patrol withdrew.

A patrol that Dutch photographer Chas Gerretsen joined got closer, but suffered casualties to do so. Numbering about one hundred-fifty soldiers, the group set out on foot from Siem Reap on July 12 to conduct a 'sweep' operation. A few were women, drafted the month before, some of whom wept on passing their ruined *lycée*, or high school, where a rocket attack had killed classmates just that day. The group proceeded along a deserted road, to the trill of countless cicadas in forests to either side. Then came an ambush. Ten metres from Gerretsen, a mortar shell severed the right leg of a soldier, who looked on uncomprehendingly as the photographer ran to him. Gerretsen could do nothing for him but shout for a medic. The group kept going, sustaining two other attacks, and finally arrived after six hours at Angkor Wat's entrance causeway. And there – peace and silence, under a cloud-speckled sky.

From the entrance complex across the moat, civilians peered out. Then a monk emerged from among them and walked in the direction of the patrol. Soldiers gathered about him and accepted the blessing that he offered. One can imagine that they felt it to be a strong one, bearing the power and authority of the temple's guardian deities in a time of grievous danger. Peace and silence continued. The soldiers remained in the area for close to an hour, some of them flopping down in grass by the moat to rest. Then came an order to leave. It took just an hour to walk back to Siem Reap. Not a single shot was fired.

* * * * *

At the conservation compound in Siem Reap, a new kind of normal had taken hold. In July, Groslier showed a French television journalist, René Puissesseau, around it. Gunshots sounded from somewhere beyond; Groslier paid them no mind. The compound now resembled a make-shift fortress, with its storage buildings' walls armoured with concrete construction slabs and upended wheelbarrows to protect the treasures inside. Stray shells and bullets had occasionally hit, but without doing serious damage, the conservator calmly explained as a camera rolled. One had exploded near a row of large statues, scarring a wall behind them but leaving them unharmed. 'We have a new miracle of the Buddhist world,' Groslier remarked. 'They endured their baptism of fire…Not a single fragment touched them.'

Several hundred Cambodians were living inside the compound, hoping for safety. Life seemed almost routine – one was getting a haircut.

* * * * *

Inside the temple zone, the North Vietnamese soldiers were settling in for a long stay. For many of Angkor's residents, the new reality meant putting up with a few of them as long-term house guests. Soldiers slept in hammocks they strung beneath family dwellings. Their days were variously taken up with patrols and training exercises, sleep, and cooking. A few expressed an interest that did not go down well with local sensibilities, that interest in dogs as food. But some of them wore buttons bearing the image of Prince Sihanouk, intended to convey to Cambodians that they were the forces of the still widely popular leader, though in fact he had scant control over what they did.

The war had brought uneasy alliances among historical enemies on both sides of the lines at Angkor, as it had all over the country. The few armed Cambodians who were present around the temples, the nascent Khmer Rouge army, were accepting help from a power and people that many Cambodians feared wanted to swallow up their country. Neither side fully trusted the other. There were reports of periodic fighting between them.

The Lon Nol side, meanwhile, had entered into an equally fraught alliance with Cambodia's other historical enemy, Thailand, which was providing it diplomatic recognition, supplies, and military help, sometimes with its own armed forces. In July 1970, the Royal Thai Air Force began staging strikes in western Cambodia, U.S. State Department records from the time show. A Thai liaison group of about twelve men was ordered to Siem Reap, mostly to coordinate Thai air operations.

Thai help was a big part of why Lon Nol's forces were able to hang onto one big gem of Khmer antiquity, Preah Vihear, the temple that the World Court had awarded to Cambodia eight years earlier. The cliff-top location that had been so spiritually

With the start of hostilities in 1970, thousands of Cambodians took shelter inside Angkor Wat, some forced there by Khmer Rouge and Vietnamese soldiers, others coming voluntarily in belief they'd find safety. During one of his bicycle visits, Conservator Bernard-Philippe Groslier took this photo of people camping out in a bas relief arcade. Photo courtesy of EFEO.

attractive to its ancient builders made it readily defendable as a military redoubt. Soldiers of a Lon Nol garrison there, peering down on a plain that came to be dominated by Vietnamese and Khmer Rouge forces, had a natural advantage against any attack up the slopes. But that garrison's long-term survival also depended on the fact that the temple's northern entrance abutted on Thai territory, from which food, ammunition, and other supplies passed freely into the grounds.

* * * * *

In the first weeks of the occupation, Angkor Wat began a chilling new chapter in its existence. The great monument that had been built as a place of prayer and ritual for kings and priests became a combination prison, haven, and refugee camp for thousands of ordinary Cambodians. It was some of these people whom photographer Chas Gerretsen had seen peering out from Angkor Wat.

Following the initial attack on Siem Reap airport, Ronnie Yimsut, then a boy of about eight, spent weeks sheltering in terror from shelling with his family at a house midway between Siem Reap and Angkor Wat. They were virtually starving. Then Vietnamese and Khmer Rouge came during a break in the fighting and told everyone to leave within thirty minutes for Angkor Wat. There would be food and supplies there, the men promised. Yimsut today believes their intention was to use them and other people as a human shield, to ward off the Lon Nol side. The family did as they were told, taking pots and pans and what little food they had, then trudging up the road toward the temple. At the junction where the road reached the southern moat, they came upon thousands of other civilians. Shells began falling again. Rather than fight their way through the crowds to the temple's west or east gates, where causeways spanned the moat, the family chose to go down into the water. The children clung to a log, and the family struggled across the moat and up on the far shore. There, exhausted and picking leaches off their skin, they took stock outside the temple's three and half kilometre-long perimeter walls.

Not all the civilians had come on orders from the Vietnamese and Khmer Rouge. With shells still falling on Siem Reap, some decided on their own to go to Angkor Wat, where, they believed, they would be protected both by the Hague Convention and the temples' resident spirits, notably one known as Ta Reach. With so many heading to Angkor, Siem Reap was acquiring a half-deserted look.

Ronnie Yimsut's family was soon established inside Angkor Wat on the floor of an outer gallery, alongside some of the famous bas-reliefs. They slept on mats, they burned candles at night, they said prayers to Ta Reach at their own tiny shrine, a milk can in which they stuck sticks of incense. All around the temple people were living in similar crisis, a sad community of the displaced. Everyone wanted to go home, but in the meantime, everyone tried to make do. People put up metal roofing and straw mats between columns to deflect the sun and provide some privacy. They stored water in jars, and fashioned makeshift ladders to give access to their claimed bits of arcade space from the ground.

Ronnie's family was safe from shelling in this place, but it had many other kinds of terror. One was a constant fear of hunger. The supplies of food that the soldiers had promised did not exist. When the food the family had brought ran out, Ronnie and others waded into the moat to hunt for frogs or snails – or snakes. Boiled with water hyacinths, snakes were turned into soup. There were no latrines available; people simply walked into the wooded area on the temple's eastern side, which was also a source of firewood.

Another form of terror was Khmer Rouge soldiers, who stood guard at the gates and periodically came in unannounced, sometimes to seize young people for forced service. Ronnie's older brother and sisters hid, and escaped their attention.

Desperation was so strong that from time to time, someone would climb to the temple's third tier and jump off. A quick cremation within the temple walls followed. Ronnie sometimes had thoughts of whether he might die this way – all he would have to do was jump, and his problems would end. But he put these thoughts aside, knowing that even as a child he had an obligation to help his family.

During the war, Cambodian civilians sought protection at other major temples of Angkor, including this one, the East Mebon. (John Burgess)

Growing up in Siem Reap, Ronnie had visited Angkor Wat many times before the war, often just to mess around with friends. But during his time living in the temple, he recalls, he paid no attention at all to the glories around him. His attention was consumed by questions of survival.

There were constant new arrivals at Angkor Wat – many members of the conservation staff ended up there – but also departures. Some people escaped on their own across the moats. Others were released to people from the Khmer Rouge zone who could vouch for them. That is how Ronnie's family left after several months. An uncle who had been living in a nearby Khmer Rouge village arrived, searched through the crowds to find them, and took them to the village. The family later found a way to cross the lines back to Siem Reap, where they lived for the rest of the war.

The French managed to get quantities of humanitarian aid to Angkor Wat. There also was a school for the countless children sheltered at the temple and a small clinic. But given the limitations on transport, the aid was nowhere large enough to keep up with the sheer numbers of people.

Similar scenes of desperation could be found at other Angkor monuments. Frightened people took refuge at the Bayon, Pre Rup, and the East Mebon, among others. Any large piece of Khmer antiquity was presumed to offer some measure of protection from the shells and rockets that continued to fall. In interviews at Angkor around the year 2000, the anthropologist Keiko Miura heard accounts of constant movement in a search for safety. One woman told her: 'I ran to Prasat Banteay [a temple north of Angkor Thom] and stayed there for ten days, and then went to Angkor Thom, where Wat Tep Pranam now stands, and stayed for two weeks.' Later she and her husband, five children, and four cows set off for another district to the southeast, stopping on the way at Pre Rup.

As of early July 1970, Groslier estimated to the journalist Puissesseau, that 3,000 people were inside Angkor Wat. The temple 'sustains a life which no one could want, and is quite distressing,' he said. Can we go there? the journalist asked. 'Not now,' Groslier calmly replied. 'But maybe in a few days it will be possible.' Puissesseau and his team nonetheless went down a road toward Angkor. At a Lon Nol checkpoint, he faced the camera to say that they would cross into no-man's land to try to reach the temples. The film ends there. Puissesseau, cameraman Raymond Meyer, and sound engineer Alain Clément were fired on near Angkor Wat, then captured by communist forces. Puissesseau and Meyer died of their wounds. Clément was detained for a month and a half, then released.

* * * * *

News of Angkor's capture was reported around the world, and concern mounted that the monuments would be damaged, even destroyed in fighting. In October 1970, delegates representing Lon Nol's government at a UNESCO conference in Paris cited danger from the vibration of bombings and shelling, and damage that refugees in the temples might do to them inadvertently. Chemical reactions caused by the smoke of cooking fires and the remnants of butchered animals might harm the stones, it was said.

The U.S. Air Force never bombed Angkor, but it did major damage to monuments built in contemporary times in Vietnam—the My Son complex, masterwork of the Cham civilisation. Many bombs fell on My Son in August 1969 at a time when it was being used as a guerrilla camp. Today, like Angkor, it is a UNESCO World Heritage site. MH0646/Shutterstock.com.

The Vietnamese and Khmer Rouge never formally agreed to abide by Hague Convention protections, but neither did they turn the temples into long-term armed redoubts. Nor did they loot antiquities in any organized way. Their soldiers did go inside the temples, as Ronnie Yimsut found, but generally to manage and oppress the people taking shelter there. A few of those visits seem to have been for old-fashioned sightseeing and tourist misbehaviour. One Vietnamese carved the following bit of graffiti into stone on Angkor Wat's third tier: 'H. Cing, 7-6-70, Hanoi.'

Still, the Vietnamese seem sometimes to have tested the limits of the unspoken agreement on what they would do. Boulbet later recounted that at one point the Vietnamese tried to put heavy weapons at the Phnom Bakheng temple, which stands on a hill that overlooks Angkor Wat – and the Siem Reap airport, Lon Nol forces' lifeline to the outside. With a few shells fired from atop the hill, the Vietnamese would have no trouble closing the airport. Alerted that something was going on, Boulbet went up the hill and found Vietnamese soldiers already there, in freshly dug holes. By his account, he told a Vietnamese commander that he had learned that the U.S. Air Force had already spotted the men and was going to attack. Better to get them out and save their lives, he said. They were gone when Boulbet next visited.

As the stand-off progressed, the Lon Nol government called for turning Angkor into a neutral, demilitarized zone, under international control. The communist side rejected the idea. That was no surprise, as neutralization would have meant its forces retreating, relinquishing land they had captured. Their response was that the danger to Angkor was not from them, but from U.S. bombers and the Lon Nol army.

In fact, U.S. bombers never attacked in Angkor, Boulbet's warning to the Vietnamese notwithstanding. They stayed away for the full duration of the war. But not so the Lon Nol forces. In May 1971, the western news media learned that shells from the Lon Nol artillery had exploded inside Angkor Wat some months earlier and a cover-up had ensued. The Associated Press said the barrage killed or wounded ten refugees and did 'severe' damage to the temple and some of its bas-reliefs. The third floor of the southern gate had been destroyed, the report said. It quoted sources saying that a local Lon Nol commander had ordered the shelling without authority from his superiors, but would not face discipline out of fear of harming the army's morale. Lon Nol's military command eventually confirmed that its howitzers had fired about ten shells toward the temple. The goal, it said, was to destroy an enemy firing position that threatened Siem Reap.

In discussions with the U.S. Embassy's deputy chief of mission, Thomas Enders, in late May, Groslier laid out details of the shelling. On the evening of 14 February, he said, a handful of 105mm shells struck Angkor Wat's southern edge. Two landed at the foot of the bas-relief gallery, causing two deaths and damage to bas-reliefs, a third shattered the top of a square column, and a fourth ricocheted off the roof of the 'inner portico.'

Groslier described another incident, on 14-15 May, in which shells landed in a settlement by the Angkor Thom moat. Vietnamese units had been in the area earlier but had left by the time the shells fell, he said; a few pigs and chickens were the only casualties. Later on, three shells struck the moat itself and two hit the city's walls. Groslier showed the American diplomat a photo of a crater about two metres across in the wall.

The gunners, he said, then shifted their attention to areas along the Siem Reap River, with a few shells falling on the Neak Pean temple grounds, though without causing much damage, and two just outside the East Mebon temple, causing one death and one serious injury. Perhaps 150 shells in total were fired during these two days. In sum, the damage of the February and May incidents was not so bad, he said, 'much less than is done in a normal tourist season.'[3] Around this time, the U.S. Air Force took reconnaissance photos of Angkor Wat at the request of the embassy in Phnom Penh, and reported back that no damage was visible from the air.

3   In a conversation with the Australian ambassador in Phnom Penh, however, he was said to have described the damage as 'irreparable.'

In his meeting with the American diplomat, Groslier expressed worries over the future, in part because the Vietnamese units with whose officers he had built a basic understanding appeared to be withdrawing. The numbers of Khmer Rouge were rising and they were less disciplined. Sometimes they 'borrowed' his tractors and returned them only on protest. They had begun digging fortifications outside the entrance of Angkor Wat.

Though the Vietnamese were organized in a chain of command, seeking approval for decisions from above, the Khmers seemed not to have any fixed structure. They told Groslier that decisions were made locally. They expressed guarded resentment over the presence of the Vietnamese. In the future, he was told, Cambodians would make the decisions, 'because after all it is our country.' Groslier was left suspecting that new fighting might break out between the Khmer Rouge and the Vietnamese.[4]

Boulbet experienced similar problems in his own work inside Angkor. The Khmer Rouge began operating their own checkpoints. The black-clad soldiers were rude, unresponsive, and prone to bullying. One day, Boulbet stumbled upon a makeshift prison that they had built inside Angkor Thom – a long shelter in which men were being held in chains in appalling conditions. Before he could say anything, he heard the menacing sound of rifle bullets being chambered and was hustled away by aggressive men.

In his conversation with the American diplomat, Groslier said the Cambodian army was unlikely ever to regain control of Angkor. It was confined to Siem Reap and could do little more than fire its artillery (and not accurately).[5] Its soldiers were corrupt, shaking down residents of the town and prices were headed up. Groslier was also pessimistic about his own future. 'Speaking emotionally,' the cable reported, 'he said that he did not believe that he could carry on very much longer and is ready to decide to close up the Angkor workshop.'

But carry on he did, even with the burden of mistrust from the Lon Nol side as well. 'We have long avoided talking about the treacherous activities of the French,' wrote a columnist in the Phnom Penh newspaper *Prayouth* in 1971, 'but we cannot be silent today because the preservation of Angkor is a stark example.' The writer claimed that under Groslier, who was meant to be neutral, cement and iron reinforcement intended for monument preservation had been handed over to the Vietnamese, who used them in military positions against the Lon Nol army.

Soldiers of the Lon Nol army held the north end of the airport road, with Angkor Wat in the distance. AP photo.

4   The embassy reported this conversation to Washington in a lengthy cable, which was later declassified and made available to the public in the U.S. National Archives.

5   In the cable, Enders told Washington that the embassy would urge the Lon Nol army to be more careful with artillery fire in the Angkor area.

*****

On 20 January 1972, the arrangement abruptly ended. Communist authorities at Angkor Wat used loudspeakers to denounce Groslier to refugees camped there. His Cambodian foremen were arrested; families of conservation workers were blocked from leaving for Siem Reap. Some twenty workers, it was reported, were executed for allegedly aiding the other side. The agreement's violent demise appeared to reflect the rising influence of the Khmer Rouge inside Angkor. This was in line with a pattern in many parts of the country as the Vietnamese role in the Cambodian war waned.

Groslier himself was not present at the time. But he did not ride his bicycle north again. He shifted conservation work to one of the few Angkor-era temples still in government hands, Wat Athvear, just south of Siem Reap. Later he left for Phnom Penh. The helm of the conservation team went to his Cambodian deputy, Pich Keo, who had trained as an archaeologist at the royal university in pre-war days.[6]

Once again, the Lon Nol government appealed to the United Nations to internationalize and demilitarize the ruins. But if there was 'no other choice,' the government said, it would be justified under the Hague Convention in launching a military operation to reclaim Angkor.

That statement signalled that a decision had been made: the spiritual heart of the Cambodian nation must remain no longer in enemy hands. Within days, Lon Nol's forces launched Operation *Angkor Chey* (Angkor Victory) with a goal of encircling the temple zone and taking it back. Troops moved east and west from Siem Reap on Highway 6. Others advanced slowly north on the road from town to temples. The attackers employed artillery and T-28s, propeller-driven trainer planes retrofitted for bombing. The defenders resisted. The column trying to go north got only about as far as the ancient levy that had fascinated Victor Goloubew in the 1930s as a boundary of his theorized giant city with Phnom Bakheng at its centre. By the end of February, stalemate had settled in.

In the meantime, the Lon Nol government was trying to obtain special capabilities for the operation. In a 26 February 1972 letter to the U.S. government, Prime Minister Sirik Matak asked for 'anti-riot bombs,' declassified U.S. State Department documents show. He seemed to mean some form of strong tear gas. His troops, he explained, were at a disadvantage and suffering high casualties because of orders not to harm the monuments. He apparently imagined using a cloud of gas to

6 Groslier later left for France, never to return to Cambodia. Before his departure, he faced down another life-threatening confrontation, this time with a thief who entered his house at night. Like his predecessor Jean Commaille six decades earlier, Groslier refused to back down. He accosted the man and suffered severe stab wounds, but survived.

drive off the defenders. His own soldiers, wearing gas masks, would move in with no harm to the stones.

The U.S. Embassy in Phnom Penh was sceptical. Perhaps diplomats there were failing to grasp how much Angkor meant in the hearts of their Cambodian clients. In cables to Washington, the embassy opposed not only providing gas but attempting to recapture Angkor at all. In its view, this effort was draining men and equipment away from more important battlefield objectives elsewhere in the country. In any case, training troops to work with gas would be problematic, the embassy said, and controversy would inevitably arise abroad from the use of what it termed 'chemical warfare agents.' A 13 March cable noted that 'any short-term tactical gains that might accrue would be of minor consequence when compared to possible long-term political costs in terms of Free World sympathy and support.' It's unclear whether the Cambodians ever got a direct answer from the Americans. The embassy alternated between saying no and delaying replying at all, in the hope that the idea would die out. Whichever it was, the United States never provided those 'anti-riot bombs.'

In May, Lon Nol was ready to try again, with conventional force. There were said to be two reasons for the decision: intelligence reports that some of the communist troops in the temple zone were moving elsewhere, and advice from spiritual aides to Lon Nol that he could win the Cambodian war only if Angkor was in his hands. An election was coming up in June. There was talk that Lon Nol would be sworn in at the old capital for a new term of office.

So under cover of darkness, government soldiers stole down the road that links the airport and Angkor Wat. Moving off to the left, they passed through fields and forest to reach the base of Phnom Bakheng, the hill topped by the tenth-century temple. They moved up its slopes and routed a force of Khmer Rouge and Vietnamese at the top. They raised their flag at the temple, and as the sun rose gazed across at Angkor Wat. Twenty-four hours later, soldiers continued with stage two of the bold operation. Moving again at night, one group hurried along the temple's north moat, then turned right to reach its eastern causeway. Another made its way to the western causeway, the main entrance. Troops were now in position for an attack from both sides. The goal was to secure Angkor Wat, then to assess whether to try to take Angkor Thom.

The scene at the western causeway was essentially a replay of what had taken place in 1946 – one force on the outer side of the moat, determined to get inside, a defending force inside determined to hold out. The outcome this time was the opposite. In his book *Road to the Killing Fields*, Wilfred P. Deac recounts that the din of weapons suddenly replaced the silence. Flares filled the night sky as communist forces in concealed positions began inflicting grievous casualties on Lon Nol's men. Twenty-one of thirty soldiers who tried to get through the western entrance were killed, according to a source quoted by the UPI news agency. Survivors fled. In the ensuing weeks, fighting continued west and south of the temple, but Angkor Chey had lost its momentum. In August, communist forces shelled Phnom Bakheng and recaptured it. The old battle lines were being restored.

We know little of what went on in the Khmer Rouge and Vietnamese side during this fighting. But one hint comes from the 'confession' of a senior Khmer Rouge official, Koy Thuon, who years later was arrested by his own movement and held at its notorious S21 prison in Phnom Penh. There he was forced to write a lengthy account of his supposed crimes. In it, he accused a Khmer Rouge leader in Siem Reap province of allowing members of the old Khmer Issarak, the movement that had briefly seized Angkor in 1946, to join the Khmer Rouge ranks in Siem Reap. This leader had then failed to carry out commands to purge spies and Lon Nol agents said to be engaging in such things as sabotage and the encouragement of defection. Thuon appeared to argue that this weakened the Khmer Rouge at Angkor and helped the Lon Nol side sustain its attack there. The Khmer Rouge were unable to repel it on their own, he wrote, and had to fall back on the help of Vietnamese soldiers still in the area. The accuracy of all this is difficult to assess. Prisoners such as Thuon were desperate, given to inventing things that they hoped would ingratiate them with their captors. He was later executed, one of many Khmer Rouge to die after coming under suspicion from a highly paranoid senior leadership.[7]

* * * * *

After the failure of the bid to recapture Angkor, the old stalemate resumed. Siem Reap struggled on as an isolated enclave of Lon Nol's Cambodia.

Transport planes landed at the airport to deliver rice and other supplies, as well as hitch-hiking passengers. When fighting made the airport unusable, planes dropped supplies over the town by parachute. The townspeople got by however they could, taking extra jobs to make ends meet. Some served

Prince Norodom Sihanouk, then the nominal head of the forces fighting Lon Nol, posed in front of Angkor Wat during his 1973 visit. Photo courtesy of Documentation Center of Cambodia Archives.

A Daring Visit by Prince Sihanouk

In the early 1970s, western intelligence agencies periodically reported that the Khmer Rouge might declare Angkor to be capital of their 'revolutionary government.' Workers were said to be putting up administrative buildings near the temples, at a time when ambassadors of communist countries at the United Nations were seeking to strip the Lon Nol government of Cambodia's seat and give it to the Khmer Rouge.

Angkor never became such a capital but it did get a visit from the revolutionary government's ostensible head, Prince Sihanouk. It was yet another audacious feat by a man long known for political theatrics. When news of the visit broke, the Lon Nol government declared it a hoax, saying it simply couldn't have happened. But happen it did.

Early in 1973, Sihanouk had been dropping hints to journalists in Beijing that he might visit the Cambodian 'liberated zone.' By this time, ceasefires were in effect in Vietnam and Laos; it would be safe for the prince to pass through communist-controlled parts of those two countries en route to Cambodia. Sihanouk later told French journalists that he travelled in a caravan of twenty Soviet-built jeeps. About 100 North Vietnamese escorted him from Dong Hoi in North Vietnam to the Cambodian border. From there, Khmer Rouge soldiers took charge—the Vietnamese had gone home from Cambodia by now.

The party set off across the north of the country, traveling by night. This was no doubt the most physically gutsy thing the prince ever did during his long political career. U.S. warplanes were no longer bombing Laos and Vietnam, freeing them up for massive attacks in Cambodia. Sihanouk later recounted feeling exposed when the group crossed the Mekong. During the month-long trip he witnessed American planes making bombing runs but, he would later say, people in his caravan suffered no casualties and the only damage

was a tyre punctured by a machine-gun bullet.

Sihanouk and Princess Monineath spent several days in Angkor. They appeared at a political rally. The prince posed smiling at Angkor Wat's western entrance, looking like a tourist save for his unusual clothing: a well cut Khmer Rouge-style black uniform and sandals. Other shots show him and Princess Monineath in what appears to be a night-time gathering at the temple. The group also went to Banteay Srei, 'citadel of the women,' where Princess Monineath posed with a group of female Khmer Rouge. There was a stop in the Kulen hills, where the prince posed again, this time with senior Khmer Rouge leaders, beneath a minor temple and a waterfall that are today busy with holiday-making locals and foreigners.

After Sihanouk arrived back in Beijing, Premier Zhou Enlai hosted him at a banquet. The prince entertained the gathering with a forty-five-minute film of his trip and rousing predictions of American defeat. In Phnom Penh, government figures and western diplomats mustered whatever arguments they could to cast doubt on the whole affair. U.S. Ambassador to Cambodia Emory Swank began a cable to Washington with these words: 'Sihanouk's visit to Cambodia, the scope of which if it did take place at all, is still questionable...'

The Phnom Penh government issued a detailed analaysis of the film. The skin tone of people in it didn't seem Cambodian, it said. A highway distance marker didn't look authentic. Conclusion: the film was faked up by the North Vietnamese and Chinese. Indeed, the nighttime photos in front of Angkor Wat did have the look of something created with the clumsy darkroom techniques that communist governments of the time employed to make image match ideology. But eventually the skeptics were forced to concede that Sihanouk had in fact gone where he'd said he'd gone.

Supplies descended by parachute into Siem Reap, when war made the airport unusable. Photo by Hervé Manac'h.

in the uniform of the Lon Nol army; others disappeared and joined the other side, whose men were to be found a short walk outside town. The Grand Hotel now housed a military command. One of the few ways to see the old capital, though just a hint of it, was to climb atop a rickety wooden structure that now stood on the hotel's roof. Off in the distance, brought closer if binoculars were used, loomed the towers of Angkor Wat.

Patterns of periods of quiet broken by skirmishes and shelling continued. In August 1973 *New York Times* correspondent Malcolm Browne stood on the airport road, looking down it at Angkor Wat. Fighters from the other side, manning a roadblock a short distance away, seemed to pay him no attention. But a few days before his visit, Browne wrote, Phnom Krom, the hill by the Tonle Sap which members of the Mekong expedition climbed in 1866, became a target of the Khmer Rouge. Lon Nol's army had held it since the start of the war, but now several hundred communist fighters scaled and seized it, only to be dislodged within twenty-four hours. During the fighting, grenades killed two Buddhist monks. A Buddhist temple at the summit sustained damage; the tenth-century Hindu temple next to it did not.

On 15 August 1973, the United States ended its bombing in Cambodia. This was at the order of the U.S. Congress, which was tired of war in Southeast Asia. But American military aid continued to flow to Lon Nol's side, which battled on.

In late 1973, a young Japanese photographer called Taizo Ichinose attempted to reach the temples from Siem Reap, in hopes of taking the first images of them in wartime conditions. He did not return. He is believed to have been captured and executed by the Khmer Rouge, who were already engaging in the brutality that the world would learn more about later on.

In August 1974, Lon Nol's troops in Siem Reap mounted a second attempt to take back ancient heritage by force. But instead of aiming, as they had in 1972, for the big prize, Angkor Wat, they went east toward an easier objective, the Bakong, Preah Ko, and Lolei temples, built in an area that was the Khmer Empire's capital from roughly 800 to 900 CE. The soldiers took the temples without serious opposition, although bunkers and some obscene graffiti were found there. Lon Nol troops settled in for a stay, relaxing on the upper tiers of the pyramid-style Bakong, inspecting sculpture, and generally waiting to see what would happen next. Some put their weapons down and went exploring like holiday-makers.

Boulbet and other EFEO people took the opportunity to inspect temples closed to them for the previous four years. Hervé Manac'h, the young Frenchman working with the EFEO, found the temples to be in generally good condition, though some were over grown. The area was peaceful, but the far-off boom of Lon Nol artillery, however, gave a reminder of the war.

Khmer Rouge official Koy Thuon's 'confession' appears to address this operation as well. He mentioned a Khmer Rouge political officer who had reportedly been spotted consorting with Lon Nol officials in Phnom Penh. This man was now a commander in the area, and his flank collapsed on being attacked. Koy Thuon seems to suggest there was some kind of battlefield deal between commanders of the opposing sides by which the Lon Nol soldiers were allowed to capture the three temples. Again, his credibility is not easy to assess. With everything he wrote in the S21 prison, he was fighting for his life.

At Preah Ko temple, Lon Nol soldiers stood behind Jean Boulbet and Kton, his wife's cousin, during a brief re-occupation in August 1974. Photo by Hervé Manac'h.

Ultimately the three temples were just a consolation prize, and a brief one at that. Scarcely a week after the troops moved in, the Khmer Rouge attacked, killing many of the soldiers. The old tense stalemate resumed, punctuated by eruptions of fighting. In August, a U.S. military transport plane was hit by ground fire in the Angkor area and made an emergency landing at Siem Reap.

As 1975 began, Lon Nol's side was near to losing the war. Its forces were gradually ceding territory in the face of escalating pressure from a well-armed and determined foe. The end came on 17 April 1975, when Khmer Rouge fighters broke through defensive positions around Phnom Penh and entered the city. The Lon Nol government collapsed immediately. Around the country, its garrisons gave up the fight one after the other. Only the contingent at Preah Vihear temple would hold out, for another month, protected by the sandstone cliffs.

In Siem Reap, people awaited the arrival of the victorious soldiers. Some were in a mood to celebrate war's end; others were deeply fearful.

It made no difference that Angkor was lost – the Lon Nol government continued to put temple images on its banknotes. (John Burgess collection)

BANQUE NATIONALE DU CAMBODGE

1000 1000 MILLE RIELS

12: A BRUTAL PEACE

**Cambodia's fanatical new rulers laud Angkor as
proof of the nation's heroic potential – but send
the conservation workers to toil in the rice fields.
Bats and tropical foliage move back in.**

In early 1945, the man who would become supreme leader
of the Khmer Rouge set out on a visit to Angkor. At the time,
Pol Pot was called by his birth name Saloth Sar and he was a
student, a member of, among other things, a theatre troupe.
He and a number of his fellow amateurs drove toward Siem
Reap in a charcoal-powered bus (wartime shortages of fuel
were inspiring special innovations in transport). Every so often,
they stopped at villages to stage skits and earn some money
toward their expenses. Once in Angkor, the group spent almost
three days wandering through the temples. 'Angkor thrilled us.
It took our breath away,' recalled Khieu Samphan, who three
decades later would be head of state of what he and comrades
called Democratic Kampuchea.

It's no surprise that these young men, born under French
rule, wanted to see Angkor. By now, Cambodians had had it
burned into them from birth. There it was on the flag; there
it was on banknotes and postage stamps. They heard of its
glories in textbooks, in films, and in the patriotic musings
of their parents. As Pol Pot biographer Philip Short would
later write, Angkor became 'both a benchmark and a
burden – the proof of what Cambodians could achieve and
a constant remainder of their failure to attain such heights
again.'

So it was that the banner of the Khmer Rouge soldiers who
entered Siem Reap in April 1975 bore an image of the great
temple a few kilometres to the north. Many of the city's people
sheltered in their homes, awaiting instructions on what to do.
Others ventured out to see what they could see. The victors
made quick work of surrendering soldiers and other people
deemed to be servants of the old regime: they were rounded
up and held in a Buddhist monastery next to the ancient Lolei
temple east of Siem Reap, then taken out for mass execution.[1]
Luckier people were turned out of their homes and sent to the
countryside.

Opposite page: Khmer Rouge
soldiers marching at Angkor Wat
in this undated propaganda photo.
(Documentation Center of Cambodia
Archives)

---

1 The account here makes
extensive use of a 2008 paper
written by the French scholar
Henri Locard, who interviewed
large numbers of survivors in
the Siem Reap area.

This was the pattern all over Cambodia as government-held towns surrendered to the Khmer Rouge: the quick murder of perceived enemies and enslavement for most everyone else. People were moved by foot and truck to poorly supplied communes to work the fields, overseen by all-powerful men (and sometimes boys) in floppy black uniforms. Disease, hunger, and exhaustion were soon endemic.

* * * * *

But two things happened in Siem Reap that were unusual.

The first was that on the day after the surrender, Buddhist monks in the town were mobilized for a religious ceremony. Khmer Rouge soldiers went to Siem Reap's monasteries and ordered their occupants to go to Angkor Wat. Inside the walls, in front of the temple, these monks found that large numbers of other monks had gathered, as well as senior Khmer Rouge cadres. A speaker's platform was in place, suggesting that preparations had been underway for some time. There followed lengthy rites and festivities, with revolutionary speeches and skits, folk music, and the chanting of a traditional prayer celebrating victory. 'Hurrah! This is the greatest victory of the people of Kampuchea, greater even than the towers of Angkor,' declared the presiding Khmer Rouge officer, pointing to the temple behind him.

Soon after the rite, the monks got the same treatment as everyone else. They were dispersed to rural settlements, deprived of their robes and status and put to work as part of a country-wide campaign to stamp out religion. Many were killed. But on this day, in the nation's ancient capital, a place that Cambodians believed was inhabited by myriad spirits possessing the powers of the bygone era, the new rulers chose to do something that in part seemed aimed at honouring and appeasing those spirits. Few if any ordinary people seem to have been invited to witness the celebration or take part. It was not so different, in fact, from the religious rites of the Angkor era, attended just by royalty and priests with a goal of providing a message to heaven.

The second break with patterns was that one group in Siem Reap got special treatment, or at least treatment that was somewhat less brutal than what everyone else got – the conservation workers and their families. It didn't seem so right away, however. Khmer Rouge soldiers entered the conservation compound on 17 April and tied up people they found inside, including the archaeologist Pich Keo, who had

taken charge after the departure of Bernard-Philippe Groslier.
Staff and families, roughly 750 people in all, were held in the
compound for two weeks, surviving on what food they had
with them. Then trucks transported them as group to Wat
Thmey in the Roluos area east of Siem Reap, location of three
major temples from the ninth and tenth centuries. The people
were assigned nearby plots of land and told to clear them for
agriculture. The work would be gruelling, but in general the
conservation families were to fare better than ordinary Siem
Reap people. They were treated, in fact, in a manner similar
to long-time Khmer Rouge supporters, getting access to rice
and fish and basic medical care. Almost all of them survived
the subsequent years. Some of their children even got a bit of
schooling.

Some of the conservation team did get to see the temples
again, though not to work on them. One day, a group was
sent to the moats of Angkor Thom to gather aquatic plants
for processing into fertilizer. The war was over, but its dangers
remained. One woman in the team, wielding a shovel, set off
a hidden explosive of some kind. But the shovel's blade saved
her, by blocking the blast's force.

Somewhere in the secretive Khmer Rouge leadership
there seemed to be an idea that at some point in the future,
systematic maintenance on the temples would resume, and
these would be the people for the job. Local relationships may
also have been at work. The head of the commune where many
conservation families were assigned was a friend of Pich Keo
and this could have translated into protection for his group. All
over Cambodia, survival during the Khmer Rouge years often
depended upon the luck of having such a tie.

But as months and then years passed, nothing much
happened with the temples. Though a few people were put
to work clearing vegetation, the temples were for all practical
purposes again at the mercy of nature. Vines and grasses
moved in. Clouds of bats were again taking up residence in the
cool dark chambers, leaving behind carpets of stone-dissolving
droppings.

* * * *

Selected Cambodians were brought to the temples for visits
meant to instil patriotic fervour. But one who did not come in
this period was Sihanouk. He had been living abroad when
Phnom Penh fell. He had told foreign journalists that, with
the war over, he had no wish to return to the capital, because

188

An Ideological Hijacking

At the same time as they neglected the temples, Khmer Rouge leaders in Phnom Penh placed them in service of their ideology. In keeping with their addled thinking about their movement's place in history, they depicted Angkor as only the start of what the Cambodian people could accomplish under the new leadership.

In a 1976 speech marking the first anniversary of Phnom Penh's fall, Head of State Khieu Samphan declared that 'the victory that our people, workers, and peasants of this era have scored over the most ferocious and most inhumane U.S. imperialists is even more brilliant and splendid than the Angkor temple.' In a speech the following year, Pol Pot stated that 'if our people could build Angkor, they can build anything.'

The new regime's prime project of public works was a huge network of canals and dams intended to water Cambodia's rice lands for increased production. Tens of thousands of people were mobilized with primitive tools, labouring day and sometimes night by the light of the moon. Again, the leaders in Phnom Penh found inspiration in Angkor, telling people to emulate their ancestors and become 'masters of water.'

But the work that these people were forced to carry out, sometimes at the cost of their lives, brought mastery of nothing. Designed by no-doubt ideologically pure amateurs, dams often burst under the pressure of rainy season waters, flooding out the very people who had built them. Canals were likewise dug without proper engineering, and failed to deliver water where it was needed.

At Angkor Wat, stone-faced Khmer Rouge soldiers with guns posed for propaganda shots meant to show total control of the country. Angkor graced the flag, while Bayon-style face towers appeared on bank notes that the Khmer Rouge printed up before deciding to do away with money altogether.

In government offices, paintings of Angkor brought rare flashes of colour to the walls. But the purpose, like virtually everything in Khmer Rouge society, was political, not artistic. No portraits of Pol Pot hung on those walls. Instead, it was the images of Angkor that symbolized the absolute power of 'Democratic Kampuchea.'

Members of a women's political troupe Banteay Srei, the 'Citadel of Women.' (Documentation Center of Cambodia Archives)

it had too many bad associations for him. Rather, he wanted to accompany the ashes of his recently deceased mother to Angkor, where he would oversee funeral rites and then take up a sort of retirement there. Imagining, perhaps, that he had real influence with the Khmer Rouge, he called on them to prepare the Siem Reap airport for his return. What happened instead was that Sihanouk and his wife Princess Monineath were flown to Phnom Penh and placed under house arrest in a villa. There was no further role in the new government for Sihanouk. He had served his purpose.

The Siem Reap that he did not make it to was quickly reduced to a ghost town, devoid of people except for those carrying out tasks of the revolution. Its Buddhist temples were variously used for weapons storage, military training, and vehicle repair. Others sat vacant and neglected, foliage moving in as it did at the ancient monuments to the north. The one-time colonial prison was refashioned for detention and interrogation of people deemed suspect. An area near the tenth-century temple Pre Rup became an execution ground, with bodies buried in pits.

Three Khmer Rouge caught on camera at Angkor Wat. (Documentation Center of Cambodia Archives)

In March 1976, the town briefly got some international exposure with a surprise accusation by the Khmer Rouge that the United States had bombed it a few days earlier, destroying or damaging numerous homes and buildings, including a hospital. The planes then flew off toward Thailand, the Khmer Rouge said. The United States denied any such attack; Thailand pointed out that U.S. airbases there had closed. Like many claims of the Khmer Rouge during this period, the facts and purposes of this one never came to light.

* * * * *

Following the practice of Cambodian governments before it, the Khmer Rouge took visiting foreigners to Angkor. 'Firstly, we wanted to show that Democratic Kampuchea did not destroy any historic buildings,' a man who was assistant to Khmer Rouge Foreign Minister Ieng Sary would later tell an interviewer from Mapping Memories Cambodia, a project of the Royal University of Phnom Penh. 'We took care of them, especially Angkor Wat.' That last claim by Soung Sikoeun hardly rings true, but those are his words. 'We also had Angkor Wat as a symbol on our flag.' The second reason for taking foreigners, he said, was that they asked to go. Like most everyone coming to Cambodia, they wanted to see the place.

Advisors from China visited Angkor Wat and posed for souvenir photos with their Khmer Rouge clients. (Documentation Center of Cambodia Archives)

With much of the country's highway system still in ruins from war, visitors typically travelled by train from Phnom Penh to Sisophon, then by road to Siem Reap. The Grand Hotel was open as an austere state-run guesthouse, taking in some of those who stayed the night. Others put up at Sihanouk's former villa. Advisors from China, the Khmer Rouge's most important international supporter, were frequent visitors in this time. Photos of them standing before the temples, grinning for the camera alongside Khmer Rouge officials and soldiers, were the period's version of the family photos of peaceful pre-war days. The ambassadors of Senegal, Guinea, and Egypt came, as did a few leaders from friendly foreign governments – Ne Win of Burma, Prince Souphanouvong of Laos, and Nicolae Ceausescu of Romania. During a May 1978 visit, Ceausescu and his wife Elena climbed steep rain-slicked steps to the top tier of Angkor Wat.

Western countries had no diplomatic relations with Khmer Rouge Cambodia, but a few of their citizens came anyway as private guests of the regime. Standing with his back to Angkor Wat, a camera rolling, the Swedish intellectual and writer Jan Myrdal filmed narration for a documentary. Visitors also included a handful of members of tiny 'revolutionary' groups in western countries, who in the Khmer Rouge mind represented their countries' peoples at large.

These types of visits picked up in 1978 as Vietnam became an increasing concern for the Khmer Rouge. They were fighting a low-grade border war with their more powerful neighbor and felt a need to make their case to the world. To that end, they also admitted, in December 1978, two Americans from large mainstream newspapers, Elizabeth Becker of *The Washington Post* and Richard Dudman of *The St. Louis Post-Dispatch*.[2] Their very closely controlled visit to Cambodia included two days at Angkor. There they saw a few labourers cutting back vegetation, but in general nature was winning, making damaging inroads into the temples – bat dung piling up, ant hills sticking to bas-reliefs. Skilled conservation workers were nowhere to be seen.

Elizabeth Becker, left front row, and Richard Dudman, right front row, posed with their Khmer Rouge escorts at Banteay Srei. Malcolm Caldwell, the group's third foreign member, is second from left in the back row. Photo © Elizabeth Becker.

2   Traveling with them was a more typical western visitor of the time, a leftist British academic called Malcolm Caldwell. Near the end of the visit, Caldwell was shot dead by a man who entered the Phnom Penh guesthouse where the three foreigners were spending the night. It has never been clear who the gunman was or why he acted. Many analysts believe the killing was engineered by a Khmer Rouge faction that opposed opening up and hosting foreign delegations.

Angkor Wat, shown here in December 1978, was largely deserted during the four years the Khmer Rouge ruled Cambodia, visited only sporadically by selected Cambodians and foreigners. Photo © Elizabeth Becker.

Becker asked why. A Khmer Rouge guide replied that intellectuals, unless they were dedicated to the goals of the Cambodian revolution, were not necessarily employed in their fields of expertise. 'We have not enough manpower to take care and maintain these monuments precisely,' he said. 'But no one loves Angkor better than our own people.'

At Banteay Srei, Becker was appalled to see young Cambodian women running their fingers over delicate sandstone carvings. Even worse, one of the women carelessly knocked over a statue. Becker's guide was not concerned. 'It belongs to them,' he said.

As they visited different parts of Cambodia, the journalists heard frequent allusions to Angkor as unique in world history and a great precursor to the Khmer Rouge system. 'I would like to stress to you,' said one official, 'that the civilisation of Angkor is not a copy of any civilisation, not its engineering or its irrigation. In our revolution, also, we have copied no one – and no one can say we have.' Another official asserted that the Khmer Rouge victory of 1975 restored to Cambodia dignity and honour that had been lost since the fall of the Angkor empire.

In late 1978, the Khmer Rouge made a surprise announcement: Angkor would open to foreign tourists for day trips costing $225. They would fly in from Bangkok, landing at 10 a.m. at Siem Reap airport. Under close supervision, they would visit selected temples, have lunch, and fly out in the afternoon. Khmer Rouge Cambodia was always in need of foreign currency, but perhaps the bigger motive was to improve its image in the face of the intensifying confrontation with Vietnam, show off the heritage, and court Thailand, where the flights would originate, as a balance to Vietnam. Khmer Rouge Foreign Minister Ieng Sary described the impending tours as 'friendship visits.'

On the morning of December 27, the inaugural flight landed at Siem Reap. All those aboard were supposed to be Thai travel industry people, but the people in the cabin included sixteen journalists who were not about to miss a chance to look inside the closed country. Khmer Rouge authorities at the airport seemed uncertain what to do. Everyone was held there for several hours, then allowed into a bus. It passed houses that were mostly empty and padlocked shut, standard sights in Khmer Rouge Cambodia. Once at Angkor, the 'tourists' were annoyed to find that the bus wasn't stopping – their guides' intention was to give only drive-by glimpses of deserted temples. Only after heated protests did the bus stop, at Angkor Wat. The visitors had a hurried forty-five minutes to look around the great temple. Then they were herded back to the bus and driven to the airport for the return flight to Bangkok.

A plane carrying real tourists landed on New Year's Day 1979. More flights were supposed to follow. There was talk that UN Secretary-General Kurt Waldheim would visit late in the month. None of that happened. The door to Angkor slammed shut again. The Khmer Rouge, the world was coming to realize, had bigger things to worry about. A full-scale invasion of Cambodia was underway. Along highways in the country's east, the army of Vietnam was fighting its way toward Phnom Penh, with a goal of installing in power a group of Cambodians who had defected from the Khmer Rouge. On 7 January 1979, Vietnamese troops seized the largely deserted capital. Shortly afterward, they captured Angkor. The Khmer Rouge era was over.

Workers cut grass near the Terrace of the Elephants in December 1978, apparently in preparation for closely monitored tourist visits that the Khmer Rouge were planning. Photo © Elizabeth Becker.

13: CONTINUING ISOLATION

With the Khmer Rouge driven from power, Angkor suffers further neglect as most of the world boycotts Cambodia's new government. Pleas for foreign help go unanswered.

As Lon Nol's soldiers had done a decade earlier, the Khmer Rouge gave up the monuments without a real struggle. For the second time in the long Indochina war, a Vietnamese army captured Angkor, heart of the Khmer nation, for its Cambodian allies.

Bernard-Philippe Groslier once said that Angkor was like a patient in a hospital, needing constant care and attention. It was now sicker than ever, due to a decade of neglect. The enormous task of trying to stabilize the patient would now fall onto the shoulders of the man who had taken over from Groslier in 1972. Pich Keo and his family had passed the Khmer Rouge years labouring in a commune east of Siem reap – his own job was said to include delivering fish from water to village. Three days after their Khmer Rouge overseers fled into the forest, Pich Keo caught a ride to the temples on a military truck. He had to see Angkor, he later recalled. It had been denied him for eight years. He walked the monuments, inspecting and evaluating with an expert eye. He slept in a nearby village, then did the same the next day and the next. Before long, officials of the new government that the Vietnamese installed in Phnom Penh became aware of his past work and his credentials from the Royal University of Fine Arts. Late in 1979, they appointed him as Angkor's new conservator.

It was a lofty title (and he was the first Cambodian to hold it), but it came with virtually no authority or resources. Before the war, about 800 people had tended the temples; Pich Keo now had to make do with fifty. He had no budget for hiring more hands, and almost no equipment. Cranes and other heavy gear from pre-war days lay rusting and ruined in various places around the complex. Records documenting pre-war projects had vanished. Pich Keo could not even enter the conservation compound in Siem Reap. Vietnamese troops had turned it into a military headquarters.

Opposite page: A lone sweeper in the corridors of Angkor Wat, April 1980. He was part of a small and underfunded conservation staff. (John Burgess)

196

Local Cambodians were again honouring Angkor Wat's holy image Ta Reach with offerings and prayers. (John Burgess)

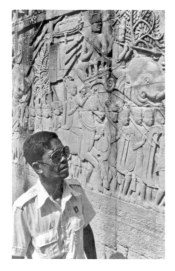

Angkor conservator Pich Keo showed the author the Bayon's bas-reliefs in April 1980. (John Burgess)

And so the conservator became a familiar, sympathetic face to the western journalists who began to visit Angkor. I was one of them, and spent a day in his company in April 1980. It was a great privilege to hear his expert commentary and personal story, but the privilege, for westerners at least, was not really so rare. Pich Keo had decided that one of the most important things he could do for Angkor was to voice its plight to the outside world, and so he sought out all its representatives. Getting us engaged was the only way that real help would arrive.

I was spending two weeks in Cambodia on a journalist visa from the new government. My government escorts and I had arrived in a Soviet Lada sedan the previous day, after passing through scenes of shocking wartime devastation along the road from Phnom Penh. We put up for the night at the Grand Hotel, which had re-opened yet again, partially at least, as a government-run guesthouse. My room resembled a monk's cell, with just a simple bed, and lights and air conditioning from 6 pm to 10 pm, after which the power went dead. But it was the height of luxury by the standards of the time. The centre of Siem Reap town remained mostly deserted; gaping entrances of old shophouses revealed there was nothing inside.

The next morning we met up with Pich Keo, who looked fresh in slacks and a crisp white shirt. But he was already fighting a familiar losing battle against tropical flora. We drove around so he could show us first-hand. 'Just one month ago,' he told me at the Terrace of the Elephants in Angkor Thom, 'we cleared this terrace of vegetation. But now you can see vegetation is already returning.' Indeed, grass and weeds were springing up between the paving stones. Nearby, a tractor stood immobilized and useless. 'We have no equipment at all,' he lamented.

At the Bayon, as we looked at the famous bas-reliefs, he remarked that the twelfth and twentieth centuries were not really so different, in terms of total war. He pointed out scenes of ancient Khmer soldiers marching toward battle, their wives and children trudging along with them.

We drove to Angkor Wat. There it was – as silent, mysterious, and glorious as ever, having come through yet another mortal threat that history had dealt up. I had wondered if the war had caused serious damage, but the temple looked virtually unchanged from my memory of 1969. But not entirely: at the western entrance by the moat, bullet scars disfigured some of the *devata* and gateways. A column was almost blown away. At the time, I didn't know about the fighting of 1946, and so

A Trickle of Tourism

The Angkor tourist trade was already sputtering back to life in April 1980. The handful of visitors who entered Angkor Wat on any given day—Cambodians, Vietnamese, and westerners—were greeted on the processional avenue by young men with Polaroid cameras. For a fee, memento photos were snapped with the great temple as backdrop, then studied with joy and pride. It felt like a conscious revival of photos that in pre-war days had signalled peace, pride, and hopefulness.

This was all by way of private enterprise, people trying to make some money to stay alive in difficult times. The Soviet-style planned economics of the new government played no role. The cameras had likely arrived illicitly from Thailand on the backs of traders' bicycles.

Later on, the government got involved in tourism, but through the '80s the flow never became more than a trickle, constrained by Cold War tensions that cut off Cambodia from most of the world.

Visitors arrived for day trips on flights from Vietnam or Phnom Penh. They saw just Angkor Wat, got a makeshift meal at the Grand Hotel, and departed from the airport before dusk. It was much the same as the Khmer Rouge tours were supposed to have been, and generated similar frustrations. Members of one group pressed their guides to go to Angkor Thom but were told that potholes in the road there would be too much for the aging vehicle they were riding. In those times, gunshots sounded occasionally in the distance—

Young men with an entrepreneurial bent obtained Polaroid cameras to snap souvenir photos of some of the small number of people visiting Angkor Wat. (John Burgess)

security concerns were clearly what were keeping tourists from the walled city. Although periodic claims by the Khmer Rouge of having captured Angkor were political fantasy, they and their guns were never far away.

assumed everything had happened in recent years. 'We don't know who did it – that's war!' said Pich Keo. An English-speaking guide from pre-war days, somehow back at his old haunt, walked us through the bas-relief galleries, exercising a language ability that he'd presumably hidden during Khmer Rouge times. Cambodians were grateful for liberation but it was common to hear, as from this man, guarded criticism of the foreign army that carried it out. 'Vietnamese soldiers bring guns in here,' he complained. 'They should leave them behind.'

We climbed to the third tier, having the huge temple almost to ourselves. Later, we strolled back down the processional avenue, which was bathed in the setting sun's rich hues. I turned around and saw some other people who were making do on their own: three young boys, carrying fish traps down the avenue. They were headed for the temple's ponds and moats, it seemed, in hopes of catching something for their families' dinner. The sight was unforgettable. Angkor was again a home, not just a heritage site.

* * * * *

198

Three boys walked down Angkor Wat's processional avenue carrying fish traps, April 1980. (John Burgess)

At the elaborately carved walls of the Terrace of the Leper King, I had counted five images that had lost their heads. The fresh and unweathered stone between their shoulders left no doubt that the decapitation was very recent.

There was (and still is) a tendency in Cambodia to blame every ill on the Khmer Rouge. Headless Buddhas and other damaged images that I saw during my two weeks in the country were invariably explained as the work of zealots out to destroy religion. 'See what Pol Pot has done!' But theft was often a more plausible explanation: perpetrators took the most valuable element (the head) of a statue that in its whole state would be too heavy to carry off.

Theft at Angkor was nothing new, of course. But the total war that beset Cambodia starting in 1970 took it to new heights. Many art experts have concluded that sometime in this conflict's early years one of the most notorious lootings in modern Cambodian history took place. The target was Prasat Chen, a temple in Koh Ker, the area eighty kilometres from Angkor that in the tenth century was briefly the Khmer Empire's capital. At the temple, an ensemble of large and near perfectly preserved statues depicted a battle in the Hindu epic the Mahabharata. The statues were anchored in stone underneath, so the looters cut them off at the ankles. Transport of statues that could weigh up to 250 kilogrammes suggests that the theft was a well planned operation involving vehicles and multiple people. The destination was the international art market. All that remained behind was the feet, embedded in the stone, signalling where the sculpted deities had stood unmolested for close to 900 years.

Things changed after the Khmer Rouge achieved victory in 1975. They banned Buddhism and killed countless monks. They destroyed or repurposed countless Buddhist temples. But the evidence suggests that while in power they did not engage in the systematic looting of Angkor-era artwork for sale abroad. And the totalitarian society they established was not a place where freelance thieves could operate.

Elizabeth Becker and Richard Dudman, the two Western journalists who visited Cambodia just before Vietnam's invasion, had been taken to the national museum in Phnom Penh. They found its antiquities collection to be largely intact but, like the temples of Angkor, uncared for. A little over a year later, the new authorities took me to the same museum. It had been ransacked. Display cases had been smashed and small items carried off. Thankfully the large statues remained, saved, I guessed, by their enormous weight. The museum was another sign that the lawlessness and civil strife that was racking Cambodia after the fall of the Khmer Rouge had opened the door again to the organized pillaging of art.

In the Angkor zone, theft would become a force of harm rivalled only by nature. Many different groups took part in a highly organized trade in which carvings were crudely hacked from temples and sent toward Thailand and sometimes Vietnam. Soldiers and officials of the new Cambodian government, receiving almost nothing in official pay, might look the other way in exchange for bribes. Refugees doubling as art traders needed money to buy exorbitantly priced food and medicine at camps that had sprung up at the Thai border. Anti-Vietnamese fighters at the camps wanted money for personal use and to keep the battle going. Of course the driving force behind the whole business was demand from foreigners, who were prepared to pay big money for art that had long been beyond their reach and would ask no questions about provenance.

As the pillage continued month after month, year after year, with virtually no opposition, the trade grew more sophisticated. Those in the know said that something resembling catalogue sales emerged, in which thieves took Polaroid photos (perhaps with those same tourist cameras?) of various art objects

Angkor Wat's 'Hall of a Thousand Buddhas' contained only about twenty-five images in April 1980, some of them broken. (John Burgess)

in situ and sent them to foreign dealers and collectors, who placed orders for specific items. Cash changed hands, then a week or two later, the requested item arrived at the Thai border. One successfully completed transaction led to another. The trade was shadowy and largely invisible, but every now and then something went wrong to briefly expose it. In 1980, for example, a fire levelled a shanty-town refugee camp on the Thai border. In the ashes were four large statues that had been lying hidden in huts, awaiting transport out.

The day I visited Angkor, Vietnamese soldiers stood guard at various points (one group was camped by the moat of Angkor Wat). Their prime mission was to block a return by the Khmer Rouge, who were still active in forests not so far away, Occasionally, however, art thieves were caught. 'They tell us only that they plan to sell the things,' said Pich Keo. 'They don't say where.' Nevertheless, I got the feeling he knew more than he was prepared to say.

* * * *

Theft was an important problem for Pich Keo. But the bigger one was getting help from abroad to care for the temples.

Over and over, to whomever would listen, he kept up his pleas for foreign help. A few journalists (I wish I had been one of them) responded personally, bringing in books about Angkor as gifts to him and his team. In 1980, he gave a visiting newspaper journalist a letter to Professor Yoshiaki Ishizawa, an Angkor specialist at Sophia University in Tokyo. It contained a plea for whatever help Ishizawa could provide. Ishizawa responded by visiting Angkor, but the continuing political turmoil blocked any significant involvement by Japan.

In the Khmer Rouge times, Angkor had been isolated because the people holding it would not let foreigners *come*. Now it was isolated because the outside world would not let foreigners *go*. The new government that Vietnam had installed was under international diplomatic boycott. It was recognized by Soviet-bloc countries, but hardly anyone else. Though the Vietnamese had stopped the unimaginable crimes of the Khmer Rouge, western governments chose to treat the invasion as a gross violation of international law and an expansion of the Soviet empire. A Khmer Rouge government-in-exile remained in Cambodia's seat in the United Nations. When it came time to decide which group should hold it, the Khmer Rouge received the votes of the United States and Western European countries, whose representatives nonetheless expressed pious revulsion over the crimes of the years in power. China, meanwhile, took on the dirty work of providing weapons to Khmer Rouge remnants.

As the boycott continued through the 1980s, leaders in Phnom Penh made their own appeals for help with, among other things, Angkor. If diplomatic relations were not possible, they argued, surely 'cultural relations' were. After all, when food ran short in 1979 in the chaos of the Khmer Rouge fall, international aid groups had launched a huge humanitarian operation in Cambodia despite lack of formal recognition of the government in Phnom Penh. But it was of course not just a question of protecting antiquity. In the new government's mind, an international presence at an Angkor under its protection would function too as de facto acceptance of sovereignty, a step, it hoped, toward eventual diplomatic recognition by the world. Western governments were determined not to cede that, but some private groups and preservationists took up Angkor's cause, urging UNESCO to rescue the monuments.

Cambodia's new government adopted a five-tower depiction of Angkor Wat as the national symbol, shown here above the gate of a political education school in Battambang. (John Burgess)

In Washington, DC, the National Geographic Society lent its weight to the argument for giving help. A team of writers and photographers visited Angkor in 1981 and the following year published a long and beautifully illustrated article in the society's famous journal laying out the perils that the world treasure faced. In April 1982, the society and UNESCO staged an elaborate photographic exhibit of Angkor at UN headquarters in New York.

But over and over, UNESCO declared itself powerless to work with a government that was not a member of the world body. At the same time, it campaigned jointly with the geographic society for a compromise plan by which Angkor would be demilitarized, with help from UNESCO to follow. The plan had no chance. Just as had been true in the early '70s, the Vietnamese and their Cambodian allies were in no mood to pull their soldiers out of the heart of the Khmer nation. Holding it was an essential part of their case that the new administration in Phnom Penh was Cambodia's legitimate government. Demilitarization would only work to the advantage of the Khmer Rouge, they said, adding that in any case there was no need for such change. The monuments were secure – UNESCO could come in at any time in full safety.

For their part, the Khmer Rouge delegation at the UN demanded that the Vietnamese get out of *all* Cambodia. The group's ambassador, Thiounn Prasith, denounced the Phnom Penh government as barbarians, saying that in contrast his own side represented 'magnificent cultural patriotism and the brave fight of the people for the several thousands of years-old civilisation and their national identity.'

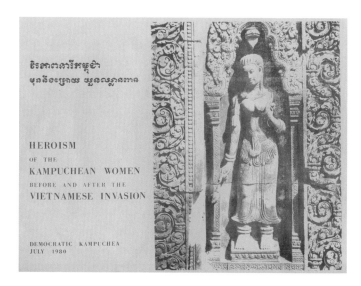

The Khmer Rouge, fighting a guerrilla war against the government in Phnom Penh, published a propaganda pamphlet comparing present-day Cambodian women to the *devata* of Angkor. (John Burgess collection)

In some of their propaganda, the Khmer Rouge depicted today's Cambodian women as contemporary versions of the *devatas* of Angkor. The cover of an English-language pamphlet featured a photo of one such image. 'A beautiful and prosperous Kampuchea will be built up on the land of Angkor, the three main most beautiful towers of which, embody the soul of the Kampuchean people on their precious national flag,' the pamphlet declared. 'Like the stones of Angkor, the race of Kampuchea will be there forever!'

* * * * *

As the impasse lengthened, Angkor did get some limited support from the Soviet Union. Pich Keo flew to Moscow, where officials organized a small program of training and financial support. Poland gave help too. But the biggest international aid in this period came from India, which was generally friendly toward Moscow at the time and had recognized the new government. India also had a special qualification, experience with its own very large collection of ancient stone temples, cultural cousins of Angkor's. The first team arrived in 1981 to conduct a survey. Later the two governments signed a six-year agreement by which a dozen or so Indian experts came to work on Angkor Wat each dry season, with help from about 200 Cambodian labourers.

India felt some pride in this project. 'After almost 800 years, the Indians are back,' wrote journalist Raj Chengappa in *India Today* magazine after a visit in 1988. 'Not as seafaring tradesmen or as saffron-clad missionaries, but as restorers.' He interviewed an Indian engineer working to right a tilting column in the temple's western gallery, another extracting a shrub that had sent out roots beneath a stone slab, and a chemical specialist removing moss from a bas-relief. In the 1960s, the French had disassembled an unstable section of the bas-relief gallery, but left the job unfinished when war began. Now the Indians were putting the pieces back together. Pich Keo was on the scene, and, eight years after I had visited, was sounding his appeal to yet another foreigner. With the Indians taking care of Angkor Wat, he told Chengappa, the world should 'come forward to restore the other monuments in the region.'

That wasn't going to happen, not yet, but as word spread of the Indian work, many foreign preservationists were aghast at the techniques being applied in what little help Angkor was getting. The removal of moss, a key aspect of the Indians'

204

Vietnamese soldiers prepared to
leave Angkor in September 1989.
Photo by Roland Neveu.

work, drew special criticism. Cambodian labourers were
wetting moss-covered walls with an ammonia solution, then
scrubbing them down with hard-bristled brushes. Sandstone
is one of nature's softer stones; often the workers rubbed away
shards of stone underneath the moss, dulling or eliminating
the features of carved surfaces. The critics – and their
voices grew increasingly loud and emotional – asserted that
priceless heritage was being ravaged with outdated techniques.
Moreover, workers were getting little training and working
exposed to harmful fumes.

The Indians responded, often with exasperation, that they
were proceeding carefully with necessary steps to stabilize the
temple, using methods that had been fine-tuned in the care of
temples in their own country.

The Indians drew further criticism concerning their use of
cement at a monument that had been built without it. Critics
called this material a visual blight, pointing to a replacement
pillar that the Indians had cast in cement, rather than repairing
the original damaged one. The Indians responded that the
great majority of the cement they used was invisible, placed in
foundations. That was not so different from what the French
had done for decades with anastylosis. No one questioned the
devotion and good intentions of the Indian team, but protests
continued. So did the Indian work.

Pich Keo was among the people who would turn against the Indian methods. 'I see this work and I think, no good,' he told a correspondent from *The New York Times* in 1992. It was another measure of his powerlessness that he, as conservator, was not able to stop it. To the government in Phnom Penh, India's work seems to have been too politically important to interfere with.

* * * * *

Ultimately it was shifts in world geopolitics that brought the breakthrough that Angkor – and Cambodia at large – needed. As the 1980s neared their close, the Cold War was winding down. The Soviet Union was losing interest in financing an endless war in Cambodia. The Vietnamese were tired too. The three major Cambodian factions resisting them, the Khmer Rouge included, had come together as a coalition, bolstered by western recognition and aid. So the Vietnamese decided to go home. They would continue to give material aid to their client government in Phnom Penh, but it would have to carry out the fight itself.

On 21 September 1989, the pull-out of the final group of Vietnamese troops still in Cambodia began at Angkor with the ceremonial departure of about 2,000 soldiers. Speeches, friendship banners, and the music of a local pop band sent the convoys of soldiers on their way. Many of the Cambodians who waved from roadsides as military vehicles passed were glad to see the foreign troops go, but they worried about future protection from the Khmer Rouge.

That same year, Norodom Sihanouk, now chairman of the anti-Vietnamese coalition, appealed to the director general of UNESCO for help with Angkor. UNESCO sent a fact-finding mission to Angkor. But again, no real action followed. Diplomatic isolation continued to block the way. The departure of the Vietnamese had not closed out the civil war, but slowly hope was building for its end. Peace negotiations in Paris turned serious. On 23 October 1991, the Phnom Penh government and the three-member coalition signed an accord to conclude the war and bring in the United Nations to oversee disarmament, elections, and the formation of a unified government of Cambodia.

A month later, UNESCO Director-General Federico Mayor was at Angkor. There he and a newly returned Sihanouk jointly appealed to the world to mobilize to save the ancient capital.

14: REOPENING

As Cambodia rejoins the world, foreign peacekeepers arrive to patrol Angkor. It becomes a UNESCO World Heritage Site. Long-delayed conservation resumes – and so does tourism.

The Paris-based agency UNESCO has countless functions, but one of the most consequential is its World Heritage program. After lengthy study, consideration, and debate, the agency declares certain landmarks, places, and institutions to be of 'outstanding value to humanity.' They 'belong to all the peoples of the world, irrespective of the territory on which they are located,' the agency declares, and deserve special aid and protection. Countries queue up to win this recognition for sites within their borders, variously for the prestige, UN aid, and tourist dollars that will follow. In return, they pledge to respect UNESCO guidelines on such issues as conservation, habitation by local people, commercial development, and tourism. As of 2020, UNESCO had conferred the status more than 1,100 times. Sometimes it was for natural wonders, such as Australia's Great Barrier Reef, but the majority are 'cultural sites' such as the Saint-Sophia Cathedral in Kiev, the Red Fort in Delhi, and the Mayan city of Chichen-Itza in Mexico. Sometimes the term 'cultural' is stretched, to include such places as the Bikini Atoll Nuclear Test Site in the Marshall Islands.

In the early 1990s, with peace returning to Cambodia, Angkor emerged as a logical candidate for World Heritage status. The program had not existed in 1970 when the temples were swallowed up by war. Conferring the designation now, advocates said, would open the door to the conservation work that had been delayed for so long. There was a strong political motive as well. UNESCO would be lending its shoulder to what would become one of the UN's largest-ever peacekeeping and nation-building operations. 21,000 military and civilian personnel from more than a hundred countries would deploy to Cambodia to support the United Nations Transitional Authority in Cambodia, or UNTAC. World Heritage status would signal to the world that Cambodia was rejoining the community of normal countries. It would bolster economic development by drawing tourists and their spending back

Opposite page: Leading Aircraftwoman Michelle Stevens, an Australian peacekeeper, walks with Cambodian children at Angkor Wat in 1993. Photo courtesy of Australian War Memorial.

Prince Norodom Sihanouk (left) and Yasushi Akashi (right), head of the UN mission in Cambodia, came to Siem Reap in August 1992 to officially open the mission's office there. UN photo/Pernaca Sudhakaran.

to a place that had been largely off-limits for more than two decades.

In November 1992, following a survey mission to Angkor, a team from the International Council on Monuments and Sites (ICOMOS) reported to UNESCO. In view of the legal requirements of World Heritage consideration, much of the report consisted of statements of the obvious, that Angkor met the program's standards of having outstanding artistic and historical significance. Give it heritage designation, the report's authors urged. But do it only when the new government of Cambodia has created the basic elements of the program's conditions: a framework of preservation law; an oversight agency staffed with qualified experts; boundaries and buffer zones around the monuments; and a system for international monitoring of compliance with the program. The authors viewed rapid creation of the buffer zones as particularly important. 'The impact of increased tourist facilities (hotels, restaurants, shops, an extended airport, car parks, etc.) around the monuments could be catastrophic if they are allowed to encroach too closely.' Already, they noted, a restaurant was operating on a bank of the ancient reservoir known as the East Baray and new houses were springing up closer and closer to the monuments.

Things did in fact proceed on the fast track. On 14 December 1992, UNESCO's World Heritage committee, meeting in Santa Fe, New Mexico, approved Angkor for the list, placing it in a special category of 'World Heritage in Danger.' It did this though Cambodia had not met the program's conditions, citing the 'unique situation' in the country, which had come under temporary UN administration pending a national election. Cambodian authorities were called on to take quick action to meet the program's conditions.

* * * * *

By now every town of any size in Cambodia was hosting a force of UN peacekeepers. The one that came to Siem Reap included personnel from France, Australia, India, Poland, and Bangladesh. The French had quickly treated everyone to some serious religious-military pomp. The occasion was Michaelmas, 3 October 1992, the Christian festival that honours the archangel Michael and other angels. Young French parachutists, bedecked with medals, stood on parade with their rifles at Angkor Wat's western causeway. Inside, a Catholic priest said a mass, attended by people of many nationalities and faiths – Christian French, Muslim Bangladeshis, and Buddhist Cambodians. Then two UN helicopters appeared overhead. Five skydivers jumped from one of them. Opening brightly coloured parachutes, they wowed the crowd below with some precise aerial navigation. One by one they touched down at a coloured cloth that had been laid down near the temple's processional avenue as a target. Then came a speech by a French colonel, the pinning of medals onto chests, and more French soldiers gliding down from the sky.

Foreign soldiers were now occupying houses and buildings in many parts of Siem Reap. They established guarded compounds, but for the most part, there wasn't much to guard against – peace was the new normal. Cambodians were friendly. The soldiers patronized the few local businesses that were cropping up, sometimes in response to their presence: tailor shops, jewellers, bars, and restaurants. A handful of adventurous foreign tourists began turning up as well.

Chatting with comrades, drinking beer, and watching movies on videocassette players were common means of passing the time off duty. But not a few of the peacekeepers felt drawn to the site to the north. Michelle Stevens, a communications specialist holding the rank of Leading Aircraftwoman in the Royal Australian Air Force, worked hard during her duty shifts on such jobs as stringing wires for computer networks and staffing a communications centre. But when she was off duty, she often changed into civilian clothes and went to Angkor. She had read up on Cambodia before deploying in late 1992, but like most everyone wasn't prepared for the scale and beauty of the real thing. Her near weekly trips took her to Angkor Wat, the gates of Angkor Thom, the Bayon, and the Terrace of the Leper King, among others. She had no guidebook; Cambodians who were working for the peacekeepers often came along and related stories they'd learned growing up. Many of the Buddha statues at Angkor Wat had lost their heads to thieves and desecrators, she noticed, but otherwise the atmosphere was magical. Stevens was free to walk all over, to take a rest in the shade, to enjoy peace and quiet, watching monks come and go. Some of the old entrepreneurialism was showing itself too. Cambodian vendors sold bottled water, soft drinks, and flower garlands with which to honour religious images. When a senior Australian air force officer came to Siem Reap, Stevens played tour guide herself, showing him Angkor Wat.

On paper, things were going well in Cambodia, but the on-the-ground realities were troubling. Despite patrols by peacekeepers, much of the country remained insecure. The Khmer Rouge disavowed the peace agreement and in 1993 began staging attacks.

The biggest one to hit Siem Reap began shortly before 5 a.m. on 3 May 1993. Stevens was pulling a night shift in the communications centre. There was no work, so she and others were watching one of the *Die Hard* movies, which are heavy on gun play. Standing at the door for a cigarette, she became aware that real gunfire was sounding outside. Bullets began striking nearby. Stephens rushed to load rifles. Soon she and several others were returning fire, aiming at muzzle flashes in the dark. Stevens fired fifty-three rounds, she later recorded in her diary. Gunfire and explosions died out at about 7:30 that morning. None of the Australians was injured. Stevens took away a souvenir bullet that had hit a filing cabinet that she had been sitting in front of moments earlier.

The Australian compound was targeted as part of a general assault on Siem Reap by an estimated 200 Khmer Rouge fighters. They also attacked the city's power plant, a garrison of government troops, and another site housing UN troops. They briefly captured the town's airport and destroyed an ammunition depot. Dozens of foreign tourists took shelter at UN installations near the centre of town. And some Cambodian families flocked to Angkor Wat, laying out their bedding in the bas-relief galleries. As in 1970, they believed they would be safe due both to the rules of war and the protection of the spirits.

Shelling and rocket attacks continued in Siem Reap in following days. The Australians got to work better fortifying their compound. They continued trips to Angkor, but now had to wear uniforms and carry weapons (as Stevens is doing in the photograph at the start of this chapter).

The Khmer Rouge eventually gave up their attacks in Siem Reap. The peacekeepers went home. But in 1997, violence came to town again as the Cambodian People's Party, heir to the party that the Vietnamese had placed in power in 1979, battled it out with its supposed partner in a coalition government, the royalist party known as FUNCINPEC. In Siem Reap province and elsewhere in Cambodia, the violence was short-lived. The upshot was that the CPP and its leader Hun Sen became the country's dominant political force.

Work continued on a job that had begun under the UN administration, the clearing of dangerous relics of war. Land mines, laid deliberately to cause harm, got broad media attention, but much of the danger came from unused

munitions — mortar rounds, rocket-propelled grenades — that one side or the other had carelessly cast aside during the many years of war. Soil or foliage quickly covered them over. Farmers, children, and buffaloes, stepping in the wrong place, fell victim to them on a tragic regular basis. Now the job was to remove them safely. Around the country, the Cambodian Mine Action Centre and international groups trained people for this dangerous job. Wearing helmets and protective vests, these men and women bravely cleared land inch by inch, locating old munitions and painstakingly digging them out for disposal.

It was dangerous work, all the more so because of continuing violence by the Khmer Rouge. In 1996, they kidnapped British demining expert Christopher Howes and his Cambodian team a few kilometres north of Angkor. Howes bravely refused an offer to go to safety to arrange a ransom for the group. Instead, the Khmer Rouge released most of the group and murdered him and his interpreter Houn Hourth.

Thankfully that kind of threat ended as the Khmer Rouge movement dwindled down to a collection of corrupt warlords reigning in scattered border zones. But key temples of the Angkor era remained in their hands for years, notably Banteay Chhmar and Preah Vihear. The latter became sort of a private retreat for one of the warlords, Ta Mok. He is said to have held court in a wooden pavilion built there on his orders; walls in his principle residence in the town of Anlong Veng were painted with primitive murals of various Angkor temples. As the Khmer Rouge movement headed toward its final disbandment in 1999, Preah Vihear began to function as a parade ground where its fighters formally surrendered to the government and were officially integrated into the national army.

* * * *

The Khmer Rouge warlord Ta Mok, one of the movement's final hold-outs, had this mural of Preah Vihear temple on the wall of his house in Anlong Veng town. (John Burgess)

ប្រយ័ត្នគ្រាប់មីន!!

Danger!! Mines!!

The UN Development Programme and other foreign aid groups helped the Cambodian Mine Action Centre clear up munitions that littered the country. Photo: UNDP Cambodia/ Chansok Lay.

Despite uncertainties like these, international groups that had been locked out of Angkor for decades arrived back in force in the '90s. In 1992, the EFEO reoccupied its shady riverside campus in Siem Reap. Japan's Sophia University and Waseda University set up shop in town as substantial Japanese conservation aid began flowing in. The U.S. National Park Service, the World Conservation Union, the Angkor Foundation of Hungary, Thailand's Department of Fine Arts, the UN Development Programme – these and other overseas groups were soon funding Angkor projects or sending people to help on the ground.

With so many foreign experts at the temples, with so many more weighing in from afar, there were inevitable conflicts, overlaps, and miscommunications. So in 1993 UNESCO created an International Coordinating Committee in which the many different governments and organizations with an interest in Angkor would be represented. Delegates would sit down together periodically to try to establish and act on common objectives. France and Japan assumed the role of co-chairs of the group; King Sihanouk acted as honorary chairman.

On the Cambodian side, a government body called the Apsara National Authority came into being in 1995, with a writ to oversee the heritage zone. The renowned and revered architect Vann Molyvann was put at the helm.

In the years ahead, the ICC and Apsara Authority would become forums for the inevitable conflicts between the goals of conservation and maximization of tourist revenue. Lines were never precisely drawn, but in general foreigners tended to place conservation ahead of tourism. Cambodians, while eager to preserve the monuments of which they were so proud, often had their eyes on the income to be gained from one of the few things their war-devastated country could sell to the world, vacation time amidst the relics of a magical 'lost civilisation.'

* * * * *

The scourge of art theft remained unchecked in the '90s, fuelled by foreign demand, corruption, and lawlessness born from continuing skirmishing with the Khmer Rouge. In 1993, the UN reported that thieves had taken eleven statues, together worth as much as $500,000, from the conservation compound in Siem Reap. In a 1998 World Heritage meeting, the South Korean delegate called for new commitment by the Cambodian government and international parties to prevent the trafficking of cultural property from Angkor. In

New Tensions with Thailand

Mistrust of historical rival Thailand remained common among Cambodians after Angkor reopened. Every so often, old tensions flared into the open with Angkor-era temples at the centre.

In 2003, a Thai soap opera actress was quoted (falsely, it turned out) as saying that she would perform in Cambodia only after it returned Angkor Wat to Thailand. Many Cambodians perceived this as a grave insult, even a call for aggression against their country. It became a subject of national conversation, with Prime Minister Hun Sen joining in on television with a remark that the actress was not worth even 'blades of grass' at Angkor Wat.

On 29 January, a mob appeared at the Thai embassy in Phnom Penh and set it on fire. Elsewhere in the city, Thai-owned businesses were attacked. Violence reached the point that Thai military transport aircraft flew in to evacuate Thai citizens. Cambodia eventually paid $20 million in compensation, and Thailand lifted diplomatic and economic sanctions that it had imposed.

Five years later, there was new trouble with Thailand concerning Preah Vihear, the cliff-top edifice that Cambodia had won back in the World Court decision of 1962. Cambodia had now persuaded UNESCO to make it the country's second World Heritage site. That riled Thai nationalist groups, which called it a bid to grab land that Thailand continued to claim adjacent to the temple. In 2008 and again in 2011, the armies of the two countries traded fire at and around the temple for days at a time. Scores of soldiers and civilians died.

Peace slowly settled back over the temple. Tourism resumed. Most of the visitors were Cambodians, riding up a frighteningly steep access road on the backs of motorbikes and pick-up trucks. Some presented policemen and soldiers up top with instant noodles and cigarettes as thanks for what was seen as defence of Cambodian soil.

The conflict with Thailand over Preah Vihear temple raised patriotic pride in Cambodia. This sign greeted temple visitors in 2010. (John Burgess)

a meeting the following year, similar complaints got another frustrated airing: there were 'alarming reports' of widespread art trafficking, the group was told.

Some brazen thefts came to light in this period. In December 1998, the late Claude Jacques, a renowned French expert on Cambodian inscriptions, visited an upscale antiques store in Bangkok's River City shopping mall. There he found a metre-tall inscription stone, missing its lower section, on sale for $8,000. This was no fake aimed at gullible tourists. It had come from the temple of Banteay Chhmar. 'I know that inscription perfectly well, because I worked on it,' he later told *The New York Times*. 'I could not stay calm.' After Jacques reported the stone's presence, the Thai government's archaeology department seized it.

The stone turned out to be part of the haul in the largest known single theft of Khmer antiquities. In late 1998, men equipped with cranes and pneumatic drills dismantled a twelve-metre section of the western wall, which included world-famous depictions in bas-relief of the multi-armed Bodhisattva known as Avalokiteshvara. Trucks carried pieces

214

This large bas-relief of the Bodhisattva known as Avalokiteshvara was among those that thieves took from Banteay Chhmar in 1998. Intercepted by Thai authorities, it was later returned to Cambodia and went on display at the National Museum in Phnom Penh. Photo by Paisarn Piemmettawat.

Above right: Banteay Chhmar temple, scene of a huge art theft in 1998, is known for its rich collection of bas-reliefs. In this one, King Jayavarman VII rides a chariot. (John Burgess)

toward Thailand with a goal of onward sale to art dealers. Thai authorities intercepted two trucks at the border. Eventually two of the Bodhisattvas and the inscription stone that Claude Jacques rescued were returned to Cambodia. Other of the Bodhisattvas have never been found.

* * * * *

After the overthrow of the Khmer Rouge in 1979, many of Angkor's long-time inhabitants had moved back to their old villages. Other people arrived from other parts of the country, hoping for peace and a modest livelihood. Before much time passed, old patterns of life had resumed in the land between the temples, and sometimes within their walls. Farmers planted rice on the beds of ancient reservoirs. They grew cucumbers inside Ta Prohm. Children and water buffaloes lolled in the moats of Angkor Wat. Trees were felled to be turned into charcoal, which went by bicycle or oxcart for sale in Siem Reap. And young men were again going to Angkor Wat for ordination as monks at its monastery.

All this was set to cause the same type of friction that had followed the French takeover eight decades earlier, if not more of it: World Heritage status was going to subject Angkor to a far larger and more complex set of rules, drafted half a world away, to govern zoning, development, administration, and, indeed, the lives of people for whom Angkor was not an archaeological site but home. As the World Heritage program spelled out, places like Angkor were deemed to belong to 'all the peoples of the world.'

In 1997, the Cambodian government created the Heritage

Police, a force tasked with enforcing the program's rules. However, those rules did not appear to apply to everyone. Military officers managed to build houses and karaoke clubs on restricted land near the temples. Developers often feigned ignorance of zoning and preservation rules; one narrowed an Angkor-era canal, filling in part of it with concrete, in order to make a parking lot for a hotel.

Angkor's village residents, in contrast, were expected to follow the rules. The Japanese anthropologist Keiko Miura, who conducted months of on-the-ground research in Angkor in this period, watched as tough new regulations were implemented in 2000. Villagers were forbidden to cut trees, collect firewood and resins, release buffaloes at Angkor Wat's moats, or plant rice in certain ponds and lakes. The following year, fishing was banned inside Angkor Thom. Typically no compensation was offered, Miura found. People were simply expected to find other livelihoods. But often they did not just roll over and accept. They filed petitions with senior officials, going over the heads of lower-ranking ones. They tried to play on rivalries between different Cambodian government agencies and political parties. Sometimes they obtained partial relief; other times they simply ignored the rules. To avoid the Heritage Police, local people took to passing in and out of Angkor Thom through two gaps in its walls for firewood collecting, cattle grazing, and other traditional activities.

With tourist numbers heading slowly up, local people were turning out at the temples to sell such things as bottled water and postcards. Others were tending informal shrines, collecting a bit of money for incense sticks and blessings. Miura reported that police officers seemed to view it as their right to pocket some of the take in return for allowing the activity.

In July 2000, Miura attended a morning-long meeting convened at Ta Nei temple to discuss the restrictions and local objections. From the very start, the meeting was organized in a way that emphasized the hierarchy at play: Officials sat comfortably at a table, while local people had places on backless benches or on the ground or large stones. For most of the meeting, officials dominated the talk. They alternated between expressing sympathy for the villagers' complaints and warning of the penalties for violations. What people had to accept, they said, was that Angkor did not belong to them. 'It is not in the interests of some twenty families, but in the interests of ten million Cambodians and the two billion people of the world that they regard Angkor as world heritage,' said a Heritage Police official.

Thieves chipped off the head of this deity at the East Mebon temple. (John Burgess)

There was periodic tension in this period between international groups and the Cambodian government as well. In 1999, the government awarded a private conglomerate five-year rights to collect tourist entry fees at Angkor. The company was Sokimex, whose founder Sok Kong was widely viewed as close to senior government figures. The initial contract provided for Sokimex to pay the government a flat fee of $1 million a year and keep whatever else it collected – a deal sharply in the company's favour in view of rising tourist numbers. Many foreign officials questioned why administration of one of Cambodia's biggest sources of foreign currency did not remain in government hands. These concerns did not prevail, though the terms of the contract were later modified to channel more

Angkor and the Long-Distance Runner

Yuko Arimori came to Angkor with a special perspective—what would it take to stage a long-distance race among the monuments? In 1996 the Japanese Olympic runner organized what would become an annual event, the Angkor Wat International Half Marathon. With starting and ending point at Angkor Wat's western causeway, runners followed a route that took them by many other monuments and in and out of the gates of Angkor Thom.

About 650 people took part in that first race. In later years turn-out grew to the many thousands, Cambodians and foreigners. Some were weekend runners who flew in for this unusual way to commune with the ancient grandeur. Others were dead-serious international competitors. Among the runners in 2006: Nary Ly, who would go on to become Cambodia's first

female Olympian marathoner, competing in the 2016 summer games in Rio de Janeiro.

The races' goal was to publicize and raise money for the cause of banning anti-personnel weapons and to help the many Cambodians maimed by munitions that still litter the country. To highlight their country's urgent need in that regard, the half marathon had a side event of a ten-kilometre race for people with artificial legs.

In 2014, the Khmer Empire Marathon was added, a full 42-plus kilometre event with children's hospitals and other Cambodian charities as the beneficiaries. Runners gather in pre-dawn darkness, then set off down the course amidst cheers, pop anthems, and the special celebratory gush that only a marathon can generate.

In 1996, the Japanese Olympic runner Yuko Arimori organized the first Angkor Wat International Half Marathon to promote the banning of landmines and raise funds for their Cambodian victims. Photo courtesy of Angkor Wat International Half Marathon.

money, based on percentage figures of the total take, to the government and conservation. In 2016, the government took back the job of ticket sales.

The holy images Preah Ang Chek and Preah Ang Chorm draw the Buddhist faithful to their shrine in Siem Reap. Photo by Mister_Knight/Shutterstock.com.

* * * * *

With the departure of the peacekeepers, Siem Reap was looking more and more like an ordinary town. Near its center there now stood a permanent home for Preah Ang Chek and Preah Ang Chorm, the holy images once possessed by the warlord Dap Chhuon. They had passed the Khmer Rouge years submerged in the Siem Reap River, cast there by the anti-religious fanatics. Rescued from the water, the images were placed with reverence inside the new, specially built shrine. Cambodians flocked in for prayers and offerings, the air bearing the sweet scent of incense. People felt confident that the two images were bestowing protection on their town.

Before many years passed, Siem Reap beyond the shrine began getting a new face. Heritage planners had designated a 'hotel zone' on a large swathe of undeveloped land northeast of town, in hopes of preserving the centre's old character. But developers were sceptical, and turned to sites considered more commercially desirable. Before long, parts of the once quiet provincial town were turning into a giant construction site. The road linking the airport to town centre was especially busy, gaining rows of large mid-price hotels often catering to people on package tours. Backpacker hostels sprang up in once-quiet residential neighbourhoods. Restaurants, photo film processors, souvenir stands, and other establishments of the tourist trade proliferated. Sex tourism found a home as well, in seedy bars and massage parlours.

At the same time, old gems of Siem Reap got a new polishing. The Grand Hotel, pride of the French colonial era, reopened under ownership of the Raffles chain of Singapore, which spent heavily to modernize it and build a large swimming pool and new wings in a fine approximation of the 1930s style. The bird-cage elevator remained in use. Norodom Sihanouk's former guest villa, meanwhile, was reborn as the Amansara resort.

There was no revival, however, for Angkor Wat's one-time next-door neighbours, the Bungalow/Hôtel des Ruines/Auberge and the never-opened Air France hotel. Both had been lost to the war,[1] but now neither was rebuilt. No hotels, in fact, went up inside the heritage zone. Keeping this kind of development away from the monuments was a signal victory for the cause of conservation. UNESCO offered special congratulations to the Cambodian government.

* * * * *

In 2001, Angkor reappeared in the world of international film. The year before, a Hollywood team had arrived to shoot parts of *Lara Croft: Tomb Raider*, the film that launched the action star career of the actor Angelina Jolie. Ta Prohm temple was the main filming location. Local people, including Buddhist monks, took part as extras. When the film became a stand-up hit in world theatres, Cambodia and Angkor got enormous attention. And there was no distraction of a hostile media interview by the film's star, as had happened with *Lord Jim*. Indeed, the Angkor shoot was the start of a sort of love affair between Jolie and Cambodia. She returned frequently in later years and adopted a Cambodian boy.[2]

In 2017, Angkor figured in the other end of the film production process, the red-carpet premier. On a humid Saturday evening that year, His Majesty King Sihamoni stepped down from a limousine at Angkor Thom's Terrace of the Elephants. Awaiting the royal arrival were Jolie in evening gown, the adopted son, and other of her children. So was a sizeable audience that included farmers, musicians, policemen, diplomats, and a famous memoirist.

1 More than bombs and bullets, materials looting is what did them in. They were literally carried off piece by piece over the years for use in construction elsewhere. Many ancient Khmer monuments have suffered this way as well. Trapeang Roupou temple, which the EFEO successfully saved from airport expansion in the 1930s and '40s, lost much of its towers' height in more recent times as local people used it as a quarry. It is now a protected monument.

2 Something resembling Angkor had made an appearance in the 1979 war film *Apocalypse Now*, as the Cambodian hide-out of the mysterious commander Kurtz. The face towers and statues that theatre audiences saw were the creations of set builders in the Philippines, where the movie was filmed.

As darkness fell, the attention of King and crowd turned to a theatre-sized video screen that had been set up for the occasion. On it rolled the opening scene of 'First They Killed My Father,' a film version of the book of the same title by the memoirist present that night, Loung Ung. Jolie was its director. For the next two hours, the audience experienced a chilling child's-eye-view of what it took to survive the Khmer Rouge.

* * * * *

Early on, scattered attacks on foreigners – an American woman and her Cambodian guide died in an ambush on the road to Banteay Srei in 1995 – and the fighting of 1997 had hampered the revival of tourism. But by the close of the 1990s a steady upward trend had set in. Annual figures were growing so fast that each year's record was easily broken. In 2001, the official head count was 208,472. The following year it was 269,155, a 29 percent rise.

Angkor was emerging as a favoured destination for people seeking escape from the harsh winters of northern Europe and Asia. As incomes rose in China and other East Asian countries, the foreign vacation became an important symbol of success in up-and-coming communities there. A package tour to Angkor, beginning with a non-stop flight direct to Siem Reap, was often just the thing.

By 2013, the foreign tourist figure at Angkor had broken through two million. The old capital was becoming proof of the aphorism that you should be careful what you wish for.

Angkor Thom was the scene of the premiere of a major feature film in 2017. First They Killed My Father ™/© Netflix. Used with permission.

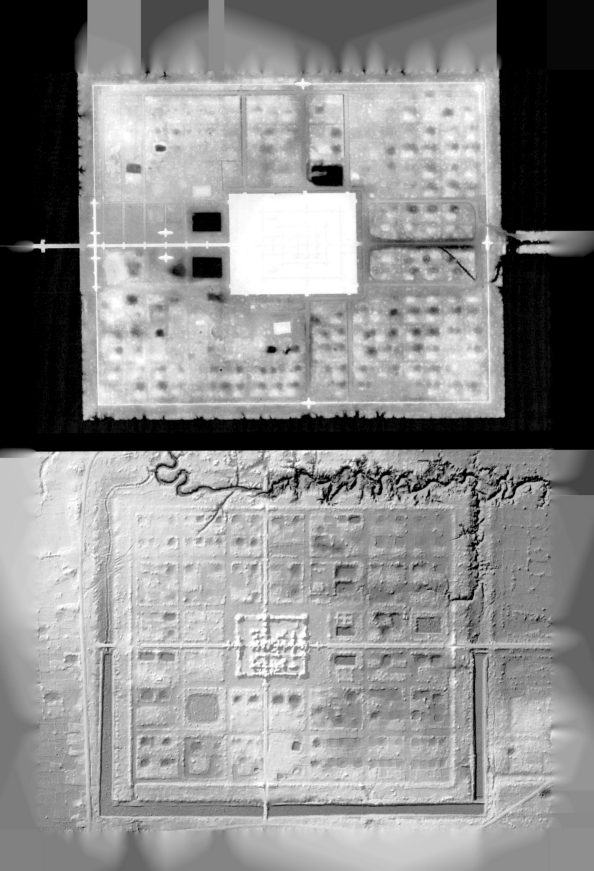

15: ARCHAEOLOGY, REDUX

Scholars employ new technology and thinking to look beyond the temples and examine daily life in ancient Angkor. Some long-accepted theories fall by the wayside.

In French colonial times, historical inquiry at Angkor focused largely on temples and inscriptions. From this approach emerged a body of knowledge with a distinctly royal bias. The names of kings, major events of their reigns, and the styles and construction sequence of their temples became known. Fame was revived for a few palace priests and military commanders. But by the late twentieth century, archaeologists were looking beyond the aristocratic. Angkor, they were coming to see, was not just a collection of temples. It was a city, one of the largest of the pre-industrial era, in population and geographical sprawl. And beyond it were equally important things, huge expanses of closely organized fields and villages where farming families had grown the rice and caught the fish that made the temples possible.

One of the minds behind the new approach was Bernard-Philippe Groslier, the last French conservator. Though war expelled him from his beloved charge in 1972, he continued to write about it after he returned to France. He had spent decades walking, driving, measuring, observing, photographing, and excavating not just at the temples but in the lands around them, in dry season and wet. He had become fascinated with the Khmers' relationship with water and their ability to make it do their bidding. He began to conceive the notion of Angkor as *la Cité hydraulique*, the hydraulic city. In 1979, he laid out particulars in a forty-two page article. The ancient Khmers, he wrote, had over the course of centuries modified the natural water flows of the region to enable massive agricultural production and urban development. The Kulen hills to the north functioned as a sort of water tower. Water flowing down the slopes to the plain below entered a complex network of canals and redirected rivers that, using gravity's gentle pull, moved this crucial resource of life to enormous reservoirs and temple moats. There it was stored, then rationed out as needed;

Opposite page: Aerial images using laser-based LIDAR technology reveal patterns of ancient habitation at Angkor Wat (top) and Beng Mealea temple. Images courtesy of the Khmer Archaeology LIDAR Consortium /Cambodian Archaeological LIDAR Initiative.

ultimately every drop was put to use. Groslier realized that the network had deep spiritual implications for the Khmers (*lingas* carved into streambeds in the Kulen hills sanctified the water passing over them) and that the Siem Reap River represented to them the holy Ganges of India. But in his article he focused mostly on its impact on agriculture. It was possible, he surmised, that the system allowed farmers to grow multiple rice crops per year. But it would have been worth the immense labour, he said, even if it guaranteed just a single crop by protecting against the capriciousness of wet season rainfall. 'The Angkorian hydraulic city,' Groslier concluded '…permitted the blossoming, then the triumph of this civilisation.'

In the two decades that conflict closed Angkor, field archaeology essentially stopped. But in the world at large, the discipline was evolving. Many of its practitioners began leaning toward studying daily existence as opposed to palaces and temples. In addition, new technology became available. From satellites, high-resolution cameras, radar, and infra-red sensors peered down. In the early 2000s archaeology would begin harnessing 'Big Data,' the collection of oceans of information points about ancient sites, to be massaged by computers into archaeological insight.

Among the new generation of Angkor scholars who arrived from abroad when Cambodia reopened, there was great respect for Groslier's lifetime of study (he had continued writing until shortly before his death in 1986). But to some people his theories didn't entirely hold up. While it was plain to see that the Khmers had built an astounding water system, its purpose, they said, was open to question. If the reservoirs were tanks for irrigation, how did water find its way from them to rice fields? There was no discernible network of locks and outflow canals, the sceptics pointed out. They did not buy Groslier's suggestion that water might have seeped, by design, through the reservoirs' levees, to be collected and directed by channels outside. In a 1998 study, Robert Acker of the University of California/Berkeley's geography department concluded that the number of fields downstream from Angkor's big reservoirs was in fact relatively small, and that, even if used for irrigation, the volume of water the reservoirs contained could have nurtured rice for only a small portion of Angkor's people. 'The idea that Angkorian agriculture needed massive hydraulic works to eke out the last grain of rice in order to survive is fundamentally wrong,' Acker wrote. 'With plentiful groundwater and multiple rice varieties at its disposal, Angkor almost certainly commanded large rice surpluses.' As with modern farming in the area, he said, water from the sky and ground was what made the rice grow.

Also undermining Groslier's thesis, the critics said, was evidence of omission. While inscriptions mentioned the big reservoirs often enough, they were silent on irrigation. Would they really have had nothing to say if the system had been the foundation of agricultural prosperity and political authority?[1] Similar points were made about the account of the thirteenth century Chinese visitor Zhou Daguan. While he did say that Khmer farmers could grow three or four crops each year (he didn't mention what was being grown), Zhou too had nothing to say about irrigation.

What, then, *was* the purpose? One proffered explanation was flood control on a plain where water drained off slowly. Otherwise the rising waters of wet season would inundate the palaces and temples. Other theories had it that, hard as it was for the modern mind to grasp, the sole purpose of the reservoirs and moats was the one that had been clear from the start – to be earth-bound depictions of heaven's perfect order. The reservoirs were the Ocean of Creation, beneath which Vishnu sleeps as he dreams a new universe into existence, the waves lapping at the base of Mount Meru, the island temples at their centres. Angkor Wat is commonly viewed as a temple bounded by moats. But it can also be seen as an island in the middle of a great rectangular sea. Perhaps the water network was in fact part of the apparatus of political power, but not due to irrigation. Perhaps it was due to the awe that arose in people's hearts as they gazed on waters that seemed as far across and as deep as an actual ocean.

The hydraulic debate concerned water's role on a macro scale. But in the '90s there also began increasing study aimed at understanding water on a micro scale – its use in daily life by ordinary people. This work, it turned out, gave insights in surprising ways as what it was to be a citizen of Angkor.

* * * * *

Ordinarily, archaeological inquiries into ancient daily life might draw on human bones and 'grave goods,' objects buried with the dead. But there were almost no bones to be found at Angkor, due to cremation and (according to Zhou Daguan) a custom of leaving bodies in the open for wild animals to devour. And there were precious few grave goods in the handful of places where ashes were found interred. Nor were there houses or palaces to examine. Beyond such clues as postholes,

1 On the other hand, inscriptions don't mention some very important things that definitely did exist – Angkor Wat, for instance.

Archaeologists began to use the view from space, such as this radar image of the Angkor region taken from the U.S. space shuttle Endeavor in 1994. NASA/JPL.

they left virtually no remains, because they had been made of wood, bamboo, and thatch that quickly perished in the region's humid climate.

What didn't perish was that most humble but important of materials, dirt. Dirt, piled up or removed, was the Khmers' main tool in controlling water, and water was the key to life and habitation. Archaeologists began paying special attention to detecting and understanding human-created variations in the topography of the Angkor area. The EFEO's Christophe Pottier conducted much of the early work and theorizing about the Khmers' etching of the landscape. Starting in 1993, using aerial photos and his own explorations on foot and motorbike, he mapped field and canal patterns south of the main temple group (the areas to the north remained insecure).

New technology was coming into play. In 2004, the space shuttle *Endeavor* produced radar imagery of the Angkor region, bringing into sharper focus ancient modifications of the region's landscape. In 2007, the archaeologist Damian Evans completed a detailed map integrating aerial photos, radar, and many other sources of data. It was becoming increasingly clear that mapping dirt meant mapping human habitation in the days of the empire.

Dirt found piled up as a mound could signal the location of a house made safe from the rising waters of rainy season. Dirt found fashioned into a berm could be a causeway over water, perhaps carrying a footpath or trapping water in a rice field. A long depression in the ground could be a village canal, while a subtle circular indentation could signal a long-ago household pond. These last shapes seemed to be remnants of something

Zhou Daguan had observed: 'Every family is sure to have a pool, or at least a pool to share among two or three families.' And then there were peculiar patterns found in many places in the Angkor area: large horseshoe-shaped indentations. These indicated the long-ago sites of 'neighbourhood temples,' small shrines with water on three sides and entrance causeways on the fourth, the eastern side.

But getting a complete picture of these formations was difficult because forest covered much of the Angkor area. Existing aerial sensing technologies had limited success seeing through it. Ground-level surveys, like one conducted inside Angkor Thom, were a costly, time-consuming process of machete whacks and insect bites. But in another sense, forest was a blessing for archaeology, because it had functioned for centuries as a protective coating over whatever lay below. It meant that modern houses or roads or fields had not disturbed the ancient underpinnings.

It would take deployment of an aerial laser sensing system to see through the forest cover and fill out the picture.

Light Detection and Ranging technology – LIDAR – was developed in the 1960s and saw early use in such tasks as weather forecasting and mapping the moon. In 2012 it became a tool of archaeology at Angkor, overseen by Evans and Tan Boun Suy of the Apsara National Authority. Its platform is not a satellite or high-flying airplane, but a standard tourist helicopter fitted with a large electronics pod. After a blessing by Buddhist monks (no serious archaeological project at Angkor begins without one), the craft takes off and flies patterns back and forth over an area of interest. The pod sends down millions of laser pulses, which strike things below and reflect back up to the pod. In forested areas, most of them hit leaves and branches. But some make their way through gaps in the foliage to the ground, just like some rays of sunlight, and reflect

Monks gather to bless a helicopter that would carry a LIDAR pod on a survey of Banteay Chhmar temple and its surroundings. Image courtesy of the Khmer Archaeology LIDAR Consortium /Cambodian Archaeological LIDAR Initiative.

back to the pod. The resulting data have been processed by computer in the LIDAR project's headquarters in Siem Reap, located initially at the University of Sydney's research center, later at EFEO's riverside compound.

The reason for going to all this trouble is that the technology can time the round trips of individual pulses, and this yields precise three-dimensional coordinates – longitude, latitude, and elevation – of the spots they strike. So far, the project has generated literally billions of these data sets. Special algorithms filter out returns from foliage. What is left is contour images of the ground below the leaves. These are nothing short of amazing, depicting minute variations in elevation. Shapes and patterns that go unrecognized even by an archaeologist walking past them on the ground show up plain as day. It has been called 'digital deforestation.'

LIDAR cannot see beneath the ground, but ancient things there often manifest themselves through minute variations at the surface. In this way, the technology has revealed the locations of some previously unknown, generally small masonry structures. But LIDAR's most important revelations concern not masonry but dirt. Virtually everywhere the technology looked, it found hints on the ground of bygone people. 'Subtle traces of these ephemeral cities remain inscribed into the surface of the Cambodian landscape even centuries later, in the form of topographic variations that indicate the former existence of roads, canals, ponds, field walls, occupation mounds, and other basic elements of the urban and agricultural networks,' wrote Evans, Roland Fletcher, and other collaborators in a 2013 article. The LIDAR surveys 'have uncovered an engineered landscape on a scale perhaps without parallel in the pre-industrial world.' The findings were confirming and elaborating on the early observations and theorizing of Christophe Pottier.

Among the first subjects of overflights were the Kulen hills north of Angkor. Some smallish temples there had long been identified as forming part of a pre-Angkor capital, mentioned in the Sdok Kok Thom inscription and known by the Sanskrit name Mahendraparvata. LIDAR peeled back the hillside forest cover to reveal the old city, showing its scale (larger than previously believed), how

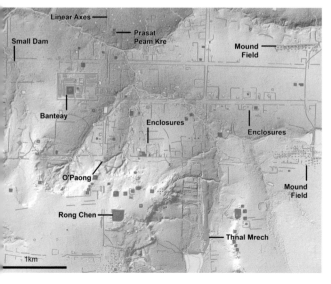

LIDAR surveys revealed a veritable street map of the pre-Angkor capital located in the Kulen hills. Cambodian Archaeological Lidar Initiative / Phnom Kulen Program (EFEO/ADF/MCFA)

its canals and roadways were laid out, and where its many temples and ponds fit in. It was as if a street map more than twelve hundred years old had been discovered.

Angkor proper also got digital fly-overs, yielding new confirmations and revelations. The big open space on both sides of Angkor Wat's processional avenue had long been known to have gentle depressions and bumps. LIDAR imaging of that area, and the much larger expanses of forested land inside the walls, revealed pond patterns that suggested orderly rows of houses. That in turn signalled that the temple grounds were a busy religious community rather than the largely empty, forbidden monument to Vishnu that early French scholars had postulated. How many people lived there? The 2013 article noted Zhou's observation that ponds were shared by one to three families. If Angkor Wat had 250-300 ponds, as LIDAR suggests, and if each household had five people, that would mean as many as four thousand five hundred people lived within its walls. LIDAR also mapped communities just outside the moats of Angkor Wat. Like those inside, they were not hodge-podge clusters of houses but carefully laid-out neighbourhoods of straight lines and right angles.

By revealing the scale to which the Khmers re-ordered their physical landscape, LIDAR and the earlier aerial work complemented a growing body of evidence emerging from modern techniques of environmental analysis. Growth rings inside thousand-year-old cypress trees in Vietnam yielded some of the most intriguing findings. By extracting tiny core samples from the trees and comparing the thickness of rings, Columbia University researchers were able to reconstruct year-to-year moisture levels in Southeast Asia from 1250 to 2008. This suggested protracted droughts from roughly 1340 to 1375 and 1400 to 1425. Crop failure and famine might have resulted (not to mention a spiritual crisis as people watched their earthbound Oceans of Creation go dry). Other studies found evidence of efforts to cope. An outflow channel at the eastern end of the huge reservoir known as the East Baray, for example, was modified repeatedly over the years, apparently as Khmer engineers struggled to deal with dwindling supplies of water flowing down from the Kulen hills. The tree-ring analysis also found that between the droughts, nature inflicted periods of intense, destructive monsoon rains. There was corroboration of this too on the ground: a metre-and-a-half thick deposit of sand and gravel in the bed of a major waterway, likely brought by a single massive flood in the fourteenth century.

Enduring Mysteries

Just as some inscriptions can be read but not understood, aerial reconnaissance can reveal things that can't be readily explained. Among these are spiral-shaped patterns of levees that LIDAR images depict just outside Angkor Wat's southern moat.

Ground-level inspection has found them to be made of sand, containing no masonry or ceramic material. Patterns of depth and water flow led to theories that the channels might have been used to grow lotus flowers for temple rituals and the banks for aromatic plants such as sandalwood trees. Or the channels might be the remains of formal gardens, perhaps with some ritual purpose connected to the temple.

For now, this remains speculation. But what is clear is that the ancient Khmers went to great effort to put the spirals there.

Spiral patterns revealed by a LIDAR survey remain difficult to explain. Image courtesy of the Khmer Archaeology LIDAR Consortium /Cambodian Archaeological LIDAR Initiative.

Elsewhere, previously unknown canals were identified. All told, the pendulum of theorizing was swinging back in the direction of Groslier's hydraulic city, with the reservoirs functioning as giant irrigation tanks, maybe not in the way he had perceived, but nonetheless playing a vital role in water management for agriculture. With the system slowly breaking down, with the plain around Angkor no longer able to support a big population, Angkor would have become more vulnerable to the armies of the ascendant kingdom of Siam.

Much of the work at Angkor took place under the auspices of the Greater Angkor Project, a research collaboration linking French, Australian, and Cambodian specialists. The archaeologist Roland Fletcher, known for his work on settlement growth and decline, played a major role as a director and organizer. Even as high-tech tools were employed, old-fashioned digs proceeded. In 2015, a team supervised by the American Alison Kyra Carter excavated a single mound inside Angkor Wat, hoping to learn more about the people who might have lived atop it. Twenty-two trenches yielded definite signs of habitation: postholes, large pieces of sandstone, burnt charcoal, and earthenware ceramics with charring on the outside, suggesting they were cooking vessels. Some of the ceramics had been locally fired, while others were Chinese, indicating international trade. The team unearthed

Technical surveys resumed in Angkor. Here a team is making scale drawings of bas reliefs at the Bayon in 1995. Photo by Brice Li, Singapore.

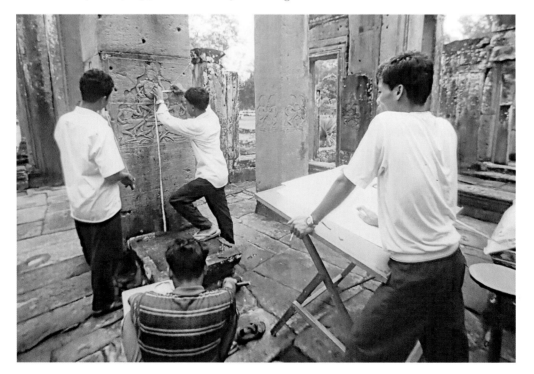

Rethinking Old Evidence

Some recent advances in field archaeology involve not new physical discoveries but new interpretation of old ones.

With that kind of approach, the Australian archaeologist David Brotherson has filled in some of the missing history of Angkor Wat. He posits that sometime between the late thirteenth and early seventeenth centuries, a period of decline and military peril for the Khmer empire, the temple was converted into a fortress.

The theory makes sense of more than six thousand holes that were created at regular intervals atop the temple's outer walls and near the top on the inner face. Brotherson argues that the holes supported palisades and platforms that allowed defenders to fight from the tops of the temple's roughly three kilometres of outer walls.

His theory also explains six anomalies in the walls – broad gaps that were bridged with mismatched stone and laterite at some point after the temple's twelfth-century construction. The idea is that the original architects intended elaborate stone gateways for these gaps, but never built them. Years later, when military threat arose, defenders hastily closed the gaps with the material we see today.

Some of the stones that filled gaps in Angkor Wat's walls were scavenged from elsewhere and include random decorative carvings. (John Burgess)

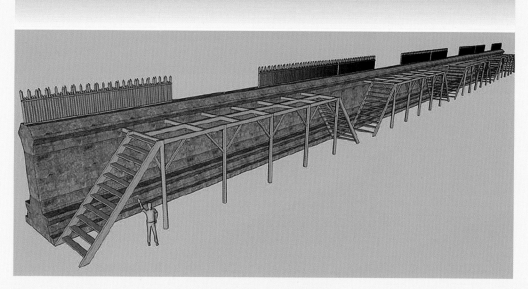

Angkor Wat's defenders may have used holes in the walls to build parapets like this one. Image courtesy of Antiquity Publications Ltd.

The 12th-century temple Banteay Kdei was the scene of a spectacular archeological find, more than 270 buried images of the Buddha. (John Burgess)

one complete vessel, a round container with a slender neck. There were also signs of the diet of the one-time inhabitants: rice grains and rind of the citrus fruit pomelo, still a common snack in Cambodia.

* * * * *

Some archaeology reveals subtle clues to history, requiring lengthy analysis and hypothesizing. Some turns up things that are immediately remarkable. That's what happened at Banteay Kdei, a temple built in the twelfth century by Jayavarman VII, who established Buddhism as his state religion. Starting in 1991, experts from Japan's Sophia University had been working with Cambodians at the temple in a project documenting how its physical structure and use had evolved over the years. In 2000, a crew excavating the foundations of a small ancillary building inside the temple's walls came upon a sitting Buddha image and pieces of sandstone half a metre down. In 2001 they returned to excavate a wider area, and unearthed a total of 273 pieces of Buddha images and a large square pillar carved with rows of tiny sitting Buddhas, 1,008 in all. These were amazing finds by any standard, but even more remarkable was the condition of the images: about eighty percent had either been deprived of their heads or divided at the torso. What the excavation crew had found was in essence a cemetery for religious images.

Archaeologists determined that the burial dated to a time of religious turmoil in the empire. In the thirteenth century, a later King Jayavarman, the eighth of that name, had disavowed the newly established Buddhism and turned the state religion back to Hinduism, sparking widespread resistance. The turmoil of this period was already known to historians through such evidence as images that can be seen today on the walls of some of Jayavarman VII's temples. Carved originally as Buddhas, the images had been modified with chisels into Hindu ascetics and other figures of that faith.

The statues at Banteay Kdei had suffered a harsher fate. One can picture a scene in which followers of the new king removed them from their niches and pedestals, then ritually broke them, to defeat their powers and demonstrate that there was no going back. But then the images received a decent burial. In newly dug pits, they were arranged in orderly rows and layers. A few were even buried with their heads put back in place. Perhaps this part of the job was conducted by different people, heartbroken devotees who gathered pieces from around the temple and buried them together, seeking to preserve and respect as best they could. But that is just a guess, one of many unknowns regarding the images' past. What, for instance, does it mean that the chosen interment place was within the walls of the temple, in ground that by centuries of Khmer tradition is sanctified? Was it intended to add to the dignity of the burial? Or was it a simple expedience to avoid the labour of transporting very heavy pieces an extended distance, or perhaps to hide the desecration from the eyes of people outside the temple's walls?[2]

Over the course of the next eight centuries, the constant temperature and humidity underground preserved the statues remarkably well. Their unweathered faces remained possessed of the same calm and detachment they had on the day they were carved. A rotating selection of the images is today on display in a Siem Reap facility specially built for them by Sophia University, the Preah Norodom Sihanouk-Angkor Museum. In piecing them back together, restorers chose not to hide their old wounds, so that their history is apparent to the viewer. With the museum's opening, the vandals' intention to forever remove the images from the public eye was finally defeated. The larger goal of restoring Hinduism as the state religion was, of course, equally unsuccessful. The kingdom soon reverted to the Buddhist faith, though today it is the Theravada strain that prevails, not the Mahayana form embraced by Jayavarman VII.

* * * * *

There remained the issue of the 'decolonization' of Angkor conservation. The 1990s reopening had brought in large numbers of foreign specialists. But slowly Cambodia was producing its own corps of experts, educated both abroad and at Cambodian institutions, notably the reopened Royal University of Fine Arts in Phnom Penh. Some, like Pich Keo, were Khmer Rouge survivors. Others had left the country before their rule began, then returned.

Current experts include people such as Im Sokrithy, who holds degrees from the *École des hautes études en sciences sociales* in France and Cambodia's Royal University. Among his work: co-direction of the Living Angkor Road Project, a years-long examination of a once well-travelled route running between Angkor and the Phimai temple, in what is now Thailand. Conducted in collaboration with Thai institutions starting in 2005, the project used digs, interviews, architectural analysis, and aerial sensing to expand scholarly understanding of the road and the people who lived along it. Researchers documented

2 There are parallels to the fate of large statues of kings of Israel that once stood high on the west façade of Notre Dame cathedral in Paris. In 1793, during the French Revolution, a mob toppled them to the ground and attacked them, apparently with shovels or pick-axes, trying with varying success to destroy them. Heads and other fragments were later taken away and buried together in the city's 9th Arrondissement. By some accounts, this was the work of an old-order loyalist. The pieces lay forgotten until 1977, when a crew renovating the headquarters of the Banque française du commerce extérieur discovered them. Today the heads, still bearing scars of the mob's anger, are one of the most compelling displays at Paris' Cluny Museum.

stone bridges, ancient villages and industries (such as metal-working), and *dharmasalas*, the twelfth-century stone chapels at way stations where people could receive medical care or a night's rest during a journey. Cultural practices of present day residents, such as use of woven fish traps, sometimes matched those depicted on Khmer bas-reliefs. The team mapped the actual roadway as well, which in many places had disappeared but in others was unmistakable these many centuries later. Following work on the Phimai road, three others got similar examination: ancient routes from Angkor to Sdok Kok Thom, Wat Phu, and Preah Khan-Kompong Svay.

At this writing, Sokrithy holds a senior post in the Apsara Authority, where among other things he serves as scientific supervisor for digs in Angkor. In 2017, one of his teams working at Angkor Thom turned up something amazing: a two-metre tall guardian statue, lying on its back just half a metre below the surface. It likely protected a hospital that stood at the north gate of the walled city. The statue was well preserved, though its lower legs were missing. The image was left in place until permission could be secured from resident spirits. With offerings of fruit laid out before them, team members knelt and recited prayers. Grid strings had already been stretched over the image to help record the scientifically executed removal that would follow.

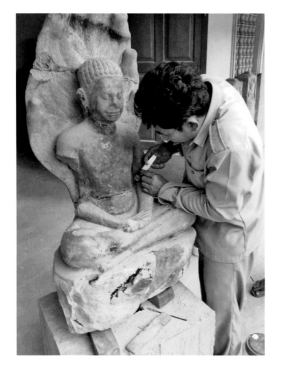

A conservation worker appliying a compound in 2017 to restore an Angkor-era image of the Buddha. (John Burgess)

The list of expert Cambodians goes on. Ang Choulean is the country's pre-eminent ethnologist, with a long career of research and writing that links present-day Cambodian society with ancient ways. Bong Sovath took part in a lengthy excavation of the Angkor Borei site in southern Cambodia in the 1990s. He later became rector of the Royal University, then Cambodia's ambassador to UNESCO in Paris.

Up-and-coming researchers include Phipal Heng, whose dissertation examines the formation of pre-Angkor states in the mid first millennium. What brought about the transition from the loosely organized societies of the 'early historic' period to principalities built around Hindu temples? His fieldwork focused on a little-studied site on the Mekong near Laos, Thala Borivat. Detailed excavations there produced large numbers of artefacts, including stoneware, a brick floor, charcoal, and Chinese 'tradeware' ceramics. Drawing in addition on inscriptions, accounts from Chinese archives, and the work of other scholars, Phipal Heng filled in blanks about this period of Khmer history. Among his findings: early Hindu temples were built atop ancestral burial sites, suggesting the builders saw continuity between the old and new faiths.

* * * * *

Other recent work focuses on words from the past. Though the Sdok Kok Thom inscription has been known for close to one hundred thirty years, ever since Aymonier made his stampings in 1883, its full meaning remains elusive. A new translation was published in 2005 by Dr. Chhany Sak-Humphry of the University of Hawaii with the assistance of Philip N. Jenner.

Other inscriptions that had never been formally analysed also got their due attention, such as a five-liner in Sanskrit and Old Khmer from Banteay Chhmar temple. It is written in the first-person voice of a man identifying himself as Sri Madhurendrasuri, who relates a personal experience to explain the deity enshrined in the structure where the inscription was found.

I have seen the Fire lighting up the directions of space [and] falling from heaven into the kingdom of Sri Jayavarman, a great wonder, which I believe will entail good results, [namely] high birth, two [good] eyes, and eminent family. May these be mine!

Sri Jayavarman refers to Jayavarman VII, the builder king of the late twelfth century. The inscription was introduced to the world of Khmer scholarship by the scholar Thomas S. Maxwell, who devoted sixty-seven pages to the five lines, giving exhaustive treatment to their historical, religious, and linguistic context.

And new inscriptions continue to come to light. In January 2013, a team from the Archaeological Survey of India unearthed a four-sided inscription stele under a paving stone on the grounds of Wat Phu, an early Khmer temple in what is now southern Laos. Despite a handling mishap – the 2.4-metre-tall stone was dropped on being moved, damaging places on its corners – the text remained clear and legible. Translated by Claude Jacques (one of the pre-eminent Khmer epigraphists) and Dominic Goodall, it yielded new understanding of how

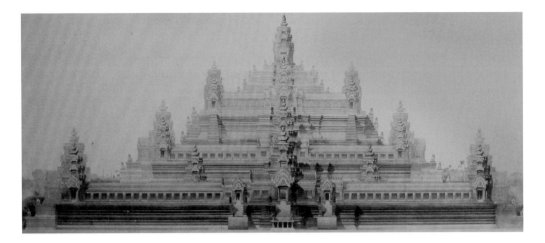

Lucien Fournereau published this not entirely accurate rendering of the Baphuon's original form in the 1890 book that he co-authored, *Les Ruines d'Angkor*.

Reconstruction work on the Baphuon, delayed for decades by war and political isolation, was finally completed in 2011. (John Burgess)

the Khmer empire collected taxes without having a currency. Among the items that seem to be listed as accepted forms of barter payment: gold nuggets, rhinoceros horns, peacock wing feathers, boar skins, camphor, crossbows and arrows, parasols, garments, pine resin, ginger, and rice.

* * * * * *

With the restart of archaeology came a parallel resumption of reconstruction. Conservation teams returning in the '90s faced a big question: what to do about the 300,000 blocks? These were the sandstone and laterite elements of the disassembled Baphuon, the eleventh-century pyramid temple. They remained where cranes and labourers had placed them in the 1960s, in rows near the temple's exposed inner core, becoming pieces to a puzzle with no known solution. Records that Groslier's team had carefully kept during the temple's disassembly to show what went where had vanished in 1975 in Phnom Penh, where they'd been taken for supposed safe-keeping. In the subsequent years of neglect, vegetation had spring up to cover the stones. But experts examining them in the '90s were happy to find that they had been little harmed by the elements or art thieves.

At this point, the EFEO stepped forward. It would be a point of honour to finish a job that the institute had begun. The French government would provide funding. Put in charge of the project was a thirty-year-old architect called Pascal Royère. Such was the depth of interest in bringing the Baphuon back to life, that Norodom Sihanouk, who had reassumed the throne of Cambodia, came to Angkor in 1995 for a ceremony officially restarting the work.

Royère and his team weren't working entirely from scratch. French engineer Jacques Dumarçay, who had supervised the 1960s work (and done his own writing about Angkor hydraulics), emerged from retirement to offer help and his powers of memory. So did about thirty Cambodians who had worked on the original project. Careful examination of close to a 1,000 technical photographs of the temple in pre-war days helped establish which stones had already gone missing at the time of disassembly and which were awaiting identification among the storage rows. A final boost came from the aesthetic inclinations of the ancient architects themselves: they had covered virtually every exposed surface of the Baphuon with bas-reliefs and carved ornamentation, which made it easier to pair up adjacent stones.

Blocks were winched back into place one after the other,

236

By the 2000s, French reconstruction work at the West Mebon was showing its age, as with this leaning section of its east wall. The wall was dismantled as part of a complete restoration of the temple.
(John Burgess)

Old-fashioned hammers have been important tools in rebuilding the West Mebon, where replacements were made on site for stones that were damaged or missing.
(John Burgess)

hiding modern concrete foundations but not touching them and their potentially corrosive chemicals. As another safeguard for the future, Royère installed something the original architects had overlooked, a drainage system to move rainwater quickly off the structure. Gradually the great pyramid began taking form again. Along the way, Royère was gaining new understanding of the temple's long and complex history of modification, in which it had been converted from Hinduism to the successor faith, with an enormous reclining Buddha built across its west side from repurposed stones. Work finally wrapped up in 2011. There was royal attention again, this time from Sihanouk's son and successor, King Sihamoni, who came to Angkor for rites of completion.

Given Angkor's size, there is always a new project to turn to. Royère took charge of restoration work at the West Mebon, the island temple at the centre of the eight kilometre-long West Baray. The Mebon was originally a square structure with twelve towers, enclosing a watery courtyard with a platform at its middle. On that platform had reclined the large bronze Vishnu statue that was found in 1936. Statue, temple, and *baray* together made up what was perhaps the Khmers' largest and most spiritually compelling evocation of Vishnu a-slumber in the Ocean of Creation. Maurice Glaize had rebuilt the temple's eastern wall in the 1940s; it was now leaning, and the rest was barely recognizable. Stones had collapsed into the *baray* or were carried off by local people for use elsewhere. Some became foundation stones in modern-era Buddhist temples (a common practice, in the belief that the stones would impart special sanctity to a new place of worship). Others became property markers on parts of the *baray* bed that were exposed in dry season.

In 2012, Royère began a full reconstruction. Sadly he was not able to finish the job. He succumbed to cancer in 2014 at the age of forty-eight, after having worked virtually his entire career in Cambodia. He is remembered today as one of the great figures of Angkor conservation. A memorial stone to him in Angkor Thom, a new honouring there of a fallen French devotee, notes that he devoted 'eighteen years of his life to transforming a ruin into a prestigious temple.'

In 2017, the island was a busy work site, employing technology both modern (diesel-powered cranes) and ancient (hammers and chisels). About 125 people were carrying out work costing about $700,000 per year. Directing the work on one morning that year was a French architect called Simon Leuckx, who in addition to ancient building techniques took a deep interest in the spiritual universe that the West Mebon occupied.

Steps leading from the eastern wall down into the central area were mostly back in place, now well anchored. Roughly ninety percent of their original elements had survived. Work was underway on the northern steps, sheltered from sun and rain by blue plastic sheeting. A pump was running continuously to drain water from the central area into the baray.

Reconstruction of this type turns up artifacts that would otherwise remain hidden. At the West Mebon, probably the most interesting are what appear to be fragments of a large Shiva *linga*. Leuckx believes it measured about a metre in diameter by five to ten metres tall and was encased in metal. Evidence suggests it stood on the temple's central platform (there is a large circular hole there) and was tall enough to be visible from outside the temple. But it was later supplanted by the bronze Vishnu. All told, reconstruction workers collected about five thousand kilograms of these fragments from scattered spots around the courtyard structures, including between and under the stones of the steps. Leuckx concludes there was a deliberate, methodical destruction of the *linga*. Was it done to destroy Shiva's power in this location, or, just the opposite, to distribute it all over the temple?

In 2018, EFEO's funding for the West Mebon project ran out and work was suspended. The Apsara Authority made funds available from its own budget and resumed the job.

Restoration work proceeded in 2012 at Ta Keo temple. Photo by De Visu/ Shutterstock.com.

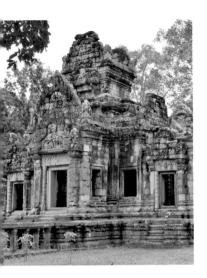

The temple Chau Say Tevoda was rebuilt by a Chinese-led team. Photo by Gonzalo Buzonni / Shutterstock.com.

In the meantime, reconstruction work had transformed many other monuments. Often national teams (whether from governments or non-profits) were assigned specific monuments – the Americans at Phnom Bakheng, for instance. Other national teams worked on specific elements rather than whole monuments. The German Apsara Conservation project, for instance, focused on safeguarding the many bas-relief deities at Angkor Wat and other temples. National teams tend to do their work based on standard practices at home, leading sometimes to disagreements and debates, but usually good-natured resolution. Cambodians are officially in charge of all work at Angkor, but overall, foreign conservationists work with a freedom of action that they enjoy in few other countries.

One country whose presence is growing is China. Chinese teams rebuilt the Chau Say Tevoda temple, then began a restoration of the much larger Ta Keo, a thousand-year-old temple that for unknown reasons never got its decorative stonework. Plans call for Chinese-funded work to begin at the royal palace compound in Angkor Thom. These projects reflect China's ever-closer relations with Cambodia in politics and economy; China is the place where the money comes from these days.

At set dates on the calendar, Angkor specialists sit down together in meetings of the International Coordinating Committee, the group that UNESCO created in 1993. The gatherings are now huge. Archaeologists put on long-neglected neckties to rub shoulders with cabinet ministers and diplomats who fly in from Phnom Penh. Local journalists come to report. Laptops, smart phones, and the earpieces of simultaneous translation devices are much in evidence.

At a meeting in 2017, attended by close to 400 people, the committee heard reports on projects to refurbish Angkor Wat's western causeway, restore the water system at Chau Srei Vibol, a rarely visited temple about fifteen kilometres east of Angkor Wat, and improve traffic patterns on Angkor roads. It was told that some small artifacts had been found at Phnom Bakheng, that researchers had followed 106 groups of people visiting Angkor Wat to find exactly where they went and by what routes (among the conclusions: gravel pathways aren't optimal, because pebbles get tracked into the temple). A German expert explained the special challenges of preserving ancient brick structures. Other presenters brought the group up-to-date on plans to rope off a ledge where people often sit, to upgrade an Angkor website, and to create a digital archive of inscriptions.

Differences within the international camp occasionally came to the surface. Considerable time went toward discussing an Italian project that had replaced stones edging Angkor Wat's west moat. By some accounts, the stones had quickly become unstable, with gaps opening between them. 'I am not criticizing the Italian way,' said a Japanese expert, who went on to propose that the work be redone with new technologies.

* * * * *

Through all of the research of the last thirty years, there wasn't much motion forward on answering the question of how the Hindu faith and culture came to Southeast Asia. No inscriptions recounting major migration (or lack of it) have surfaced, certainly no tell-tale swords dropped on the battlefield by those mythical Brahmin warriors.

But world archaeology has acquired in recent years a technology that could eventually give some answers, DNA analysis. It has been used to examine such fundamental questions of pre-history as who settled the South Pacific islands and when. In Cambodia, 'archaeogenetics' might examine how and whether the genetic make-up of modern citizens matches up with that of people in southern India, particularly members of the Brahman class there. Are there enough Indian markers in the DNA of men and women in the communities around Angkor to suggest a sizeable migration from India in the first millennium? Or perhaps just enough to suggest that just a few priests picked up and moved, intermarrying with the royalty of early Cambodian mini-states?

In the meantime, the trove of academic research about life in Angkor continues to grow. And digital technology is allowing us to *see* that life. A team at Australia's Monash University led by Senior Lecturer Thomas Chandler has created a remarkable collection of 3D computer animations depicting life in the empire's golden age. The clips synthesize the Bayon bas-reliefs, archaeological excavations, textile analysis, LIDAR surveys, and other disciplines of Angkor study. We see an aristocrat arriving on a palanquin at Angkor Wat, his retainers hustling to keep him shaded by the parasols they are bearing. In a village, two priests stroll past a shrine. A fly-over of Angkor Wat reveals its grounds to be a vibrant community of people and houses – and its towers covered in gilding. Until the invention of a time machine, these tableaux will give us the best feeling of what it was to be a resident of the old capital.[3]

3   Many of them can be viewed online with a simple search for 'Monash Angkor animation.'

16: Angkor and the Multitudes-2019

Tourists arrive in stellar numbers, bringing jobs for many, wealth for some, and new challenges for the temples' decorum and physical integrity.

If you get out of bed at 4:30 in the morning to see something special, you might expect to be largely alone. Unless the something special is sunrise at Angkor Wat. Early bird tourists arriving at the temple in near darkness find that they are joining a march of the multitudes. Crowds press through the stone entranceways and build up by the ancient pools located off the temple's processional avenue. Trod-upon toes, flashlight glare, and sharp elbows as people jostle for position with cameras and selfie sticks – these are all part of the experience. Yet once the sight begins, once the solar disk edges above the five towers as it has for close to nine centuries, the sight unfailingly dazzles. People fall silent, or let out oohs and ahhs. It is truly a moment to savour – and share. Within minutes, photographs start popping up all over the world on Facebook and Instagram, relayed by a nearby mobile phone tower disguised to look like a tree. Twenty-four hours later, the process starts up again, with a whole new crowd.

The reopening of the 1990s set in motion the realization of the old dreams of tourism promoters: Angkor as one of the world's most popular travel destinations. Close to two million foreigners visit each year—Chinese office workers, Israeli backpackers, German factory hands, Japanese retirees, American honeymooners. Occasionally there's a VIP mixed in. In 2015, visitors were startled to see American First Lady Michelle Obama taking in Angkor Wat. In 2019, South Korean President Moon Jae-in gave politician-style handshakes through one of the temple's windows to delighted tourists who'd recognized him.

About forty percent of the foreign visitors are Chinese, making them the biggest nationality group by far. That rank is due in part to long-term tourism cooperation between the two countries, with a goal of more than doubling the Chinese number alone to two million. More Chinese signs, more non-

Opposite page: Tourists throng the processional avenue of Angkor Wat. Photo by Vassamon Anansukkasem/ Shutterstock.com.

American First Lady Michelle Obama takes in Angkor Wat with a guide in 2015. Official White House Photo by Amanda Lucidon.

stop flights to Siem Reap, more Chinese-speaking guides are among the steps taken to bump the figures upward.

The airport that the French opened outside Siem Reap in 1932, having expanded and re-expanded repeatedly over the years, seems to be finally nearing its end as the prime gateway to Angkor. UNESCO has long warned that aircraft noise undermines spiritual decorum at Angkor and could even damage the temples' stones. But what seems finally to have turned idea into actual project is the reality that the existing airport is too small for the hoped-for numbers of arrivals in the years ahead. At a site about forty-five kilometres southeast of Siem Reap town, construction teams are at work on a seven-hundred hectare facility tentatively called Siem Reap New International Airport. On completion, planned for 2023, it will be the largest airport in Cambodia, ultimately able to handle ten million travellers annually. To no surprise, Chinese capital and technical expertise are at the heart of the project. The Cambodian government signed an $880-million agreement with the state-owned Yunnan Investment Holdings to build the airport, operate it for fifty-five years, and then transfer it to Cambodian ownership.

The higher tourist numbers seem set to bring yet more development to a town that is already dotted with construction sites. Take a walk and you see cranes lifting building materials, labourers spreading concrete. The streets below are clogged with cars, tour buses, and tuk-tuks, the ubiquitous motorbike-

and-cart combos that function as taxis. Crossing the street safely requires fleetness of foot and good timing.

Siem Reap offers all manner of diversions for people returning from sightseeing at the temples. There is the Angkor National Museum, which despite its name is privately owned, and whose numerous displays include pieces from the nearby conservation compound. For a sampling of the history and horrors of Cambodia's quarter century of conflict, there are a landmine museum and a war museum. Classical dance can be enjoyed at any number of stages or hotels around town. And for a plain old good time, there is the Cambodian Circus Show, which combines feats of acrobatic daring with tales and costumes from the Cambodian tradition and modern era. It seems always to be full – tickets are hard to come by.

Food in Siem Reap ranges from high-end French cuisine to cut papaya on the street to mass-produced Chinese buffet. A thriving artisanal coffee scene has taken root. Beer and things stronger can be had in countless joints along the loud and garishly lit Pub Street. Also available are massages, pedicures by nibbling fish, and souvenir tee-shirts sold in a busy night market.

When it is time to turn in, tourists can retire to a top-rated suite at the Amansara resort – if they're good for $2,100 a night (plus fees and taxes). With that price they also get such

Pub Street in Siem Reap includes countless restaurants, bars, and souvenir shops for the diversion of Angkor tourists. Photo by Baiterek Media/Shutterstock.com.

Some Siem Reap artisans have found work as makers of religious images for sale to visitors. Photo by posztos/Shutterstock.com.

package pluses as a meditation walk led by a monk or a class in Khmer incense. If all they have is $5, they can bunk down in a hostel room shared with fellow budget travellers and prowling mosquitoes.

Those who don't care for the bustle can 'glamp' in a fancy tent set up among rice fields outside town or check into an eco-lodge that pledges to respect the environment. They can ride oxcarts little different from those of the ancients or steer all-terrain vehicles down trails crossing plots that the ancient Khmers farmed. For those wanting a view of Angkor from above, the choices include helium balloon, hot-air balloon, ultra-light aircraft, and helicopter—and the Angkor Eye. This eighty five metre-tall ferris wheel, taking tourists aloft in forty-eight air-conditioned cabins, completes a rotation every eighteen minutes, but giving more a look at Siem Reap town than the big temples, which stand several kilometres away.

Bit by bit, the scale of development has been straining Siem Reap's supply of water. Each of the town's countless swimming pools, fountains, ornamental lawns, fish tanks, and hotel room showers needs water, some of it drawn from wells sunk legally or otherwise into the local water table. Civil engineers worry about a long-term threat to the temples themselves, that a slowly declining water table might undermine their foundations and make them shift and subside. One of the potential solutions to this problem, and the related challenge of flooding: restore as best possible the hydraulic system that the ancients built. Archaeologists have concluded, after all, that at the empire's zenith the system had assured that water was never in too large or too small a supply. Helping water flow smoothly down from the Kulen hills and out to the Tonle Sap would help control flooding and assure the replenishment of the water table.

* * * * *

Many thousands of Cambodians find gainful employment and economic advancement providing the many tourist services. Workplaces train local people as chefs, flower-arrangers, accountants, hotel managers, wood carvers, swimming pool cleaners. For a price, additional skills and qualifications can be obtained at commercial schools that have popped up in many places around town. Tourism is bringing people hope for financial stability, education, and general advancement, following their country's decades of conflict and isolation. The noise and diesel fumes that can appal foreign visitors are to many Siem Reap residents welcome signs of peace and prosperity. But sometimes they too can feel that environmental strain has gone too far, and they act with public spiritedness. For instance, volunteer groups turn out to clear up plastic bags and other litter along the town's streets and river.

As its tourism-based economy has grown, Siem Reap has turned into a sort of United Nations of languages, in the form of the cadre of official tour guides, recognizable by their blue and yellow uniforms. These men, and occasionally women, hit the books to qualify in foreign languages – English, French, Chinese, Japanese, Thai, Korean, Vietnamese, Portuguese, and more – so as to take around tourists who speak those languages. Guides also study deeply into Khmer heritage. They gather periodically to hear speakers who further advance their appreciation of what their forebears accomplished. At the temples, guides go about their jobs with discernible pride, tasked with introducing the great tradition to one more group of people from far away.

On days off, the architectural creations of the forebears serve as recreation spots for their present-day descendants. Moat-side picnics and family gatherings on temple lawns are a common sight. (One privilege accorded to Cambodian citizens is no-charge entry to the heritage zone.) At wet season, with the West Baray faithfully again filling up with water a thousand years after its construction, Siem Reap residents flock to make-shift beaches on its banks. Mothers and fathers swim, children splash about on tire-tube floats. Vendors sell snacks and soft drinks, hammocks rock the weary to sleep. Local farmers, meanwhile, find benefit from the baray's original practical purpose: a spillway built in modern times on its southern levee supplies water to fields downstream.

But despite the tourism boom, only a few of Siem Reap's residents do truly well economically. Standards of living, though headed upward, remain low by international measures. The few well-to-do often live in walled-off villas on side streets. More typical are the wooden or rough concrete houses of people who are struggling to advance themselves.

Around the world, tourism generates foreign exchange that pays wages, as it does for the many thousands of people in the trade in Siem Reap. But part of the funds can also be invested to upgrade education, public health, and civil infrastructure. In Siem Reap, long-term improvements like those have been stubbornly slow in materializing. Many of the town's sidewalks remain cracked and broken, its state schools sadly under-funded and equipped. Visitors going a few kilometres beyond its limits can easily think the war ended just yesterday. Many

246

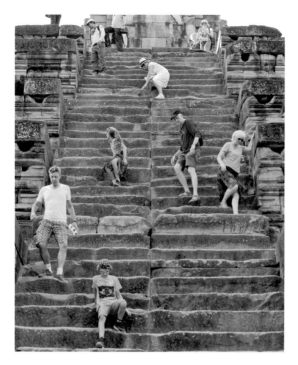

Tourists negotiate a very steep stairway at Ta Keo temple, stepping on the original stone. Photo by puyalroyo/Shutterstock.com.

people are still living in primitive thatch houses. Motor vehicles raise clouds of dust because generally it's just the main roads that are paved.

Old tensions smoulder on between authorities and people for whom Angkor is not a heritage zone but home. House construction is an issue that won't go away. The rules are complex, but in general they allow people to keep old houses and improve them in certain ways, but not to build new ones on new sites, unless they have permits. During election campaigns, officials can be unusually willing to issue permits, with an apparent objective of harvesting votes. Just before the local elections of June 2017, close to five hundred new houses appeared almost overnight in restricted parts of the heritage zone. The Apsara Authority, with the concurrence of UNESCO, demanded they be demolished. Local people mounted protests, at one point blocking the road linking the airport and Angkor Wat. Some displayed letters from local officials that they argued gave them permission. But police mobilized in force, and before long bulldozers were flattening brand-new houses.

International reconstruction efforts that began with the UN mission in the 1990s continue in Siem Reap, to the point that it can seem that every street has a non-profit with a focus on education, nutrition, or health. One of the most successful is the Kantha Bopha hospital for children. It was founded by the late Swiss physician and musician Beat Richner, who for years applied the healing arts there. On weekends, he charmed patients and tourists alike with professional-grade recitals on his cello. Tourists in the audience were asked to make a contribution to the hospital – their choice of cash or blood.

Ideally, foreign aid groups nurture skills and institutions, then turn things over to local people and pull out. But in Cambodia, poverty, corruption, and the lingering effects of the Khmer Rouge's near total eradication of the educated class have kept many international organisations operating with no end in sight. And Siem Reap's aid world has at times been tainted by corruption of its own. In what amounted to orphanage tourism, foreigners were lured to visit and

financially support institutions whose children weren't parent-
less at all, but human props in a cynical game of deception.

* * * * *

Out at the temples, the human congestion at an Angkor Wat
sunrise is nothing unusual. The other major monuments are
heavily trafficked as well. Corridors whose floor stones felt just
a smattering of bare feet in ancient times are crossed daily
by many thousands of pairs of shod feet. Apsara Authority
employees labour on in valiant efforts to protect the temples.
They have installed wooden steps on many staircases to reduce
wear on original stone steps, and have made some precarious
places off limits. But there remain a great many spots where
tourists can legally tread, a boon for them and their photos,
but sometimes not for the integrity and decorum of the
monuments.

Fortunately, a design decision by the original architects
of Angkor Thom restrains the numbers inside the old city:
The only ways in and out are its five gates, which were built
wide enough for royal elephants and their riders, but not the
lumbering air-conditioned coaches that many tour companies
operate. As a result, some tourists never see the Bayon, the
Baphuon, and the other monuments inside Angkor Thom.

Here and there, modern authorities have applied social
engineering to calm the human flow. Phnom Bakheng temple,
the favoured hilltop spot for viewing Angkor Wat at sunset, is
restricted to three hundred people at a time. But initiatives like
that can have scant effect on an overall sensation of human

Cameras and phones in hand,
tourists crowd the courtyard of an
Angkor temple. Photo by rodcoffee/
Shutterstock.com.

inundation at many places. Guides develop work-arounds for clients who want a taste of the old solitude. One is to enter Angkor Wat from the back or wait until midday, when bus groups retreat to Siem Reap to have lunch and avoid the worst heat of the day. Phnom Bakheng, so busy at dusk, can be all but deserted at noon. Plus there are the numerous lesser-known temples to be found inside the heritage zone or a few kilometres beyond it. Visitors unconcerned with their small scale (and they are small only by the standards of the ancient Khmers) can have them more or less to themselves at basically any time of day.

* * * * *

When visiting the Angkor monuments, many tourists show due respect. They realize they are privileged to be experiencing one of humankind's greatest creations. They read up before they come. They dress modestly and keep their voices down. They listen intently to their guides. Others jump queues, shout, wear the skimpiest of clothes, and climb to precarious heights. A few seem determined to set new records of bad holiday behaviour. In 2015, two foreign women were reportedly arrested and accused of making nude photos of themselves in an Angkor temple and posting them online. They escaped jail time but were deported.

Incidents like that helped bring on an official code of

Good News on Art Theft

Through diplomacy, legal action, and public shaming, Cambodia has reclaimed some of the art treasures that left the country under murky circumstances.

Among the most spectacular returns were large tenth century statues that had vanished from Koh Ker and come to be in major foreign museums. In 2013, the Metropolitan Museum of Art in New York returned two that it had displayed as 'Kneeling Attendant'. In explanation, the museum said it had recently obtained ownership information that it lacked when the pieces were acquired. In 2014, the Norton Simon Museum in Pasadena, California sent back a large piece it had called 'Temple Wrestler'. The museum said it had properly acquired the statue from a reputable art dealer in New York in 1976, but had decided to give it back to Cambodia as a gesture of friendship. It was reunited there with its feet, which the thieves had left behind.

In 2019, a prominent collector and dealer living in Bangkok was indicted by U.S. authorities in connection with the traffic in Khmer antiquities, including items from Koh Ker. Prosecutors alleged that Douglas Latchford, a dual British and Thai citizen, had over the course of years provided foreign auction houses with looted artefacts and false information on provenance. He died in 2020 with the case unresolved.

In the meantime, the supply of stolen antiquities had been squeezed hard. The wholesale pillaging of major monuments had stopped. Thieves continued to try their luck at small sites in remote areas of the countryside, probing for buried treasure with hastily dug holes. It was unlikely they would find anything of market value, but success seems to come often enough to keep them trying. A rare glimpse of this largely invisible trade came in February 2020, when Cambodian authorities presented to the media five men who they said had been arrested for using metal detectors to hunt for ancient items at Prasat Khna, a small temple from the early Angkor period in Preah Vihear province.

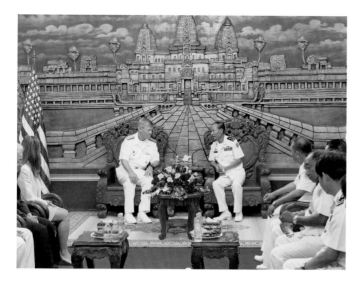

Angkor images remain a fixture of pride in offices of the Cambodian government. Here Cambodian Navy Vice Admiral Ouk Seyha receives U.S. Navy Vice Admiral Robert L. Thomas at Ream Naval Base in 2014. U.S. Navy photo by Lt. Andrew Orchard.

conduct that all tourists are supposed to follow. 'Revealing clothes such as shorts and skirts above the knee and showing bare shoulders are prohibited in sacred places,' it declares. Other acts that were officially banned: touching carvings, smoking, talking loudly, and photographing monks without their permission. And buying things from children who should be in school.

The message is laid out in a clever video that the Apsara Authority commissioned depicting an ancient prince arriving in the present day atop an elephant and reacting with shock at the behaviour of tourists around him. The video closes with a slogan: 'It's our heritage now. Let's respect Angkor together.'

Still, some people have begun to wonder if the issue is not bad tourists but too many tourists. A few travel websites began labelling Angkor as a place to avoid. 'The literal wear and tear brought on to the 900-year-old temples [by their huge popularity] is having damaging effects on its foundations and structural integrity,' Fodor's said, listing Angkor among 'thirteen places to reconsider in the year ahead.' In raw numbers, Angkor with its two million-plus foreign visitors a year remains far below some of the world's hottest tourist spots. Paris, for instance, is said to draw twenty million in a typical a year, Singapore fifteen million. Still, to anyone caught in one of its many bottlenecks – the line to buy a heritage zone pass, the corridors of the Bayon bas-reliefs, and those coveted sunrise-viewing spots at Angkor Wat – Angkor can *feel* like it's at the top of the list.

* * * * *

Foreigners spend a few days at Angkor and sample its magic. Yet for most Cambodians, and not just the people who live there, the stay lasts a lifetime, if you consider the place that the temples occupy in the national psyche. No matter how tough life might be, no matter how much richer neighbouring countries become, Cambodians can take comfort in knowing that their forebears built a place of glory unrivalled in history, and that maybe, maybe, today's generation will achieve something similar. Angkor remains on the country's flag, banknotes, and postage stamps – no government would want it any different. Politicians continue to come to the old capital in pilgrimage to signal that they understand the place it holds in the Cambodian heart. In 2013, opposition leaders Sam Rainsy and Kem Sokha staged a large rally at Angkor Wat days before a national election. In 2017, Prime Minister Hun Sen led two days of ceremonies there intended to underline his party's claim to be the key to stability and prosperity in the long-troubled country.

Though most studies of tourism focus on foreigners and the hard currency they bring, there is also a huge flow of Cambodians who live elsewhere in the country but are eager to see the things they've learned about since childhood. Countless homes around Cambodia have family photos with temple towers in the background. Others have wedding pictures – Angkor has become a favourite place for tying the knot. As Ang Choulean once told a documentary film interviewer, 'It can be a little bit like Muslim people who go to Mecca. You wish that at least once in your life you have to see Angkor Wat.' For many Cambodians, it is much more often than once.

And of course Angkor retains its central place in Cambodian spiritual life. In the western entrance complex of Angkor Wat, there stands the large, four-armed stone image of the god Vishnu. But it is not only Vishnu. It is Ta Reach, prime deity of the temple, possessed of such power that it is said that a bird that dares fly overhead may die and fall from the sky. It was Ta Reach who was deemed to offer protection during the war. Today foreign tourists often walk past the

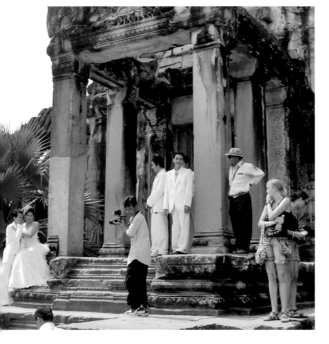

Foreign tourists and a guide look on as a Cambodian wedding party poses at Angkor Wat. (John Burgess)

great image unknowing, but Cambodians take care to stop to light incense sticks and kneel in prayer. On festival days, they bring offerings of music, rice wine, food, and the cooked heads of pigs. Lesser, but still powerful, deities are understood to preside at Angkor Wat's three other gates.

Buddhist monks gather in 2016 for prayer on Angkor Wat's second tier. Photo by Darren Wilch.

Each year, at the Visakha Bucha festival, which commemorates the three major events in the life of the Buddha – his birth, his enlightenment, his death – more than a thousand monks and nuns gather at Angkor Wat for a spectacular rite of meditation by candlelight. Closed off to tourists, the great temple regains, however briefly, the identity that its builders intended, supreme place of worship. In the grounds in front of the temple, monks sit in rows in meditation, each with a candle and mat. Their robes become indistinguishable from the orange flicker of their candles' flames. Up inside the temple, other monks sit around its stone pools as they strive to focus their practice and improve their chances, ultimately, of attaining the enlightenment that the Buddha achieved.

With the festival completed, business as usual resumes. Angkor Wat reopens in its other identity – secular symbol of the Cambodian nation, destination of mass holiday travel. At dawn, another throng of tourists arrives, intent on catching the ascent of the sun over the five towers.

POSTSCRIPT

Angkor, tranquil again.

When I began work on this book, it seemed a sure bet that the final pages would mention foreign tourist arrivals reaching some new record high. The world had not yet heard of COVID-19. When it struck in early 2020, the impact on the old capital was quick and dramatic. China, first to face the virus, began shutting off the largest flow of visitors. International travel in general contracted. Cambodia imposed inward restrictions, blocking entry by people from various COVID flare-up countries. Within weeks it became essentially impossible to reach Angkor from abroad. Statistics reported by Angkor Enterprise, the temples' gatekeeper, told the tale: In April 2019, 185,403 entry passes were sold. In April 2020 the figure was 654.

People began to say that history had repeated itself – Angkor had again been abandoned. Certainly there was some resemblance to what Father Bouillevaux and Henri Mouhot had encountered a century and a half earlier. Mammoth stone temples lying silent in the forest, eliciting an ancient civilisation's glories. But, then as in 2020, Angkor hadn't really been abandoned. In between the temples were communities of people for whom the old Khmer capital was simply home. They tended their gardens, they herded their buffaloes. In the monasteries of Angkor Wat, monks chanted prayers as before, continuing the search for enlightenment. And, like pilgrims in centuries earlier, Cambodians came from around the kingdom to see the great stone creations that embody Khmer civilization. It could almost feel like Angkor was back in the hands of its original owners.

The handful of foreigners who did come, purchasers of those 654 passes, were mostly long-term residents of Cambodia. Many were eager to experience Angkor in a way that had been impossible for decades. They could now stroll the corridors accompanied by only the sound of their own footfalls on stone. Viewing the sun rise over Angkor Wat could again be an occasion for solitude.

Many of those foreigners felt misgivings that their mystical encounters were coming at the expense of economic disaster a few kilometres away. In Siem Reap, restaurants, souvenir shops, and hotels closed and laid off staff by the thousands. Pub

Opposite page: Angkor Wat in April 2020. Photo by Nick Sells.

Street became a row of shuttered shophouses. Barriers blocked entry to the Grand Hotel's front parking lot, signalling that until further notice no one would be checking in. Education largely stopped as schools closed in anti-virus precautions. All over Siem Reap, dreams of secure incomes and better futures were snuffed out. Yet there were few signs of panic or despair. Cambodia's modern history has had more bad times than good. People have learned the skills and frames of mind necessary to stand up to adversity. And there was an important saving grace: Siem Reap and Cambodia as a whole were largely escaping the biological ravages of the virus. As of June 2020, the government had reported just one hundred twenty-six cases of COVID-19 for the entire country and not a single death.

As it happened, Angkor had had a sort of preview in 2019. In a process so gradual that people barely noticed at first, foreign tourist numbers began to dip. Month after month, arrivals were lower than in that month the year before. By the end of 2019, it had added up to a fifteen percent drop for the year as a whole. It was largely attributed to Chinese groups being channelled elsewhere by tour companies, notably to Sihanoukville, the seaside town where Chinese investment had erected a plenitude of high-rise hotels and casinos. Westerners being frightened off by reports of over-crowding may also have lowered the numbers. The decline prompted alarm in Siem Reap. There was hope that Angkor Eye, the enormous ferris wheel, and other initiatives would give tourists new reasons to come and nudge the numbers up. But within a few months, with the town idled by COVID precautions, steps like those seemed hardly relevant.

Once again, Angkor's modern history had veered off in a direction that no one saw coming.

Three months into the restrictions, a tentative loosening was tried. Siem Reap began coming back to life, as shops and restaurants reopened, albeit without foreign patrons. It remained unclear how long would pass before all controls came off and people would again be free to fly in from abroad.

Under a business-as-usual recovery scenario, hotels, restaurants, and tour companies would resume operating as before as clients materialized. The monthly counts would climb back to pre-virus levels, however long that might take, and keep going. Sunrise at Angkor Wat would again draw crowds. Cambodia would do all it could to drive the rise, feeling pressure to make up for time lost to the 2020 cratering of its economy. In a country short on export industries that can compete globally, Angkor would remain one of the few things that could bring in foreign exchange.

But under another scenario, perhaps, the hiatus could serve as a chance to rethink the temples' future. Tourists would return, but to a new sort of Angkor. One in which the monuments were more assertively protected, in ways that would let them function as a sustainable economic driver for improving the lives of Cambodia's people at large. For physical preservation, many steps might be considered, such as covering bas-reliefs with transparent screens, ending foot traffic on more stairways and corridors, and metering the number of people who can enter a temple at one time. Encouraging visits to lesser-known temples – and the myriad natural and cultural attractions beyond Angkor – could help smooth out tourist flows and relieve jams. Steps like these could be accomplished fairly easily, at low cost. The more difficult challenge would be in directing a larger share of Angkor's earnings to development projects and the household budgets of the millions of Cambodians who get by with so little. Coming up with the right mix of initiatives would not be easy, whether from a planning or political point of view, but Cambodia has taken on many arduous tasks in its recent history. The COVID-19 pause could give it time to consider the many different paths that might be possible.

While the people of Siem Reap and Angkor awaited whatever was coming next, some things continued as before, including conservation and archaeology. In April 2020 at the Srah Srang reservoir, a team from the Apsara Authority began reconstructing a small temple that had stood surrounded by water at is centre. Over the centuries, it had tumbled down to the point that many people didn't know it was there – its fallen stones showed only when the reservoir dropped to dry-season lows. Now workers built dikes around the temple, drained out the water, then got to work sorting out the stones. Soon there was an exciting buried discovery: a meter-long stone sculpture of a turtle, possibly Kurma, one of the avatars of the god Vishnu. With it were holy artefacts – two metal tridents and the carved head of a Naga. All had been placed there to assure heaven's blessing on the temple and the Khmer people in general.

One more piece of the Angkor puzzle had been solved.

ACKNOWLEDGEMENTS & REFERENCES

The research for this book stretched out over three years, conducted in Cambodia, Thailand, France, and the United States, where I live. I walked through the doors of a good many libraries and archives, and spent a good many hours doing that remotely through the computer screen on my desk. Quite a few obscure journals and books from the nineteenth and early twentieth centuries that help fill out the Angkor story have made their way to the Internet in full text, searchable form.

I'm indebted to Michelle Vachon in Phnom Penh, Jean Coyner in Paris, and Osamu Aridome in Kanoya City, Japan for ferreting out documents and images that otherwise I would have lacked. Thanks go to my wife Karen, for helping me in research and writing and putting up with my long absences. Special help came from Elizabeth Becker, Alison Kyra Carter, Kent Davis, Ricardo J. Elia, Sadao Fujihara, Chas Gerretsen, Don Guiney, Christine Hawixbrock, Stephen Heder, Julio Jeldres, Pierre Le Roux, Simon Leuckx, Hervé Manac'h, Joel Montague, Magali Morel, Roland Neveu, Isabelle Poujol, Michelle Stevens, Lynda Trouvé, Minja Yang, and Ronnie Yimsut.

Any and all mistakes of fact or analysis in this book are of course my own responsibility entirely.

Chapter 1

The account of Father Bouillevaux's 1850 visit to Angkor is drawn from two books that he published in later years, *Voyage dans l'Indo-Chine* and *L'Annam et le Cambodge: Voyages et Notices Historiques*, as well as writing about him in *Mémoires de la Société académique indochinoise de France*. *The Journal of the Royal Geographical Society* describes a British visit around 1859.

Mouhot's two weeks at Angkor in 1860 were first documented in the now-famous 1863 article in *Le Tour du Monde*, 'Voyage dans les Royaumes de Siam, Cambodge, de Laos et Autres Parties Centrales de l'Indo-Chine' and subsequent book versions drawing on the same material. Bernard-Philippe Groslier gives an account of earlier European visits in his book *Angkor and Cambodia in the Sixteenth Century*. The 1926 exchange between Félicien Challaye and Gosselin Quertier can be found in 1926 editions of the newspaper *L'Oeuvre*. John Thomson's time in Angkor is described in *Siam: Through the Lens of John Thomson 1865-66*. The Mekong Commission's work is documented in *River Road to China* by Milton Osborne. In addition, commission members including Charles Garnier left personal accounts.

Chapter 2

The prime source for this chapter is Delaporte's own account, *Voyage au Cambodge*. Other material comes from the biography *Louis Delaporte, Explorateur, ses missions aux ruines khmères* by René de Beauvais. Also useful was writings on the mission by the scholars Michael S. Falser and Julie Philippe. Delaporte's report to the French government can be found in two 1874 editions of the *Journal Officiel de la République Française*. Published in connection with a 2013-2014 exhibit in Paris, *Angkor: Naissance d'un Mythe, Louis Delaporte et le Cambodge* contains a wealth of information on the man and his work. The chapter also draws on *Cambodge et Siam: Voyage et Séjour aux Ruines des Monuments Kmers*, by August Filoz, who immediately followed Delaporte's team at Angkor.

Chapter 3

The initial founding of the Angkor Archaeological Park is recounted based on material in the Bulletin of the *École française d'extrême-orient (EFEO)* and in EFEO's massive three-volume *Le Temple d'Angkor Wat*. Langdon Warner's visit is recorded in a report he filed to Charles Lang Freer, founder of the Freer Gallery of Art in Washington, DC. Governor General Antony Klobukowski's report on the 1909 festivities at Angkor is found in the EFEO archive in Paris. George Groslier's work in Cambodia is described in *Cambodian Dancers: Ancient & Modern*, a 2011 English translation of Groslier's 1913 work of that name. Penny Edwards' book *Cambodge: The Cultivation of a Nation, 1860-1945* contains extensive analysis and insights on the *mission civilisatrice*. Garnier's views on Khmer art are found in his account of the Mekong commission, while Paul Claudel's are in his diary. *Angkor: Naissance d'un Mythe, Louis Delaporte et le Cambodge* was very useful in recounting the spread of Khmer art in France in the late nineteenth and early twentieth centuries.

Chapter 4

The account of Étienne Aymonier's work with inscriptions is distilled from my earlier book, *Stories in Stone: The Sdok Kok Thom Inscription and the Enigma of Khmer History*. Aymonier's letter about the inscription was viewed at the Paris archive of the *Société Asiatique*. Various articles by and about Victor Goloubew can be found in the EFEO Bulletin. Sappho Marchal's book, published in translation as *Khmer Costumes and Ornaments of the Devatas of Angkor Wat*, gives an understanding of how bas reliefs reveal new things about Khmer civilisation. Zhou Daguan's account of Angkor has been translated by Peter Harris as *A Record of Cambodia: The Land and Its People*. The account of early aerial photography draws on articles in the EFEO Bulletin and a magazine of colonial times, *Indochine Hebdomadaire Illustré*.

The discussion of other early scholarly works arises from Aymonier's *Le Cambodge* and other books and journal articles. Outlines of pseudo-scientific analysis of Angkor's rise and fall can be found in many non-academic works by early western visitors.

Chapter 5

The account of Charles Carpeaux's work at Angkor is taken from a book of his letters, diary, and photos that his mother published after his death, *Les Ruines d'Angkor, de Duong-Duong et de My-Son (Cambodge et Annam)*, as well as an elaborate photo book that the French government brought out in 1913, *Le Bayon d'Angkor Thom, Bas-Reliefs*. Parmentier's assessment of archaeological work at Angkor was published in the EFEO Bulletin. The account of the discovery of the Vishnu statue at the West Mebon is taken from Jean Laur's *Angkor: An Illustrated Guide to the Monuments*. The account of Henri Marchal's reconstruction of Banteay Srei draws on articles by and about him, including one quoted in 'Imagined Pasts: Anastylosis and the Creation of the Thai National Past,' a 2006 article by John Victor Crocker.

Chapter 6

The verse of Oknya Suttantaprija is quoted in Penny Edwards' book *Cambodge: The Cultivation of a Nation, 1860-1945*. The book also contains a detailed account of the murder of Jean Commaille. Commaille's obituary in the EFEO Bulletin was another major source. The full text of the 1949 letter protesting the export of Khmer art work can be found in the EFEO archive, along with various official French letters about it. The account of French sales of Khmer artwork draws on Pierre Singaravélou's book, *L'École française d'Extrême-Orient ou l'institution des marges (1898-1956)*. Disputes within the French community are documented in letters and reports in EFEO's archive. Henri Marchal's unpublished memoir can be found at the French Overseas Territories Archives Department in Aix-en-Provence.

Chapter 7

Therese Yelverton's account of Angkor was published in the American journal *The Overland Monthly*. Pierre Loti described his visit in his book *Un pèlerine d'Angkor*, the Duke of Montpensier in *La ville au bois dormant, de Saïgon à Ang-Kor en automobile*. The account of early tourism and the opening of the Bungalow hotel draws variously on the EFEO Bulletin, documents in the EFEO archive, documents at the National Archive of Cambodia, and articles in colonial newspapers. Helen Churchill Candee published her account, *Angkor the Magnificent*, in 1924. Lucille Sinclair Douglass's life was recounted in a 2006 article in *Alabama Heritage* by Stephen Goldfarb, while Jeanette Reid Healy's time at Angkor is described in her diary. André Malraux's escapade gets a full examination in *André Malraux: The Indochina Adventure* by Walter G. Langlois. Arthur Davison Ficke's account of putting back a stolen piece of sculpture was published in *The North American Review*. Angkor postcards are described based on cards in the author's collection. The opening of flying boat service to Angkor was reported in the French aviation publication *Les Ailes*. The passage describing the sensations of an Angkor Wat landing is from *The opening of Aerial Tourism in Indochina: From Saigon river to Angkor-Vat on a straight wing* by Henry Bontoux. Details of Antoine de Saint-Exupéry's abortive effort to fly to Angkor come from *Saint-Exupéry: A Biography* by Stacy Schiff. Max Ernst's time in Indochina is described in *Ghost Ships: A Surrealist Love Triangle by* Robert McNab. Alfred Messner's work at Angkor is documented in the EFEO archive and in contemporary colonial publications.

Chapter 8

Monthly reports filed to EFEO headquarters in Hanoi by conservator Maurice Glaize were an invaluable source in reconstructing the 1941 war with Thailand affected Siem Reap and Angkor. The account of the talks in Tokyo that ended the war drew on telegrams and affidavits on file at the French National Archive in Paris, as well as French newspaper reports and official statements of the time. An article in *Indochine Hedomadaire Illustré* describes French efforts to retain control of Banteay Srei.

Chapter 9

EFEO conservator Maurice Glaize's monthly reports to Hanoi were a major source for this chapter. The EFEO archive also has extensive material on Victor Goloubew's visit to Japan in 1941, including a transcript of the radio interview that is quoted. *The Melancholy of the Orientalists* by Sadao Fujihara of Ibaraki University describes Japanese actions and interest in Angkor during the war and the exchange of art work by EFEO and Japan's Imperial Museum. Ricardo J. Elia of Boston University kindly provided material from his research into U.S. occupation authorities' investigation of that exchange after the war. *Indochine Hebdomadaire Illustré* published a lengthy article about a visit by Admiral Decoux to Angkor in 1942. Joseph Schilling's account of life in wartime Siem Reap was published in 1999 in the French Roman Catholic newspaper *La Croix*. David Chandler's article *The Kingdom of Kampuchea, March-October 1945: Japanese-sponsored Independence in Cambodia in World War II* provided an account of the late war period. The 1946 attack in Siem Reap by Khmer Issarak guerrillas is described in EFEO documents and the French newspapers *Combat* and *France Libre*.

Chapter 10

The filming of *Lord Jim* at Angkor was reported in *Life* magazine, the *Saturday Evening Post*, and the *Phnom Penh Post*. Various of the late King Norodom Sihanouk's films can be viewed in whole or part at YouTube.com. The account of the dispute over Preah Vihear temple is taken from the author's earlier book, *Temple in the Clouds: Faith and Conflict at Preah Vihear*. Reconstruction work at the Baphuon temple draws on EFEO Bulletin articles and Michelle Vachon's account in *The Cambodia Daily*. The account of Jacqueline Kennedy's visit in 1967 is based on media reports, the oral history of American diplomat Daniel Oliver Newberry, and *Jackie: Beyond the Myth of Camelot* by K.L. Kelleher. The description of Angkor's Air France hotel draws on documents from the Air France Museum in Paris. The post-Sihanouk government's condemning of the kings of Angkor was reported in *The Washington Post*.

Chapter 11

The Gate by François Bizot contains Bizot's account of witnessing the Vietnamese take-over of Angkor. In an interview, Ronnie Yimsut recounted his experiences at wartime Angkor (he also describes them in his book, *Facing the Khmer Rouge: A Cambodian Journey*). Jeff Williams, then of the Associated Press, recounted his experience at Siem Reap by email and in a book that he co-authored with Kurt Volkert, *A Cambodian Odyssey and the Deaths of 25 Journalists*. Bernard-Philippe Groslier's account of Angkor to an American diplomat is found in declassified embassy cables at the U.S. National Archives, as is the Cambodian government's request for tear gas for use at Angkor. EFEO ethnologist Jean Boulbet's book *De Palmes et d'Épines* contains extensive material about events of this period. Hervé Manac'h, who worked in Siem Reap for EFEO during the war, provided his own memories by email, as well as photographs. René Puissesseau's interview with Groslier can

be viewed at the website of France's *Institut national de l'audiovisuel*. Stephen Heder provided translations of 'confessions' of Khmer Rouge prisoners who mentioned Angkor. The account of the Lon Nol government's attempt to recapture Angkor Wat in 1972 was based on *Road to the Killing Fields* by Wilfred P. Deac and journalistic reports of the time. Norodom Sihanouk's 1973 visit to Angkor was recounted using his own account, media reports, and U.S. embassy cables, some of them provided to me by Julio Jeldres. Other information about wartime Angkor was drawn from articles by Elizabeth Becker of *The Washington Post*, Malcolm Browne of *The New York Times*, and other correspondents.

Chapter 12

Pol Pot's experience in Angkor as a young man is recounted in *Pol Pot: Anatomy of a Nightmare* by Philip Short. The account of events in Angkor and Siem Reap immediately after the Khmer Rouge victory in 1975 draws heavily on interviews conducted by French scholar Henri Locard and published in his paper 'Siem Reap-Angkor During the War (1970-1975) and Democratic Kampuchea (1975–1979): From Violence to Totalitarianism.' Mapping Memories Cambodia, a project of the Royal University of Phnom Penh, interviewed the Khmer Rouge Foreign Ministry assistant who took visitors to Angkor in Khmer Rouge times. Elizabeth Becker's newspaper articles and book, *When the War was Over: Cambodia and the Khmer Rouge Revolution*, illuminated Angkor's condition late in the Khmer Rouge period. The account of the Khmer Rouge's abortive effort to open Angkor to tourists comes from media accounts.

Chapter 13

The account of post-Khmer Rouge Angkor draws heavily on the author's own visit there in April 1980. The account of art theft is based on media, academic, and museum reports and official statements, and the author's observations in refugee camps. A 1988 article in *India Today* article gives a detailed description of Indian restoration work at Angkor Wat. Diplomatic negotiations toward peace in Cambodia are recounted based on media and official reports.

Chapter 14

The ICOMOS report on Angkor gives a detailed look at the old capital as it reopened to the world. Michelle Stevens recounted her experiences as a United Nations peacekeeper at Angkor in a Skype interview. The parachute display at Angkor Wat is described by Amélie de la Musardière, who was there that day, in her book *Quatre années au Cambodge*. Numerous UN and NGO documents and reports provided material concerning the return of foreign specialists. Claude Jacques' discovery of a stolen inscription stele in Bangkok is recounted in articles in *The Phnom Penh Post* and *The New York Times*. Keiko Miura's 2004 paper 'Congested Heritage: People of Angkor' gives a detailed account of Cambodian society at Angkor in this period.

Chapter 15

Groslier's article *La Cité hydraulique* was published by the EFEO Bulletin in 1979; it was translated into English and republished with commentary in 2007 by Terry Lustig and Christophe Pottier. Robert Acker's 1998 study 'New geographical tests of the hydraulic thesis at Angkor' took issue with Groslier's theories about the Khmers and water. The findings of LIDAR surveys are described in a collection of papers authored by Damian Evans, Roland Fletcher, and collaborators, beginning with 'Uncovering archaeological landscapes at Angkor using lidar,' published in *Proceedings of the National Academy of Sciences* in 2013. Sophia University's discoveries at Banteay Kdei are described in an article by Yoshiaki Ishizawa and Masako Marui in a 2002 edition of *Arts*

Asiatiques. The writings of Im Sokrithy, David Brotherson, Alison Kyra Carter, and Thomas Maxwell can be found with online searches, as can the computer animations of Monash University.

Chapter 16

This chapter draws heavily on the author's own experiences in recent visits to Angkor and Siem Reap. The return of Khmer artwork from the United States has been reported in statements from the museums involved. Media reports, official websites, and other sources were drawn on for the discussions of house construction in the Angkor zone, accusations of misbehaviour by tourists, the price of nights in Siem Reap, and Visakha Bucha at Angkor Wat.

BIBLIOGRAPHY

André Malraux: The Indochina Adventure. Walter
G. Langlois. Frederick A. Praeger, New
York. 1966.

*Angkor and Cambodia in the Sixteenth Century,
according to Portuguese and Spanish Sources.*
Bernard-Philippe Groslier. Orchid Press,
Bangkok. 2006. Originally published in
French by *Presses Universitaires de France.*
1958.

Angkor: An Illustrated Guide to the Monuments.
Jean Laur. Flammarion, Paris. 2002.

Angkor and the Khmer Civilization. Michael
D. Coe and Damian Evans. Thames &
Hudson, London. 2018.

Angkor: Cambodia's Wondrous Khmer Temples.
Dawn Rooney. Sixth Edition. Odyssey
Illustrated Guides, Airphoto International
Ltd., Hong Kong. 2011.

*Angkor: Naissance d'un Mythe. Louis Delaporte et
le Cambodge.* Under the direction of Pierre
Baptiste et Thierry Zéphir. Gallimard/
Musée national des arts asiatiques Guimet,
Paris. 2013.

*Angkor the Magnificent: Wonder City of Ancient
Cambodia.* Helen Churchill Candee,
DatASIA Inc., Holmes Beach, Florida.
2008. Originally published by Frederick A.
Stokes Co., New York in 1924.

'The Angkorian Hydraulic City: Exploitation
or Over-Exploitation of the Soil?'
Bernard-Philippe Groslier. *Bulletin de
l'École française d'Extrême-Orient*, 66, pp
161-202. 1979. Translated into English,
with commentary, by Terry Lustig and
Christophe Pottier in 2007.

Bulletin de l'École française d'Extrême-Orient.
Paris. Various issues.

Le Cambodge, Étienne Aymonier. Ernest
Leroux, Éditeur. Paris. Three volumes,
published between 1900 and 1904.

*Cambodge: The Cultivation of a Nation, 1860-
1945*, Penny Edwards. University of
Hawai'i Press, Honolulu. 2007.

Cambodian Dancers, Ancient & Modern. George
Groslier. DatASIA, Holmes Beach,
Florida. 2011. Originally published in
French by Augustin Challamel in Paris in
1913.

'Cambodian Sunset.' Arthur Davison
Ficke. *The North American Review*, Vol.
214, no. 788, 1921, pp. 50-61. Cedar
Falls, Iowa. 1921. *JSTOR*, www.jstor.org/
stable/25120779.

*A Century in Asia: The History of the École
Française d'Extrême-Orient 1898-2006.*
Catherine Clémentin-Ojha and Pierre-
Yves Manguin. Editions Didier Millet,
École Française d'Extrême-Orient, Paris. 2007.

*Challenging the Mystery of the Angkor Empire –
Realizing the Mission of Sophia University in
the Asian World.* Yoshiaki Ishizawa. Sophia
University Press, Tokyo, 2012.

*Colonial Cambodia's Bad Frenchmen: The Rise of
French Rule and the Life of Thomas Caraman,
1840-87.* Gregor Muller. Routledge
Studies in the Modern History of Asia,
Abingdon, UK. 2006.

Contested Heritage: People of Angkor. Keiko
Miura. Thesis for Doctor of Philosophy
degree, School of Oriental and African
Studies, University of London, London.
2004.

La découverte de 274 sculptures et d'un caitya
*bouddhique lors des campagnes de fouilles de
2000 et 2001 au temple de Banteay Kdei à
Angkor.* Yoshiaki Ishizawa and Masako
Marui. *Arts Asiatiques.* Vol. 57, 2002.

*'Discovering' Cambodia: Views of Angkor in French
Colonial Cambodia (1863-1954).* Jennifer
Lee Foley. Cornell University, Ithica, NY.
2006.

*'Les échanges entre le Japon et l'Indochine française
durant la seconde guerre mondiale: aux origines
de la collection d'art khmer du musée national
de Tokyo.'* Sadao Fujihara. *Ebisu Études
japonaises. Institut français de recherche sur le*

Japon à la Maison franco-japonaise. Tokyo. 2015.

L'École française d'Extrême-Orient ou l'institution des marges (1898-1956). Essai d'histoire sociale et politique de la science coloniale. Pierre Singaravélou. Éditions l'Harmattan, Paris. 2000.

Excursions et Reconnaissances, Saigon. Various issues.

Facing the Khmer Rouge: A Cambodian Journey. Ronnie Yimsut. Rutgers University Press, New Brunswick, New Jersey. 2011.

'The filming of a motion picture can be an adventure in itself, just as exciting as the original story. This is what happened with Lord Jim.' Pete Hamill. *The Saturday Evening Post*, The Curtis Publishing Company. Philadelphia. 21 November 1964.

'The first plaster casts of Angkor for the French *metropole,* from the Mekong Mission 1866-1868, and the Universal Exhibition of 1867, to the *Musée khmer* of 1874.' Michael Falser. *Bulletin de l'École française d'Extrême-Orient*, Paris. 2012-2013.

'The fortification of Angkor Wat.' David Brotherson. *Antiquity.* Volume 89, Issue 348 Durham, United Kingdom. December 2015.

'From America to Angkor: The Artistic Odyssey of Lucille Douglass.' Stephen J. Goldfarb. *Alabama Heritage,* Birmingham, Alabama. Issue 81, Summer 2006.

The Gate. François Bizot. Alfred A. Knopf, New York. 2003.

Ghost Ships: A Surrealist Love Triangle. Robert McNab. Yale University Press, New Haven and London. 2004.

A History of Cambodia. David Chandler. Westview Press, Boulder, Colorado. 2008.

'Household Archaeology at Angkor Wat.' Alison Kyra Carter. *Khmer Times,* Phnom Penh. July 7, 2016.

'Jackie Kennedy fulfills a lifelong wish…to see ancient Cambodia.' *Life* magazine. Time Inc., New York. 17 November 1967.

'Japan's Angkor art: Booty or fair exchange?' Julie Masis. Asia Times Online. 23 December 2013.

'A Journey in a Junk: The Ruins of Angkor Wat.' Therese Yelverton. *The Overland Monthly.* John H. Carmany & Company. San Francisco. Pp 30-43. Volume X. 1873.

Khmer Costumes and Ornaments of the Devatas of Angkor Wat. Sappho Marchal. Orchid Press, Bangkok. 2005. Originally published in French as *Costumes et parures khmèrs d'après les devatâ d'Angkor-Vat* by Librairie Nationale d'Art et d'Histoire, Paris and Brussels, in 1927.

'The Kingdom of Kampuchea, March-October 1945: Japanese-Sponsored Independence in Cambodia in World War II.' David Chandler. In *Journal of Southeast Asian Studies*, Cambridge University Press. Cambridge, UK. Vol. XVII. No. 1. March 1986.

'The landscape of Angkor Wat redefined.' Damian Evans and Roland Fletcher. *Antiquity.* Cambridge, UK. 2015.

'Lord Jim: The Perils of Peter O'Toole in filming a classic.' *Life* magazine. Time Inc., New York. 22 January 1965.

Louis Delaporte, Explorateur, Ses missions aux ruines khmères. René de Beauvais. Imprimerie des Orphelins d'Auteuil, Paris. 1929.

The opening of Aerial Tourism in Indochina: From Saigon river to Angkor-Vat on a straight wing. Henry Bontoux. Les Éditions d'Extrême-Asia, Saigon. 1929.

Orientarisuto no Yuutsu (Melancholy of the Orientalists) by Sadao Fujihara, published in Japanese by Mekong Publishing, Tokyo, 2008.

Overbooked: The Exploding Business of Travel and Tourism. Elizabeth Becker. Simon & Schuster. New York. 2016.

De Palmes et d'Épines: Vers le Paradis d'Indra. Jean Boulbet. Seven Orients, Paris. 2002.

Phnom Penh – A Cultural History (Cityscapes). Milton Osborne. Oxford University Press. Oxford, UK. 2008.

A Pilgrimage to Angkor. Pierre Loti, translated by W.P. Baines and Michael Smithies.

Silkworm Books, Chiangmai. 1996. Originally published in French as *Un Pèlerin d'Angkor* in Paris by Calmann-Levy in 1912.

Pol Pot: Anatomy of a Nightmare. Philip Short. A John Macrae Book, Henry Holt & Co., New York. 2004.

Quatre années au Cambodge. Amélie de la Musardière. Société des Écrivains, Paris. 2014.

A Record of Cambodia: The Land and Its People. Zhou Daguan. Translated by Peter Harris. Silkworm Books, Chiangmai. 2007.

'Prince Sihanouk: The Model of Absolute Monarchy in Cambodia 1953-1970.' Weena Yong. Trinity College, University of Cambridge, Cambridge, UK. 2013.

River Road to China: The Mekong River Expedition, 1866-73. Milton Osborne. Liveright, New York. 1975.

Road to the Killing Fields: The Cambodian War of 1970-1975. Wilfred P. Deac. Texas A&M University Press, College Station, Texas. 1997.

Les Ruines d'Angkor, de Duong-Duong et de My-Son (Cambodge et Annam), Charles Carpeaux. Published by Mme. J.-B. Carpeaux. Augustin Challamel, Éditeur. Librairie Coloniale. Paris 1908.

Les Ruines d'Angkor: Étude artistique et historique sur les monuments khmers du Cambodge Siamoise. Lucien Fournereau and Jacques Porcher. Ernest Leroux, éditeur, Paris 1890.

Saint-Exupéry: A Biography. Stacy Schiff. Alfred A. Knopf, New York. 1994.

The Sdok Kak Thom Inscription. Chhany Sak-Humphry with the assistance of Philip N. Jenner. Buddhist Institute, Phnom Penh. 2005.

Siam Through the Lens of John Thomson, 1865-66. Paisarn Piemmettawat, translated by Narisa Chakrabongse. River Books, Bangkok. 2015.

'Siem Reap-Angkor During the War (1970-1975) and Democratic Kampuchea (1975-1979): From Violence to Totalitarianism.' Henri Locard. In *Siksacakr/The Journal of Cambodia Research.* No. 10. Phnom Penh. 2008.

'Some Evidence of an Inter-Relationship between Hydraulic Features and Rice Field Patterns at Angkor during Ancient Times.' Christophe Pottier. *The Journal of Sophia Asian Studies.* No. 18. Tokyo. 2000.

'Souvenirs d'Angkor avant la tourmente.' Joseph Schilling. La Croix, 9 March 1999.

Souvenirs d'un ancien conservateur d'Angkor. Henri Marchal. Unpublished memoir.

Stories in Stone: The Sdok Kok Thom Inscription & the Enigma of Khmer History. John Burgess. River Books, Bangkok. 2010.

Le Temple d'Angkor Wat, Mémoires Archéologiques publiés par l'École française d'Extrême-Orient. Les Editions G. van Ouest. Tome 2 in three volumes, 1929-1932. Reprinted by SDI Publications, Bangkok in 1995.

Temple in the Clouds: Faith and Conflict at Preah Vihear. John Burgess. River Books, Bangkok. 2015.

'Travels in Siam and Cambodia.' D.O. King. *Journal of the Royal Geographical Society,* London. 1860.

'Uncovering archaeological landscapes at Angkor using Lidar.' Damian Evans et al. *Proceedings of the National Academy of Sciences of the United States of America.* Washington, DC. 2013.

La Ville au Bois dormant: de Saïgon à Ang-Kor en Automobile. Duc de Montpensier. Librairie Plon, Paris. 1910.

'Voyage dans les Royaumes de Siam, de Cambodge, de Laos.' Henri Mouhot. *Le Tour du Monde.* Librairie de L. Hachette et Cie., Paris, 1863.

Voyage dans l'Indo-Chine, 1848-1856. Charles-Émile Bouillevaux. Librairie de Victor Palmé. Paris. 1858.

Voyage d'Exploration en Indo-Chine, Francis Garnier. Librairie Hachette, Paris. 1885.

When the War Was Over: Cambodia and the Khmer Rouge Revolution. Elizabeth Becker. Public Affairs, New York. 1998.

INDEX